Coalition Politics and Economic Development

Coalition Politics and Economic Development challenges the conventional wisdom that coalition governments hinder necessary policy reform in developing countries. Irfan Nooruddin presents a fresh theory that institutionalized gridlock, by reducing policy volatility and stabilizing investor expectations, is actually good for economic growth. Successful national economic performance, he argues, is the consequence of having the right configuration of national political institutions. Countries in which leaders must compromise to form policy are better able to commit credibly to investors and therefore enjoy higher and more stable rates of economic development. Quantitative analysis of business surveys and national economic data together with historical case studies of five countries provide evidence for these claims. This is an original analysis of the relationship between political institutions and national economic performance in the developing world and will appeal to scholars and advanced students of political economy, economic development, and comparative politics.

IRFAN NOORUDDIN is Associate Professor in the Department of Political Science at The Ohio State University where, in 2007, he was named Distinguished Undergraduate Research Mentor of the Year. His work has been published in multiple journals including *Journal of Politics, International Organization, Journal of Conflict Resolution, International Studies Quarterly, Review of International Organizations, Comparative Political Studies*, and *International Interactions*.

Coalition Politics and Economic Development

Credibility and the Strength of Weak Governments

IRFAN NOORUDDIN

CAMBRIDGE
UNIVERSITY PRESS

CAMBRIDGE
UNIVERSITY PRESS

University Printing House, Cambridge CB2 8BS, United Kingdom

One Liberty Plaza, 20th Floor, New York, NY 10006, USA

477 Williamstown Road, Port Melbourne, VIC 3207, Australia

314-321, 3rd Floor, Plot 3, Splendor Forum, Jasola District Centre, New Delhi - 110025, India

79 Anson Road, #06-04/06, Singapore 079906

Cambridge University Press is part of the University of Cambridge.

It furthers the University's mission by disseminating knowledge in the pursuit of education, learning and research at the highest international levels of excellence.

www.cambridge.org
Information on this title: www.cambridge.org/9780521138758

First published 2011

A catalogue record for this publication is available from the British Library

Library of Congress Cataloging in Publication data
Nooruddin, Irfan.
    Coalition politics and economic development : credibility and the strength of weak governments / Irfan Nooruddin.
        p.   cm.
    Includes bibliographical references and index.
    ISBN 978-0-521-19140-1 (hardback)
    1. Developing countries–Economic conditions.   2. Coalition governments–Developing countries.   I. Title.
    HC59.7.N65 2010
    338.9–dc22   2010035946

ISBN 978-0-521-19140-1 Hardback
ISBN 978-0-521-13875-8 Paperback

For Heidi, unerring muse

Contents

Figures

Tables

Preface

All over the world people eke out existences on the edge of subsistence. For these members of the "bottom billion," the difference between survival and desperation is razor-thin. Policymakers and academics alike have expended considerable energies identifying policies that might raise the standard of living of the poorest members of our societies, as well as those that provide a partial safety-net against the worst outcomes. Yet, in spite of its obvious importance, we know very little about why some societies are more prone to the types of economic crises and recessions that threaten to plunge one-sixth of humanity below subsistence. This book seeks to add to our understanding of the determinants of such growth-rate volatility, and, by doing so, to change how we think about where economic development might come from for those currently mired in poverty.

Research on economic development is necessarily interdisciplinary, drawing insights from economics, sociology, history, geography, and, more recently, political science. Understanding the economic foundations of economic development is a prerequisite, but, as countless examples suggest, politicians do not heed economists' advice. What is rational for economists is not necessarily optimal for politicians whose incentive structures are influenced more by the imperatives of retaining power than of maximizing economic growth. Where these incentives overlap good things can happen. Indeed a primary insight behind those who advocate the adoption of democratic governments in the developing world is that, by making leaders accountable to their publics, democracies build in a motivation to promote economic development. Yet the most recent research on democracy and development finds no evidence that democracies grow faster than their non-democratic counterparts.

The absence of any relationship between democracy and development bolsters the case of those who defend a form of "benevolent dictatorship," the exemplar of which is supposedly Singapore. Economic reform requires difficult choices and an attention to long-term prerogatives, both of which election-minded politicians are ill-suited to provide. Insulating decision-makers from societal pressures therefore becomes crucial to the adoption of the appropriate policies for economic development. But what such arguments can't explain is why we should expect unaccountable politicians to use their unconstrained power to enact policies in the public interest rather than to enrich themselves and their cronies.

In this book, I offer an alternative to these theories. I come down in favor of democracy, but with an important caveat. The true democratic advantage, I argue, is in its encouragement of political competition and the representation of multiple viewpoints in the deliberative process. When governments are forced to accommodate diverse positions in order to reach policy consensus, the resulting policies are more stable – if (or maybe because?) less radical – than when governments can make changes unilaterally. This stability bolsters confidence among private economic actors who fear policy change, and encourages them to make longer-term investments that they would hesitate to make in a riskier environment. More stable investments in turn lay the foundation for stable economic growth and long-term economic development.

What institutions of democracy promote such policy stability? I argue that institutions that diffuse policymaking authority across multiple actors responsible to different societal constituencies are the key. A perfect example of such an institution is a coalition government in a parliamentary democracy, in which the survival of the government requires cooperation among the members of the coalition, which necessitates compromise and fosters policy stability. In this book, I use a combination of macroeconomic and micro-survey data to test this argument, both cross-nationally and in individual country case studies. The evidence overwhelmingly supports the argument.

A word about my approach is in order. For some readers, the framework developed here will seem too sparse. I do not advocate a "silver bullet" that countries can adopt to reduce growth-rate volatility and increase economic growth. Rather the contribution of my research is to identify the central dynamic of interest: what configuration of institutions works best to harness this dynamic is an empirical question, albeit one whose answer is guided by theory. In the developed North, for instance, independent central banks are the norm, yet there is little evidence that statutory independence for central bankers has yielded any benefits in the global South. Similarly, policy stability via "gridlock" has been good for parliamentary India and Italy (as I will argue in some detail), but scholars of Latin America bemoan the negative effects of gridlock in the presidential systems they study. I believe that my "credible constraints" theoretical framework can help explain these differences, but understand if my answers are unsatisfactory to some. In that case, my sincere hope is that my work encourages others to tackle these same questions in order to yield better answers. The stakes of getting them right are too high not to try.

Academic projects, much like economies, experience highs and lows. This project began after an earlier effort at a dissertation imploded when I learned of the existence of the about-to-be-published and obviously bound-to-be-seminal work by Przeworski *et al.* (2000) that made my efforts at answering related questions seem quite pointless. But, taking inspiration in the fact that I had been thinking along the same lines (albeit not nearly as clearly) as those eminent scholars, I used their work as a starting point for my inquiry into yet unexplored territory in the relationship between political institutions and economic volatility. Little remains of the dissertation in which I first explored the main ideas that underpin this book, but the influence of my advisors at the University of Michigan – Pradeep Chhibber, Rob Franzese, John Jackson, and Michael Ross – is evident on every page of this manuscript. To each, once more, I express my deepest gratitude. Most of all, for his steadfast mentorship and encouragement as the dissertation made its halting metamorphosis into a book and as I moved from graduate student to tenured professor, I thank Pradeep. If I can mean to my students a fraction of what he has meant to me, I'll consider my career a success.

Writing the book required considerable research assistance, and I was lucky to be able to draw on the help of a remarkable group of graduate students: Quintin Beazer conducted the preliminary analyses of the EBRD-World Bank enterprise surveys utilized in Chapter 4 and helped prepare the index in addition to providing comments on the entire manuscript; Autumn Lockwood Payton helped construct the bibliography (aided by Brooke Keebaugh); Michael Cohen offered detailed comments on the Italian case study; Sarah Wilson Sokhey was instrumental in the completion of the comparative case studies for Chapter 6; Amanda Yates (with Xiaoyu Pu's help) constructed

Appendix A. Daniel Blake, Scott Powell, Allyson Shortle, and Dana Wittmer, along with Sarah, Quintin, Autumn, and Michael, were a constant source of support and encouragement; I am fortunate to have had these scholars as colleagues and even luckier to count them as friends.

The book is much better for the comments received over its long gestation – so long in fact that I'm sure I've forgotten some whose names should appear below. Audiences at Washington University in St Louis, the University of Notre Dame, Ohio State, University of Chicago, Yale University's Macmillan Center, Stony Brook University, American University, Penn State, and the APSA, Midwest, and Southern meetings provided useful feedback. Nathan Jensen and James Raymond Vreeland went far beyond the call of friendship to offer extremely careful and helpful comments on the entire manuscript; my debt to each is beyond words. Mark Souva, Eddy Malesky, Tim Frye, Pradeep Chhibber, Joel Simmons, Ken Kollman, and Ashu Varshney commented on earlier papers that ended up as part of the book. Daniel Corstange, Daniel D'Souza, Amaney Jamal, Zaheer Nooruddin, and Joel Simmons read multiple chapters of the manuscript and asked difficult questions; for their time and honesty, I am deeply appreciative. Carew Boulding, Emily Beaulieu, and Susan Hyde endured more conversations about the book than I'm prepared to admit, always asking the right questions and offering helpful advice. Considerable thanks are due to the two anonymous reviewers at Cambridge University Press (and the six anonymous reviewers and four editors of other presses that considered the manuscript) for their excellent comments on the entire manuscript; these anonymous scholars exemplify the best of this profession. Finally, John Haslam and Carrie Parkinson have been exceedingly generous and patient editors for Cambridge. This book would be much better had I been capable of addressing all the helpful advice I've received, and I beg these scholars' indulgences for the shortcomings that remain in spite of their best efforts.

My parents and brother have been a constant source of support throughout my life, and their love and encouragement made negotiating the book and tenure process easier. My daughter Esme arrived in May 2009, changing my life forever; her smile makes her the most delightful – if distracting – writing companion. Most importantly, I thank my wife, Heidi Sherman; for nothing I have accomplished, not

least this book, would have been possible without her constant friendship. A consummate intellectual, she influenced every page of every
draft, beginning with my dissertation seven years ago, and engaged
me (often against my will) in conversations about the main ideas that
helped me improve their clarity and presentation. She pushed me when
I needed to be pushed; supported me when I needed support; and her
unconditional love gave me the courage to finish this book when, like
an inchworm crawling on a leaf, I threatened forever to "cling to the
very end, revolve in air, feeling for something to reach to something."
This book is gratefully dedicated to her, my best friend and unerring
muse, who makes everything perfect.

1 | Introduction

Has India's political system aided its successful economic growth over the past fifteen years, or has India's rise occurred in spite of the political forces militating against economic growth? On the face of it, the picture of India's success being "In Spite of the Gods," to use Edward Luce's phrase, appears quite compelling (Luce 2008). Over the sixty years since it gained independence from British rule, the Indian political system has changed almost as dramatically as its more-heralded economic system.

The principal political change has not been to India's democratic framework. That has remained intact. Rather, if one were to use a single word to describe the modern Indian political system it would have to be "fragmentation." After continuous rule at the Center and in most states by the Congress Party, today's political system finds a multitude of regional- and state-level political parties in power or in the position of kingmaker as tenuous coalition governments are assembled.[1]

The effects of this are easy to see in the political arena: virulent anti-incumbency tendencies and high electoral volatility, which in turn affects the quality of governance and types of public policies enjoyed by citizens.[2] At the national level (or Centre), the rise of regional parties and the increasing inability of the "national" parties such as the Congress and Bharatiya Janata Party (BJP) to compete all over the country have made coalition governments a fact of modern Indian political life.

---

[1] The fragmentation of the Indian political system is documented by Chhibber and Nooruddin (2000), and explained by Pradeep Chhibber and Kenneth Kollman (1998, 2004).

[2] Linden (2004) and Nooruddin and Chhibber (2008) focus on anti-incumbency and electoral volatility respectively. Chhibber and Nooruddin (2004) show that Indian states characterized by multi-party competition provide lower levels of public services to citizens than those with robust two-party competition.

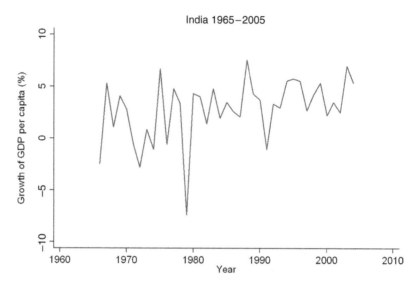

Figure 1.1 India's economy is doing better in recent years (source: World Bank 2006).

Even a brief review of the relevant scholarship in political science would suggest that the *economic* effects of such political fragmentation should be negative. Political instability is expected to cause domestic and international investors to flee a potentially chaotic situation, while coalition governments are thought to be hamstrung from providing deeper and more business-friendly economic policies. Yet, the opposite appears true (see Figure 1.1). Since 1991, when a balance-of-payments crisis and pressure from international lenders such as the International Monetary Fund (IMF) led to wide-ranging economic liberalization, India's economy has been growing rapidly. This successful economic performance, long overdue for India's immense poor majority, is puzzling in two important ways. First, the economic progress has occurred against the backdrop of minority and coalition national governments, increasing party fragmentation, and higher electoral volatility. Second, the economy has become more stable, with fewer and smaller fluctuations in its growth rate, even as it has been more exposed to the vagaries of international trade and finance.

This book seeks to resolve these two puzzles by focusing on a hitherto-ignored question in comparative and international political economy: why do some countries experience more volatility in their growth?[3] This issue is central to our understanding of the dynamics of national economic performance, and holds the key to clarifying how political institutions affect economic growth. Further, in tackling this question, the book will also shed light on other important questions in comparative political economy, such as why do some countries attract more foreign direct investment than others? Why are some more prone to destabilizing capital flight? Why are some able to encourage citizens to save more? Each of these questions has received considerable attention from political scientists and economists; this book provides an integrated framework for understanding these diverse phenomena, which affect the lives of billions of people around the world.

Good national economic performance, I will argue, is the consequence of having the right configuration of national political institutions. Specifically, I will show that countries in which policymaking authority is diffused across political institutions controlled by actors responsive to different societal constituencies are better able to make credible commitments to long-term policy stability. These commitments, in turn, engender more stable investment patterns by private economic actors, and make countries less susceptible to capital flight as investors are less likely to flee at the first sign of trouble. Taken together, such behavior by private actors leads to more stable, and higher, economic growth over the long term.

That political institutions affect national economic performance and investment behavior is not a novel argument. Over the past twenty years, even economists have come to accept this proposition, with some of the more prominent recent contributions by economists to the study of economic growth placing historical and current political institutions at the center of their investigations. Similarly, scholars have studied the effect of democratic institutions on foreign direct investment flows and on the incidence and severity of crises. So, what's new here?

The argument proffered expands our understanding of the politics of national economic performance in at least four distinct ways. First,

---

[3] Growth-rate volatility might be defined as the relative rate at which growth rates increase and decrease. A conventional measure of volatility is the standard deviation of growth rates over some period of time. I am certainly not the first to study growth-rate volatility and the past decade has seen scholars begin to focus on this important topic. Yet, compared to the vast literature seeking to explain variations in *average* growth rate, work on *volatility* is but a drop in the ocean.

the empirical implications of the argument, as will be detailed below, will strike many readers as counter-intuitive and potentially controversial. Unlike other scholars who emphasize the importance of "state strength" or "political will," I come not to bury "gridlock" but to praise it. Here, separation-of-powers institutions in which political leaders cannot make drastic policy changes unilaterally and arbitrarily are celebrated for providing private economic actors with credible information about future policy stability. Second, I seek to bring "society" back into institutional analyses of economic performance by emphasizing the importance of political parties in representing diverse societal preferences within the formal halls of power. This enriches how we think about political institutions, and moves away from overly abstract formulations of institutions in which a single policymaker responds to a single median voter in society. Rather, I argue, politics must be understood as a competition over power in which policy compromise is to be valued rather than bemoaned. Third, I identify a diverse set of empirical implications of the causal story in order to tease out the causal mechanisms at work here. Prior studies typically stop short of doing so, and as I will try to convince the reader, existing arguments linking political institutions such as democracy with economic outcomes are underspecified so that empirical correlations are consistent with several alternative interpretations of the underlying causal mechanisms. Finally, the framework developed crosses boundaries between comparative and international political economy. For modern developing countries, the dynamics of economic growth are intimately connected to those of international capital flows. International business actors must choose where to invest their capital, and this decision is conditioned in part by the political framework in place and the expected stability of the rules-of-the-game in that country. The argument thus privileges policy stability over its content. I am not sure if policy matters, or even if we know what policies are best, but a stable policy environment definitely matters, and diffuse policymaking authority is the best way to get policy stability. If there are good policies out there, the coalition form of diffuse authority is the safest way to get them. By explaining where such stability comes from, my framework can thus make explicit predictions, which I test cross-nationally, about foreign direct investment and capital flight patterns.

The remainder of this introductory chapter is organized as follows. In the next section, I establish more fully the empirical puzzles motivating this book, and explain why understanding volatility is intimately connected to understanding growth. Then I provide a synopsis of the theoretical framework developed here, summarize the main empirical results, and contrast my argument with previous research. (A fuller explication of the framework, as well as a more complete consideration of prominent alternative political and economic explanations, is reserved for the next chapter.) The final section highlights the book's primary theoretical contributions, its normative and policy implications, and concludes with a road-map to the rest of the book.

Puzzles of national economic performance

In 1999, in the aftermath of the Mexican "tequila" crisis and the East Asian financial crisis, the International Monetary Fund (IMF) published its annual *World Economic Outlook*, focusing on the importance of maintaining macroeconomic stability at low inflation. In it, the IMF concluded "the severe macroeconomic crises in Latin America during the 1980s [had] brought into sharp relief the need for deep-seated reforms to restore fiscal and monetary discipline and increase reliance on market mechanisms for resource allocation" (International Monetary Fund 1999: 52). Argentina was hailed in this report as "one of the countries where [such] structural reforms have advanced the most," the success of which was evident in the "expansion of real GDP by 5.35 per cent a year on average between 1990 and 1995," despite the severity of the 1995 "tequila" crisis (International Monetary Fund 1999: 52–3).

Three years later, the IMF's assessment appeared recklessly optimistic and inaccurate. The Argentine economy collapsed between 2000 and 2002, with devastating consequences for the population. The economic crises led to widespread unemployment and under-employment, forcing millions of people into poverty. At the height of the crisis, on September 22, 2002, the *New York Times* wrote, "Argentina's jobless rate has risen above 20 per cent and the value of the peso has fallen by more than 70 per cent against the dollar. Homelessness is on the rise, and nearly *half* the country's 36 million people now live in poverty." The *Times* article went on to tell of how previously employed residents of Buenos Aires were turned into scavengers, digging through garbage to find items to recycle for money or food to eat. Another *Times* article

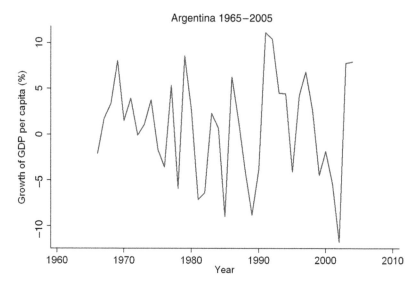

Figure 1.2 Argentina has always had extreme volatility in its growth (source: World Bank 2006).

told of old-age pensioners who turned to prostitution in Buenos Aires because their savings had been wiped out.

Today, Argentina's economy is enjoying high growth again. But the events of the past fifteen years in Argentina beg two questions: should we have been surprised by the collapse in 2001 and should we expect the good times to continue indefinitely now? A brief look at Argentina's growth patterns over the past forty years suggests that the answer to both questions is no. If anything the high rates of crises and consistently high levels of growth-rate volatility in Argentina's past caution us that the current good growth is soon to be followed by a collapse, and indeed the most recent indications are that this is precisely what is coming to pass.

Such horror stories of sudden unpredictable economic collapse are not unique to Argentina, of course. At the height of the Asian financial crisis, "World Bank assessments warned that the economic fallout could wipe out all the progress against poverty these countries had achieved during the past 25 years" (USAID 2000: 2). Korea, for instance, experienced an increase in the country's poor "from 7.5 per cent [of the population] just before the crisis (first quarter of 1997) to a peak of 22.9 per cent in the third quarter of 1998" (Atinc 2002: 123).

In Indonesia, between ten and twelve million people were forced into poverty within a year of the crisis (Atinc 2002). As in Argentina a few years later, the social crisis in East Asia was exacerbated by reductions in public spending on essential services such as health care and education, and the fall in household incomes as people lost their jobs and prices rose (Newfarmer 1998). The effects could be long-lasting. The short-term consequences in East Asia were higher hunger and malnutrition, a surge in infectious disease, and a drop in school enrollment rates. The long-term consequences are yet to be determined, but the World Bank warned that poor health and increased malnutrition would hurt worker productivity, reducing future growth prospects. Young children were likely to suffer most, with the worst-hit facing stunted growth and poor cognitive development.

The negative consequences of volatility can be thought of as reversing the positive effects of development. Indeed, World Bank economists Jorge Arbache and John Page have argued that volatility in growth had erased the gains of positive growth between 1975 and 2005 resulting from improved policy and governance in many sub-Saharan African countries. Holding all other factors steady, if African economies could have eliminated periodic collapses in growth, they would have grown at 1.7 percent a year per capita, rather than the 0.7 percent they actually realized. This might not seem like a lot, but an extra percentage point of average annual growth over the period would have added 30 percent to the region's GDP (Gross Domestic Product) (Arbache and Page 2007: 11). Sirimaneetham and Temple reach a similar conclusion, finding in their data that "a 1 standard deviation improvement in stability translates into an annual growth rate that is 0.5–0.7 percentage point higher over 30 years" (2009: 463). Averaged over the period, a 0.7 percentage point increase would result in a 23 percent higher GDP per capita.

Sirimaneetham and Temple's analysis of volatility's effects on growth rates makes two points relevant to the broader discussion on the importance of focusing on volatility as a distinct dimension of countries' national economic performance. First, macroeconomic stability dominates several other possibilities for identifying distinct growth regimes; and, second, instability appears to form a "binding constraint" on growth for countries in the less stable growth regime, by reducing the effectiveness of technology and innovation, and of investment (Sirimaneetham and Temple 2009: 475).

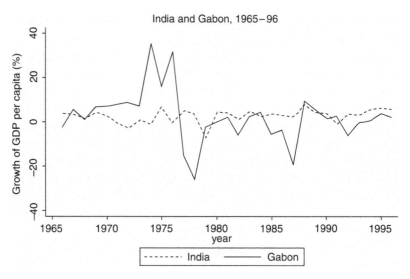

Figure 1.3 India and Gabon, 1965–96 (source: World Bank 2006).

Not all countries experience such destabilizing volatility, of course, and some countries manage to extract themselves over time from the conditions that cause it. Such variation in growth-rate volatility has received relatively little attention from political scientists, most of whom have focused instead on explaining variation in average long-term growth rates. But the almost-exclusive attention to growth averages has masked important differences in national economic performance.

Consider the different growth trajectories of India and Gabon from 1965 to 1996, just prior to India's recent rapid and sustained economic growth.

The choice of these two countries is not accidental. Both India and Gabon are developing societies but with fairly different growth trajectories. Over the thirty-year period summarized by Figure 1.3, India's average growth rate was 2.46 percent; Gabon's was 2.47 percent. That is, the two countries were indistinguishable in terms of the average growth rates they managed to achieve. However, their average volatilities are very different: while India never reached the extremely high growth rates experienced by Gabon in the early 1970s, India grew at a fairly stable rate while Gabon's high rates of growth were quickly followed by several years of devastating negative growth. The discovery of oil in the early 1970s generated tremendous income so that Gabon's per capita income doubled from $4,168 in 1973 to $8,508 in 1976. But the fall in oil prices in the mid-1970s devastated Gabon's economy so that by 1978 the per capita income had fallen 37 percent to $5,322. Per capita incomes in Gabon have fallen ever since as negative growth persisted well into the 1980s. India, by contrast, chugged along steadily at what some observers derisively termed the "Hindu rate of growth" until its recent sustained high growth.

Lest one wonder about the comparability of India and Gabon, perhaps one more example will serve to convince readers of needing to consider volatility too. Angola and Namibia, neighbors in Africa's southern cone, are both resource-rich sub-Saharan countries, albeit with different recent political histories. Angola has just ended a devastating civil war that spanned three decades, while Namibia is near the end of its second decade of relatively successful democratic self-rule. Did this difference in political past affect the economy? By one reckoning, no. If one considers only the average growth rate of both countries between 1990 and 2005, there is virtually no difference between the two countries with both showing limited evidence of growth.[4] But even a brief glance at Figure 1.4 reveals that this is misleading.

The negative effects of Angola's civil wars are quite evident in the crippling economic collapse between 1987 and 1994, in which economic growth rates never got over zero, and fell as low as negative 27 percent in 1993. Angola certainly enjoyed more years of high growth than Namibia, largely due to rising oil prices in this decade, which leads to the apparent equivalent average performance over the past twenty-five years, but one would be hard-pressed to argue that the two countries truly had no difference in economic performance during this period. Once again, looking simply at average growth masks more than it reveals.

Stepping back from the experiences of these countries to a more global perspective reveals interesting and hitherto unexplained variation in national economic performance. Figure 1.5 plots all countries

---

[4] Angola's average growth in GDP per capita is 1.68 percent while Namibia's average growth rate during that period is 1.32 percent.

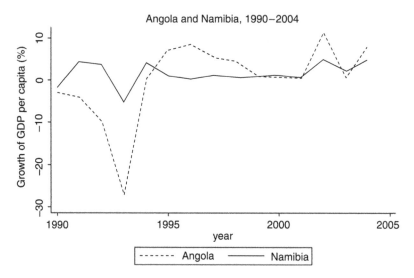

Figure 1.4 Slow growth on average in both, but Angola and Namibia had different growth trajectories nevertheless (source: World Bank 2006).

for which data are available from the World Bank in terms of their average growth rate and the volatility of that growth rate. To ease comprehension, I indicate the world averages on each axis by drawing a straight line at that point.

Countries in the lower right-hand quadrant of Figure 1.5 are those that have achieved growth rates higher than the world average over the same period but at lower-than-average levels of volatility. One might term these "sustained high-growth" countries. Those in the upper right-hand quadrant have had high average growth but at very high rates of volatility too ("unstably successful"). In the lower left-hand quadrant are states with lower than average growth, but with low instability too ("stable underperformers"). And, finally, in the upper left-hand quadrant are those stuck in a low-growth high-instability equilibrium from which it is extremely difficult to emerge ("unstable poor performers").

While most countries fortunately never experience crises on the scale experienced by the East Asian states in 1997 or by Argentina in 2002 or Angola in the early 1990s, most developing countries do go through recessions and slight crises at different points in their history.

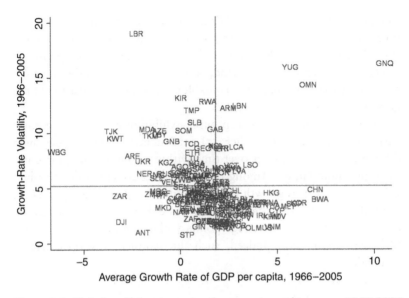

Figure 1.5 Global variation in national economic performance, 1966–2005 (source: author's calculations from World Bank 2006).

For instance, India's growth trajectory over the first fifty years after the founding of its republic can be divided into three epochs. The first was from 1950 to 1964 and reflected the initial successes of Nehru's five-year plans and the industrial revolution. An economic crisis in 1965 led to a first set of reforms. From 1967 to 1977, India's economy was more volatile than ever before, and for the first time in its history, India underwent successive years of negative growth. As anyone familiar with India's history knows, the bookend of this period was Indira Gandhi's declaration of Emergency, followed by the replacement of the Congress Party at India's helm in New Delhi. Finally, the 1980s were a period of growth in which India had a steady growth rate of around 3 percent per year. India's economy then experienced significant reform and liberalization in 1991, and the 1990s provided a mixed record with higher rates of growth although never approaching the levels previously seen in China or the East Asian Tigers.

These periods of India's growth trajectory do not differ simply in their average growth levels; they differ also in the degree of volatility. If one divides the forty-year period represented in Figure 1.1 into two, using the end of Emergency and Congress Rule in 1978 as a convenient breakpoint, India's growth-rate volatility in the first period, as measured by the standard deviation of the growth rate over that period, is 3.09 percent. In the second period, between 1980[5] and 2004 (the most recent date for which data are available), the standard deviation of the growth rate is just 1.87 percent.[6]

India is by no means an exception in exhibiting such cross-temporal variation in growth rate. Rather, as Lant Pritchett (2000) clarifies, such differences in growth rates over time within a country are quite common and quite large. "Among the developing countries the absolute value of the shift in growth rates averages 3.4 percentage points ... Growth rates in 55 of the 111 countries either decelerated or accelerated more than 3 percentage points within the period [surveyed]" (Pritchett 2000: 227). Indeed, such fluctuations cause Pritchett to conclude,

[the] fixation on differences in long-run (even possibly steady-state) differences in growth in the theoretical and empirical research explaining growth has led to an underestimation of the importance of the *instability* and *volatility* in growth rates ... Is explaining Brazil's "growth" explaining the 4.2 percent growth from 1965 to 1980 or explaining the stagnation from 1980 to 1992 (actually a slight fall of −0.2 percent) or explaining Brazil's average growth percent from 1960–92 of 3.14? (2000: 222).

To be clear, Pritchett is talking about variation in the levels of growth over different periods of a single country's history rather than variations in the volatility of growth over different periods, a subtle but crucial distinction. However, his larger point is important: to understand growth we must pay attention to fluctuations within countries as well as across them (see also Agenor *et al.* 2000).

---

[5] As with most developing countries, India had an economic crisis in 1979 as a result of the second OPEC price hike. This led to the downfall of the Janata Party government and the return to power by Indira Gandhi. I exclude this year (1979) from the analysis because it is an outlier.

[6] The average growth rates over these two periods were 1.65 percent and 3.79 percent respectively. Data are from the World Bank (2006: CD-Rom).

Growth-rate volatility, of which crises are the most dramatic instances, is understudied in political science, but as the cases of East Asia and Argentina demonstrate, the human effects of extreme volatility make understanding its political determinants a central question for comparative and international political economy.

The credible constraints argument summarized

Previous research on political institutions and economic growth has found mixed or no support for the claim that democracy generates higher average levels of economic growth (e.g., Przeworski *et al.* 2000). These weak results have arisen in part because, in seeking to explain cross-country variation in growth rates, $V_i(d(Y))$ (where i indexes countries and Y is income), as a result of cross-national variation in (the degree of) democracy, political science has generally ignored cross-national and cross-temporal variation in growth-rate volatility, $V_{it}(V(d(Y)))$ (where i indexes country and t indexes time), thereby missing an area of economic performance both critically important to long-term growth and more directly susceptible to political factors.[7] These, in turn, extend deeper than merely the degree of democracy in the abstract to its institutional and structural specifics. However, political science has as yet allocated too little effort either to explaining cross-national and cross-temporal variation in growth-rate volatility or to elaborating the specific institutional and structural features of concrete democratic regimes that underlie such explanations.

In this book, I argue that governments' inability to commit credibly to present and future policies strongly contributes to growth-rate volatility. Specifically, governments' inability to commit credibly to future and current policies, i.e., to policy stability, (1) induces investors to avoid long-term commitments in and to their investment projects,

---

[7] Przeworski *et al.* (2000) do find that democracies are more consistent in their growth performance than non-democracies. That is, non-democracies produce the miracles and failures, whereas performance among democracies is closer to the mean. Note though that this finding says nothing about growth-rate volatility *within* a country's history, only that growth performances among non-democracies are more heterogeneous than among democracies. This is an interesting insight, but conceptually distinct from the one I'm making here. I thank an anonymous reviewer for this point.

and (2) makes them, because of the nature of their investments and because they lack confidence and/or certainty regarding future government policy, more likely to abandon the country at smaller signs of economic trouble. The ability to make such volatility-dampening and growth-enhancing credible commitments is rooted in a specific configuration of state institutions that I identify. Specifically, I contend that the diffusion of policymaking authority to multiple actors with accountability to different constituencies lowers the average level of growth-rate volatility a country experiences, while increasing stable investment flows and discouraging capital flight. This diffusion of policymaking authority across different policymakers with different accountabilities provides a set of *credible constraints* on an executive's ability to change policy autonomously (and potentially arbitrarily). Such constraints from potentially arbitrary policy and from policy variability bolster confidence among private economic actors. The investor confidence engendered in countries with such institutions, in turn, fosters longer-term, more stable investment that helps those countries withstand temporary shocks, preventing them from developing into the full-blown crises that are more likely to emerge in countries lacking such institutions as panicked investors flee the likely unstable and/or poor policy-environment in the aftermath of shocks. Thus, the inability of governments lacking the credible constraints of diffuse policymaking authority and accountability to commit credibly to present and future policies induces savings and investment volatility and, thereby, growth-rate volatility.

  I test various empirical implications of this argument using two sets of data. The primary tests are conducted using cross-national political and economic data, primarily from the World Bank but supplemented by other sources where necessary. I find that states with diffusion of policymaking authority resulting from divided or minority governments, and coalition governments – each of which entails diffusion of policymaking authority across actors accountable to differing constituencies – have lower growth-rate volatility, *ceteris paribus*. On the other hand, the degree of democracy, *per se*, and other aspects of democratic regimes less connected to the diffusion of authority across differing-constituency representatives are not, or less, correlated. Furthermore, I show that these correlations of output-growth volatility and certain democratic institutions do in fact arise via the savings-and-investment-volatility channel as argued.

Advantageously, the *credible constraints* framework can also be enriched to contain case-specific detail on the nature and identity of key policymakers, moving beyond the standard (readily available) quantitative measures of a government's type, its divided or minority status, and its monetary institutions, to discuss more precisely the experiences of specific cases with their particular diffusion of authority. I demonstrate this advantage in a second set of analyses using India as an empirical test-bed for these ideas. India has experienced very high growth for the past fifteen years, which is long overdue given its previous record of slow growth with occasional bouts of volatility. To some extent, this is puzzling given economists' explanations of growth stability: in essence, India's most stable growth has been achieved at a time when its exposure to the vagaries of international trade and financial flows are at their highest. Further, contrary to the expectations derived from existing explanations but consistent with the *credible constraints* framework offered here, India's stable and high growth rates have been achieved under sustained coalition governments at the Center, while its less stable and lower growth rates were under the watch of single-party majority governments. I also leverage the inter-state variation within India to shed light on my argument since India's states vary both in their economic performance and the diffusion of policymaking authority, while allowing me to hold constant national-level political institutions and economic policies.

In a final empirical evaluation of the theoretical framework, I conduct four brief case studies of two developing states (Brazil and Botswana) and two developed democracies (Spain and Italy). The case studies demonstrate the utility of the framework for explaining national economic performance in varied settings, and indicate interesting directions for future research.

The book's argument thus advances our understanding of growth-rate volatility by specifying the institutional and economic policies that cause, and the mechanism by which they cause, growth-rate volatility, and, thereby, shape national economic performance. Four existing political explanations of growth-rate volatility offer important insights into some of the different roles democracy may play in mitigating volatility. First, Siddharth Chandra and Nita Rudra argue that institutional diversification, which they associate with democracy, leads to less volatile policy outputs through what they call "partisan mutual adjustment" and therefore lower volatility: an institutional-portfolio-diversification argument (Chandra and Rudra 2008). Next, Dani Rodrik (1998b, 2000) argues that democracies exhibit higher levels of social cooperation and compromise in the face of exogenous shocks, which allows them to navigate and ameliorate the effects of these shocks: a constituency-diversification-through-compromise argument. Third, Dennis Quinn and John Woolley argue that, in democracies, risk-averse publics are better able to constrain their more risk-acceptant leaders in democracies from making risky policies, their emphasized source of growth-rate volatility: an-assumed-risk-averse-principal-constrains-an-assumed-risk-acceptant-agent argument (Quinn and Woolley 2001). Finally, Acemoglu *et al.* (2003b) argue that societies in which executives are constrained, again more likely in democracies, have stronger property rights protections and stronger economic institutions, and therefore lower volatility: a constrained-executive argument.

While important, making contributions that have influenced my thinking here, these arguments are limited theoretically because they make strong auxiliary assumptions that may not always hold (Quinn and Woolley) and/or because they do not specify clearly what political institutions should matter for growth-rate volatility (Chandra and Rudra), what aspects or types of democracy best produce the argued effect (Rodrik; Acemoglu *et al.*), or what economic policies are "risky" and volatility-inducing (Chandra and Rudra; Rodrik; Quinn and Woolley). Empirically, the first three studies all use the same Freedom House index of political and civil liberties to measure democracy, preventing one from distinguishing among these three possible mechanisms by which regime type could relate to volatility and from exploring what specific aspects of regime type produce that relationship. Acemoglu *et al.* (2003b) use the Polity measure of "executive constraints," a closer match to their argument, except that we cannot be sure which types of constraints matter, or how this effect differs from the general 'democratic' effect since they do not include a control for the latter. This book aims to advance comparative political economy of national economic performance research by specifying the configuration of government institutions – namely the diffusion of policymaking authority to multiple policymakers accountable to different constituencies – that makes policy change more difficult and policy stability more credible. Further, where policy change is required to deal with economic shocks, diffusion of policymaking authority requires policymakers to compromise with each other if they are to enact policy. Thus, the analysis here encompasses both Chandra and Rudra's (2008) institutional-diversification argument and Rodrik's (2000) social-compromise thesis, clarifying the specific institutional sources of these effects and the mechanisms by which they obtain. Likewise, since separation of powers occurs more commonly in democracies than non-democracies, the framework can also accommodate Quinn and Woolley's (2001) risk-averse-public/risk-acceptant-policymakers argument and Acemoglu *et al.*'s (2003b) constrained-executive argument, again supplying sufficient specificity to compare effects within and across democratic and non-democratic cases. The effects will, for example, neither obtain in all democracies nor fail to obtain in all non-democracies to the same degree because the effects propagate through the nature of the division of policymaking authority and depend on the nature and on the structure and openness of the domestic economy. These more precise theoretical distinctions and comparisons, moreover, enable empirical exploration that can also distinguish between differing arguments for broader correlations of democracy and growth-rate volatility. Finally, unlike the extant theories, which do not explore intermediate connections from government policy to volatility, my theory explicitly links these specific democratic institutions and economic contexts to growth-rate volatility through cross-national savings and investment patterns, and to business decisions to engage in new ventures, so its empirics gain additional leverage explicitly testing that linkage.

Theoretical contributions and policy implications

The argument developed in this book contributes to two longstanding questions in political science. The first of these debates concerns the relationship of the state to society. I incorporate insights from statists and pluralists by suggesting that political scientists can gain from considering how societal interests interact with institutional configurations to enable policy change. Recent political economy of development research on the determinants of cross-national economic growth focuses exclusively on institutional factors (such as democracy), leaving aside questions of societal interests and how political institutions mediate these interests. Indeed, to the extent that societal factions enter such analyses, the goal is to find ways to insulate technocrat-policymakers from the corrupting influence of such special interests. The second theoretical debate to which I contribute concerns the sources of policy credibility. The core argument made here, i.e., that governments can gain credibility via "gridlock," is likely to be controversial given that scholars have argued for some time that such gridlock hinders developing countries' abilities to make needed economic reforms. The conventional wisdom is that economic reforms, such as privatization or liberalization, require "strong" governments with political "will." While this may in fact be true, my consideration of credibility raises the question of why such reforms by "strong" "willful" governments are considered credible by others and suggests insights for thinking about the success and failure of economic reforms as well as the scope of the reforms pursued.

These ideas have important policy implications, especially as they bear on the design of political institutions. For some time now, it has been conventional wisdom to encourage developing countries to bolster judicial independence, and to create independent central banks. These recommendations accord with the core argument of this book, but my research suggests we must go further and encourage developing countries to create political institutions that require the incorporation of diverse interests and societal preferences in the policymaking process. Further, the mechanism via which these interests should be represented is the political party, a political institution that has been ignored in most recent research on economic growth. But, as Samuel Huntington argued in his seminal book, *Political Order in Changing Societies*, political parties play a vital role in channeling public opinion into the policy arena. There exists a heated debate in some circles as to whether ethnic, cultural, and linguistic heterogeneity hinders growth; certainly it might, especially if some groups are excluded from the halls of power and have no opportunities for expressing themselves or for having their preferences reflected in policy. Rather than create strong executives as is being done throughout the developing world (presidential governments are the most frequently created form of new democracy), this book suggests we should heed the sage advice of James Madison in *Federalist 10*: "where there is a consciousness of unjust or dishonorable purposes, communication is always checked by distrust in proportion to the number whose concurrence is necessary"

(Hamilton *et al.* 1987 [1788]). In other words, the original insight of the framers of the US Constitution to require a system of checks and balances were sound, and must be followed as we create new institutions in new democracies. To this I will add one caveat as the book progresses: it is better to have systems that generate coalition governments than those that generate divided government, i.e., to have parliamentary democracies than to have presidential systems. In the former, I shall argue, and the evidence will show, the survival of the government depends on the cooperation of the various members of the coalition, which dynamic enables cooperation over, and the passage of, policies when necessary. In divided presidential systems, by contrast, the executive and legislature survive independently of each other, nullifying incentives for cooperation, and making policy gridlock possible even when it is imperative for the government to act. Such problems are especially likely when political parties are young, and leaders are still developing the rules and norms that will guide their behavior in office.

The next chapter situates this argument in the broader literature about how politics might affect national economic performance, and develops its underlying causal logic in more detail. The chapter concludes by identifying a set of empirically verifiable propositions suggested by the theoretical framework. Chapter 3 takes the main implications about economic growth and volatility to a cross-national time-series data set of all developing countries from 1965 to 2004, and finds strong support in their favor. This chapter also utilizes matching techniques to address concerns of endogeneity. Chapter 4 uses the same cross-national data, as well as a World Bank survey of firms across the world, to test the implied causal mechanisms of the theory. I find that firms located in countries governed by parliamentary coalitions are less likely to perceive policy uncertainty to be a major obstacle to their businesses, and more likely to consider opening a new establishment in the near future. Similarly, such countries generate higher rates of private saving and induce lower levels of capital flight. Taken together, these results suggest that the basic logic of the theory is sound, and bolster confidence in the findings reported in the previous chapter.

Having demonstrated the strength of the argument cross-nationally, Chapter 5 applies the theoretical framework to the Indian case. India is today considered to be one of the world's foremost economic engines, and is increasingly tipped to be an economic superpower in the coming century. This heady optimism is in sharp contrast to the pessimism that characterized most observers of India's "Hindu rate of growth" for the first thirty years after independence. Interestingly, the rapid increase in growth coincides with the fragmentation of the Indian political system and, increasingly, coalition politics. I argue that this is not a coincidence, and utilize variation in business attitudes and coalition governments across India's states to support the claim. Chapter 6 applies the logic to four different cases, demonstrating the flexibility of the argument as it helps explain the persistently high volatility of Brazil, and the comparative economic success of Botswana. The argument also works in developed democracies, as shown by case studies of Spain and Italy in the post-1945 period. The book concludes in Chapter 7 by considering possible extensions of the framework, as well as the theoretical and policy implications of my findings.

2 | Coalition politics and economic development
Theory

Economic growth requires unleashing the productive capacities in society. Modern growth theory suggests that growth is a function of a country's present level of output as well as its long-term growth rate. The latter is what must be manipulated in order to increase a country's economic performance.

So what affects long-term growth?

We can usefully divide the sources of long-term growth into "policy" or "luck" (alternatively, policy or nature). This dichotomy is purely illustrative, of course, but makes clear that a country's growth potential is shaped both by its natural endowments and by decisions by governments and private actors of how best to utilize those endowments.

For instance, natural resource wealth provides countries with a tremendous advantage in terms of stimulating the economy, though the jury is clearly out on whether such resource wealth is a curse or not. The resource curse literature spearheaded by Sachs and Warner and Michael Ross argues that resource wealth can hurt countries, but the tide has begun to turn as others now argue that the key is how governments choose to utilize the wealth. Thus, Goldberg *et al.* (2008) use the case of the United States to show that resource wealth did not harm either political democracy or growth in oil-rich states, just as we know that oil-rich states in the North Sea were able to use their resources to jump-start their economies.[1]

More generically, government policy is important for creating conditions under which private entrepreneurs can thrive. The Washington Consensus recommended a new government that opened the country's economies to international trade and investment, and minimized interference in the economy. A less radical notion of what governments

[1] There exists a separate and vibrant literature on whether resource wealth is good for democracy or causes civil war, but on both of these fronts as well, the debate is ongoing (Ross 2004a, 2004b, 2006).

should do might be that they use their strong "thumbs" to provide public goods such as infrastructure (roads, electricity, water, defense, etc.) that are required for an economy to run successfully.

That is, the role of government in promoting economic growth is thus twofold. First, through its own investment and demand-management policies, it can stimulate economic activity. Second, and more importantly for longer-term growth, government policies must create pro-business environments that encourage private actors to invest scarce resources in future production. In *Stages of Economic Growth*, W.W. Rostow (1971) describes this process almost formulaically: when a country's savings and investment rate exceeds 30 percent of GDP annually, the economy enters what he termed "take-off," a stage that lasts until the savings and investment behavior is normalized and surpluses are regularly reinvested into the economy, which in turn is slowly diversified as successful sectors spread out into previously undeveloped ones. Growth thus occurs when savings and investment grow, and when governments use their increased revenues wisely by developing better public infrastructure that in turn begets more economic activity, so that eventually this process becomes self-sustaining.

For less developed countries, then, growth is about mobilizing capital by (1) convincing domestic actors to forgo present consumption in exchange for future gain and (2) attracting mobile capital from foreign countries to locate within their borders. As capital flows globally have increased exponentially, the latter strategy has become increasingly popular, but the mobility of internal capital is a double-edged sword if investors choose to withdraw their capital and leave. This phenomenon of "hot" money that zips around the world at a moment's notice has received increased attention in the aftermath of the Asian Financial Flu, the Argentine Meltdown of 2002, and various speculative attacks against national currencies. The problem with such capital actually runs deeper, however, because it is less likely to stimulate long-term economic growth anyway. For that, investments must be longer-term and less liquid, which is why getting foreign direct investment can become increasingly important for developing countries' growth strategies (Jensen 2006; Markusen 2001).

To summarize this admittedly brief discussion of the determinants of economic growth literature, economic growth requires two things from governments: (1) smarter choices about what to do with investment, and (2) the ability to attract and stimulate investment. The latter in turn is a function of a government's ability to create a pro-investment environment that investors are confident will last for the duration of their investment, especially since the returns on the investment are delayed. The major concern, therefore, for investors is that governments may renege on promises made or that policy environments may change after their investments are made but before the returns are realized. The point, that the credibility of policy promises matters as much as the content of the policy, is important, and I will return to it below. For now, however, let's consider what other scholars have found to explain why some governments are better able to generate economic growth.

Politics of growth

Why are some governments able to deliver better economic performance than others? Existing arguments focus on the ability and willingness of governments to provide pro-growth policies – typically understood as pro-business or pro-market, though these are certainly not the same thing. While all explanations typically have elements of both, I would divide existing political explanations of growth according to their relative emphasis on the role of political agency versus the incentives created by formal political institutions.

Political agency

Agency-based explanations tend to be made by those who take a more historical-sociological view of things, and who are interested in analyzing the growth trajectories of individual countries. Such approaches seek to identify critical junctures in policymaking that explain the adoption of economic reform policies, or, alternatively, that derail positive economic growth. Likewise, such analyses identify the particular actors involved in critical decisions and describe why they implemented the policies they did, as well as the social conditions of coalition that enabled them to do so.

Agency-based explanations tend to share four important theoretical commonalities:

1. They recognize and emphasize the agency of political elites in choosing specific policy directions, and the role these key individuals play

in building political consensus around the policies, as well as in quelling opposition to such policies.

2. The role of "political will" is central to such explanation. Governmental leaders here are faced with a menu of policy choices, some less palatable than others. Economic growth requires encouraging private actors to defer consumption and make sacrifices in the present. Such "forced" saving historically has been encouraged by reducing the choice of goods available to consumers, which is hardly popular politically. Additionally, business investment is risky, as investors are uncertain about future prospects. Governments must buy off their doubts by providing present benefits that make the risk more palatable. One way in which this is done is by reducing tax burdens on business, but this in turn reduces revenues for the state and therefore the fiscal space from which public programs are funded, leading to periods of unpopular austerity. Finally, to increase efficiency, governments must often reduce subsidies to parastatals and divest themselves of state-owned enterprises, both of which involve angering powerful vested interests. Only strong governments willing to incur short-term political costs can make such reforms possible.

3. The political costs involved in the reform process raise a third feature of politics common to societal explanations: the importance of building pro-growth and pro-reform societal coalitions. Strong political leaders are thought to forge national consensus behind which citizens rally and for which private actors are willing to make sacrifices for the national good. Nation-building thus becomes part of the overall development process.

4. A final common feature of these arguments is often more implicit: there exists a "right" set of pre-growth policies at the center of the pro-economic growth puzzle, and the only question is whether leaders are willing to enact them. Because these policies are often painful in the short run, the argument is that strong leaders are required in developing countries to enact a form of tough love for their countries.

Explanations with these characteristics were commonly made to explain the rapid growth of the East Asian Newly Industrializing Countries in the 1960s, 1970s, and 1980s (World Bank 1993). Prominent contributions were made by scholars like Alice Amsden

(1989), Stephan Haggard (1990), and Chalmers Johnson (1982). More recently, two scholars have reinvigorated such theorizing with important books.

Atul Kohli's *State-Directed Development: Political Power and Industrialization in the Global Periphery* (2004) argues that industrialization is the *sine qua non* of economic development today, just as it has been historically. But industrialization can be a difficult process, requiring the vast mobilization of societal capital and the mobilization of an industrial labor pool. Using the cases of Korea, Brazil, India, and Nigeria, Kohli states that the "creation of effective states within the developing world has generally preceded the emergence of industrializing economies" (2004: 2). The key is the organization of state power and the direction of this power for the purposes of economic/industrial development. Where leaders were able to mobilize such power, growth resulted. Kohli identifies three ideal types of states in the developing world: (1) cohesive-capitalist, (2) fragmented-multiclass, and (3) neo-patrimonial. Of these, cohesive-capitalist states were most effective in jump-starting economies because of a consensus within the state regarding its goals and an agreement over the course to be pursued. On the other hand, states like India, which had fragmented multiclass coalitions at the helm of power, were less capable of forging consensus and, as a result, growth limped along as leaders avoided the hard decisions required to unshackle India's economic potential. Finally, neo-patrimonial states, such as Nigeria, were least effective "because both public goals and capacities to pursue specific tasks in these settings have repeatedly been undermined by personal and narrow group interests" (Kohli 2004: 9).

A similar analysis is provided by Vivek Chibber's *Locked in Place: State-Building and Late Industrialization in India.* Chibber (2003) argues that the key to successful growth is the outcome of the struggle for power between the state and capitalists in society. Where this struggle results in the state power being controlled by pro-capitalist interests, industrialization can ensue, but where the central players on each side are unable to agree on a plan for industrialization, as Chibber argues was the case in post-independence India, industrialization was hampered and the economy was constrained.

Agency-based explanations are especially useful for overcoming an institutional determinism that implies countries' economic performances are driven solely by the formal rules governing politics. Rather, these analyses make clear that leaders require coalitions within society to empower them to act, and that these coalitions are often created by artful political maneuvering. In the absence of such coalitions, politicians rarely have any incentive to act decisively to provide pro-growth economic policy, especially since such policies are often accompanied by costs to established interests in society. Yet, while extremely valuable, such arguments have two major limitations that restrict their utility for constructing a general political theory of growth. First, the emphasis on the agency of political elites and the importance of political will tends to remain silent on why and when leaders decide to use their power for "good," rather than to steal from the state's coffers. Second, and relatedly, such theories are hard pushed to make a priori predictions about the direction a country will take: how might one identify when a leader will use state power and national fervor to stimulate economic growth as happened in the East Asian states, rather than to pillage the economy for private gain as tragically occurred in Zaire or Zimbabwe? Indeed, if one considers lessons learned from the study of Africa's lack of economic progress over the past fifty years, one is hardly likely to conclude that the problem was that leaders had too little power or that political and economic elites were unable to agree with one another (Bardhan 2006, 2009). Rather, the lesson appears to be that these leaders were in fact too unconstrained and faced too few checks on the arbitrary use of power.

Institutions

A second analytical approach to understanding the politics of growth helps partially to remedy this weakness of agency-based explanations by focusing on the "structure" of political institutions that shapes the incentives for leaders to do the right thing. This literature tends to be more "economic" and "rationalist" in its understanding of the policymaking process. Here, leaders are rational actors who seek to maximize their power – whether as a means to policy, or for private gain, or as an end in itself – and respond to the incentives generated by the political institutions and context within which they operate. I do not view such "institutional" explanations as contrary to the more sociological/agency-based explanations described above, but rather argue that they are potentially complementary if used to identify whether the types of political institutions required to channel their leaders' agency for productive purposes are conducive to building strong pro-growth societal coalition.

A seminal statement of this argument is found in Robert Bates's *Markets and States in Tropical Africa* (1981). Bates examines the puzzle of urban bias in policymaking in Uganda. Why would national leaders favor urban actors in largely rural states? Bates argues that the close proximity of urban dwellers to the halls of power makes their concern more salient to politicians. In addition, industrial policy is largely pro-urban and requires a cheap and cooperative labor pool. One way to appease labor is by reducing the cost of food, which governments do by subsidizing farmers and placing price controls on so-called essential good commodities. Ashutosh Varshney, in *Democracy, Development and the Countryside: Urban-Rural Struggles in India* (1998), applies this insight to India with similar results: previously "strange" policies become explicable when one considers more fully the incentives leaders face. The issue then is: what sorts of political institutions create incentives for leaders to promote economic growth?

Posing the question thusly has led to the proliferation of an extensive research program seeking to link democratic institutions to better economic performance. Scholars in this tradition seek to (1) identify the institutional differences between democracies and non-democracies which might shape leaders' incentives differently, and to constrain leaders' excesses differently, and (2) shape national economic performance differently. Similar literatures have sprung up in other subfields of political science seeking to explain cross-national variation in everything from other aspects of development such as literacy and malnutrition (Ross 2006) to spending priorities (Bueno de Mesquita *et al.* 2001; Lake and Baum 2001) to propensity to fight wars (Russett and Oneal 2001). Given this proliferation of research on democracy's alleged effects, it's perhaps no surprise that a variety of causal mechanisms have been posited by scholars, each emphasizing different features of democratic rule.

The simplest and most common claim is that democratically elected leaders are held accountable for policies and policy performance in a way that non-democratic deciders simply are not. Elections, Przeworski *et al.* (2000) succinctly stated, are the "sine qua non of democracy." Elections are certainly not the only institutional feature of democracy, nor do elections themselves make for a good or effective democracy, but it is certainly true that we cannot imagine a democracy in which elections were not held at regular intervals to choose national leaders. What effect might this have on economic performance? The standard argument is that because leaders' ability to retain power is contingent on voters' approval, leaders work harder to satisfy voters. Assuming plausibly that voters prefer good economic growth to poor economic performance, and that they punish poor-performing leaders at subsequent elections, the election mechanism implies that, in democracies, leaders should work harder to deliver economic growth. A related argument was made recently by Quinn and Woolley (2001) to explain lower growth-rate volatility in democracies. Leaders, they posit, are more risk-acceptant than the median citizen; where leaders are unconstrained by voters via elections, leaders are free to pursue riskier policies and therefore non-democracies experience more volatility. In democracies, however, elections allow risk-averse voters to select less risk-acceptant leaders in the first place and credibly to signal that they will punish risky economic policymaking. Elections in this argument are the key to better and more stable economic growth.

Elections, others argue, are made meaningful by the presence of political competition for office. If leaders do not face competition for office, then voters have no options from which to choose at elections, so the voting mechanism loses its bite. Democratic systems allow greater competition for office than non-democracies (1) by placing few barriers to entry into the political arena; (2) by allowing freer and fairer elections, giving opponents a chance to win; (3) by permitting free media, which allows opponents to spread their message; and (4) by promoting and allowing a vibrant civic life wherein people may form associations that serve as the foundation for political opposition to elites. Irrespective of which of these particular mechanisms a scholar endorses, the key point is that elections in democracies are more likely to have genuine competition, and a credible risk of losing power for the incumbent.[2]

The existence of political competition is thought to have at least three effects on policymaking in democracies. First, because citizens care about economic performance, contenders for office compete on their records for providing better economic performance. This puts

---

[2] Przeworski *et al.* (2000) call this an alternation rule and only regard a country as a democracy once an election results in a change in power.

a premium on "good" policymaking. Second, because citizens abhor recessions and crises, leaders are less likely to take policy risks and therefore avoid volatility (Quinn and Woolley 2001). Third, political competition constrains leaders' ability to use public revenues for private gain and places a premium on the provision of public services such as education and health care, which in turn are thought to encourage growth (Lake and Baum 2001).

A third mechanism, offered by Rodrik (2000), highlights democracy's superior ability to forge social compromise in the face of economic shocks. Rodrik argues that democratic norms encourage leaders to cooperate to deal with economic difficulties, which makes policy solutions easier to forge. This theme of democratic compromise is echoed by others, and indeed my own argument will develop these ideas further, so it's worth considering the other forms the arguments take.

For instance, George Tsebelis's seminal work on *Veto Players* has been used to argue that democracies are more likely to have checks and balances on power, making policy change harder (Tsebelis 1995, 1999, 2002). Siddharth Chandra and Nita Rudra (2008) adopt a "portfolio diversification" model of political institutions to argue that democracies – states with a greater diversity of institutions – should experience more stable growth. Such explanations do not necessarily specify the particular institutions responsible for forging compromise or the causal mechanisms linking policy-compromise to stability, but their overall insight is important: to the extent that democracies permit opposition to voice its opinions and require incumbents to respond to such opposition, democratic policymaking should be more moderate (i.e., move towards the center of the ideological space) than in non-democracies where leaders are relatively unconstrained and can do as they wish.[3]

A fourth causal mechanism linking democracy to superior national economic performance was proffered more recently by Bueno de Mesquita *et al.* In *Logic of Political Survival*, these scholars argue that the main institutional difference between types of governments is the size of the eligible population (which they term "selectorate") required to support the leader for her to retain office (i.e., how large must the

---

[3] Joseph Wright (2008) argues that authoritarian leaders can and do create "binding legislatures" which enable them to claim constraints credibly. I explore this idea below.

"winning coalition" be?). For societies where the necessary winning coalition is large (e.g., in democracies, where it is some kind of majority of the voting-eligible population) leaders emphasize the provision of public goods over private goods to solidify support. Further, if the winning coalition is small, as in dictatorships, private goods are provided to pay off the small group of loyal cronies whose support is required for the dictatorship to maintain power. The public good suffers as a result. Economic growth is the ultimate public good that leaders can provide those in the selectorate, which leads Bueno de Mesquita *et al.* (2003) to expect states with larger winning coalitions to emphasize economic growth more.

At least three other sets of arguments exist in the literature linking democracy to economic growth. These focus mainly on the "indirect" effect on growth via democracy. That is, democracies are thought by these scholars not necessarily to affect "growth" directly, but through the policy choices they make. Arguably the most famous of such arguments has been made in multiple settings by North and Weingast (1989). North and Weingast, whether writing alone, with each other, or with other collaborators, emphasize the centrality of governments' ability to commit credibly to maintaining property rights in order to stimulate economic growth.[4] Governments have an incentive to promise property rights to encourage investment, but once the investment has been made, governments are tempted to renege and keep the investments for themselves. Knowing this, investors choose not to invest unless the promise to honor property rights is considered credible. The question for governments is how they might constrain themselves; democratic political competition is thought to be one such mechanism. Because the loss of investment due to a broken promise would hurt economic growth and result in punishment at the polls,

---

[4] The importance of property rights for economic development is well-developed in the political economy literature. Well-developed property rights reduce transaction costs of market exchange, leading more actors to enter into transactions as well as into larger transactions. Credible property rights encourage investors to incur risk costs in the present in exchange for future gain, an intertemporal trade that would be unappetizing if the investor feared the loss of her property rights in the interim. Interested readers can read more about why property rights are crucial for growth in North (1981, 1990, 1994, 2005) and North and Thomas (1973). Here, my point is simply that authors have identified a strong and robust correlation between democratic political institutions and the enforcement of property rights.

leaders of democracies are expected to provide stronger property rights than those of non-democracies, and consequently to enjoy higher economic growth.[5]

Another indirect mechanism emphasizes democracies' higher propensity to invest in the education and health care of their citizens, thereby increasing the stock of human capital in society, and through it the state of economic growth, since workers with higher human capital are more productive and because investors are attracted to such higher-skilled, more productive workers (Barro 1991; Lucas 1988). Matthew Baum and David Lake make such an argument explicitly in "The Political Economy of Growth: Democracy and Human Capital." Baum and Lake (2003) conceive of governments as firms who must decide how much of public goods to produce and how much of their revenues to keep for private profit or for rewarding a narrow group of supporters. Where leaders face no competition for office, they can behave as monopolists and reduce the provision of public goods while retaining what they consider their share of the revenues. Political competition in democracies, however, tempers these monopolistic tendencies of governments and so they spend more on public goods such as education and health care. Bueno de Mesquita *et al.* (2003) reach the same conclusion but by a different mechanism. Because leaders in democracies must cater to large winning coalitions, they emphasize public services.[6] And several scholars have argued that higher responsiveness to public desires for government services due to the election-accountability mechanism should lead to greater provision of education in democracies. Finally, Peter Lindert (2004) argues that an educated population is likely to be more threatening to autocratic leaders than to their democratic counterparts.

Irrespective of which of these mechanisms linking democracy to increased education one finds most convincing, the predictions of each are clear: democracies should do better at educating their citizens, and therefore reap the benefits of higher economic growth via increased human capital. Similar predictions occur when scholars link democracy to greater transparency of public policy or to more vigorous competition over ideas. To the extent that such factors – education,

[5] A similar argument is sometimes made regarding the rule of law.
[6] With Pradeep Chhibber, I apply a variety of this argument to explain variation in the provision of public services across the Indian states (Chhibber and Nooruddin 2004).

transparency, intellectual freedom – form desiderata for economic growth, the conclusion from such studies is that democracy's effect on growth is indirect and occurs through the channel of its effect on these factors. This indeed is the conclusion of a recent meta-analysis of eighty-four published studies on democracy and growth conducted by Doucouliagos and Ulubasoglu (2008).

For all the persuasiveness of the various arguments reviewed above, the debate over whether democracy is good for growth is far from settled. In fact, several of these pro-democracy arguments have an "evil twin" suggesting just the opposite.

Accountability-via-election, rather than leading to an emphasis on growth and risk-aversion, might have several negative effects. Elections shorten leaders' time horizons, as they must deliver results prior to the next election in order to be re-elected. This creates a disincentive to engage in long-term planning where the fruits of the policy might not be felt for several years. This is especially true if the policies required are likely to have costs in the interim period. To the extent that many of the economic reforms endorsed by economists over the past forty years carried with them severe dislocation costs, it's hardly surprising that leaders were reluctant to implement such programs unilaterally. Vreeland (2003) leverages this fact to suggest that leaders use the International Monetary Fund as a shield behind which to hide while pushing through domestically unpopular "shock therapy" or "austerity" reform packages. And these were the leaders with sufficient "political will" to want to reform their economies in spite of the costs. Those with weaker wills, or those reliant on support from societal groups opposed to reforms, were considerably less inclined to engage in such painful reforms, even if it meant sacrificing some potential growth in the long run. Leaders whose survival in office depends not on popular support but on a small elite group are more insulated from such backlash and so more free to engage in traumatic surgery on their ailing economies.[7] Why some non-democratic leaders use this insulation to do so – as happened in South Korea and Singapore – rather than to enrich themselves their supporters – as in Zaire – is left unanswered by such institutional explanations.

[7] Susan Stokes uses this medical metaphor in her book *Mandates and Democracy: Neoliberalism by Surprise in Latin America* (2001).

Another objection to pro-democracy arguments takes issue with the utility of the election mechanism as an instrument to hold leaders accountable for growth. Voters seek a multitude of goods from their governments, and growth is clearly one such good. But the pro-democracy arguments imply, via their emphasis of the median voter's preferences, that it is national growth that is most relevant. If, however, politics are more fractionalized and organized along group lines, political competition might result in leaders being more focused on the interests of their group relative to a more abstract "conception" of the "national interest." By this account, competition for office can have at least three negative effects. First, powerful opposition or vested interests can derail the reform process and, to the extent that getting the "right" policies in place matters, make growth less likely. Therefore, institutions that promote the fragmentation of policymaking authority (e.g., Kohlis's fragmented multiclass coalition in India) should result in slower growth. Mancur Olson articulated this position slightly differently in his seminal *Rise and Decline of Nations*. Olson (1982) argued that established democracies experience an ossification of the policymaking process as societal groups that successfully overcome their collective action problems get organized and lobby the government. The stronger such groups are, the more likely they can block policy changes with which they disagree, and since such interest groups are more likely to have free rein in democracies, Olson's theory predicts a slowdown in growth in such countries over time. More recently, Sean Ehrlich (2007) builds on this insight to suggest that among the developed, OECD states, the proliferation of "access points" (i.e., the government actors relevant to the policy) in trade policymaking has enabled societal groups to lobby successfully for additional protection. And anecdotal evidence abounds of reforms thwarted by powerful vested interests. From the perspective of such work, too much opposition can be disruptive to the growth endeavor.[8]

Pushing beyond regime type

In spite of considerable effort in developing compelling theoretical arguments linking democracy to better national economic performance

---

[8] Rock evaluates the hypothesis that democracy has slowed growth in Asia, and finds no evidence in its favor. In fact, his data show that "democracy causes growth and investment to rise" (2009: 941).

(whether positively or negatively), empirical evidence supporting any of these claims has been difficult to come by. Przeworski and Limongi (1993) illustrate this point persuasively in their review of extant literature, while their seminal contribution, co-authored with Michael Alvarez and José Cheibub, in *Democracy and Development* (2000) solidifies the point that relationships between democracy and development are spurious unless one can adequately account for the processes by which regimes survive at different levels of development. Doucouliagos and Ulubasoglu (2008) echo this pessimistic conclusion in a meta-analysis of eighty-four studies of democracy's effect on economic growth. They conclude that democracy has no clear effect on growth, though it might have some indirect and long-term effects via its provision of public services such as education and health care (much like the Lake and Baum argument discussed earlier). My own review of the past decade's growth literature reveals the same pattern. I surveyed 235 articles published between 1991 and 2008 in economics, political science, and sociology journals (see Appendix A). Political-institutional variables are included mainly in the political science articles, and most often ignored by economists. Most attention is paid to qualities of "governance" based typically on expert assessments, and to the prevalence of elections (i.e., democracy) as a way of choosing leaders. Results for the democracy variables are mixed at best.

Perhaps even more troubling than the lack of consistent evidence linking democracy and growth is the growing skepticism about two core claims that undergird the entire literature. First, and more importantly, is the proposition that democracies choose different policies than non-democracies (if policies are the source of growth, then differences in growth by regime type must occur because different regime types adopt different policies). Mulligan *et al.* (2004) study 142 developing countries between 1960 and 1990, and consider an array of possible policy variables that theory might lead us to expect should vary by regime type, but irrespective of whether they consider spending or tax policies, no differences by regime type emerge. My own research is consistent with this claim. In a study of the impact of International Monetary Fund programs on domestic social spending, Joel Simmons and I find that observed differences in policy between democracies and non-democracies diminish significantly in the presence of IMF programs, leading one to wonder whether the differences we observe "in good times" (i.e., when IMF programs are not necessary) have more to do with differences in budget constraints across regime types (say, because democracies are better at raising revenues as in Levi's work (1988) or at raising debt as argued by Schultz and Weingast, as well as David Stasavage (2003)) than with fundamental differences in the ability or incentives of democratic leaders to provide public goods (Nooruddin and Simmons 2006).

The second claim that requires rethinking is that we know which policies are required to generate economic growth. Indeed a skeptical rereading of the democracy-growth literature reveals a common formula: either we argue that democratic institutions create the right incentives for leaders to enact pro-growth policies or we argue that "too much democracy" hinders governments' ability to enact pro-growth policies. Either way, the implicit notion is that we know what constitutes a pro-growth policy, yet this is, at best, a contested assumption. Models of economic growth are notoriously fragile as Xavier Sala-i-Martin (1997) famously demonstrated in his extreme bounds exercise which involved estimating two million regression models using a set of sixty-two possible covariates of growth. Sala-i-Martin found only seven economic covariates of growth that were robust to model specification, leaving aside the many other problems that could befall a statistical model.[9] Economists Charles Kenny and David Williams build on this point to argue that we actually know little about what governments can or should do to foster economic growth (2001). Acemoglu *et al.* (2003b), Easterly (2005), and Fatas and Mihov (2005) show that policies play little role in fostering economic growth once institutions are included in the model. Biglaiser and DeRouen (2006) find that economic reforms are not essential for attracting FDI since countries that implement reforms are no more likely to attract FDI than those that do not.

Why should this be the case? After all, economic theories of growth have grown remarkably sophisticated in recent years; so why can't we

---

[9] The seven, with the direction of their effect on growth provided in parentheses, are (1) real exchange rate distortions (-); (2) standard deviation of the black market premium (-); (3) equipment investment (+); (4) non-equipment investment (+); (5) fraction of primary products in total exports (-); (6) fraction of GDP in mining (+); and (7) openness (+). He also identifies fifteen other correlates of growth that have to do with a country's region, culture, history, and political situation. See Levine and Renelt (1992) and Burkhart and Lewis-Beck (1994) for related exercises.

explain cross-national growth patterns any better? Three explanations
are most plausible to my mind. First is that we have been searching
too hard for a single policy solution to what is essentially a complex
context-conditional problem. This implies that even if we could agree
on a set of policies that were pro-growth, its implementation would at
best be a necessary, but not a sufficient, condition for growth. Kohli
articulates this critique well: "The impact of the same policy applied
in two different settings may vary because of the contextual differences, some of the more obvious being varying global conditions and
different initial conditions of the economy" Kohli (2004: 13). Lee and
Kim (2009) develop this idea to show that policies and institutions
matter differently for different groups of countries depending on the
income class in which they fall; importantly, at low levels of income,
institutions matter more.

Taken seriously, this critique suggests that we should not be looking for a "one size fits all" solution but rather tailoring solutions
to the specific needs and concerns of each state. Indeed this goal is
what guides the recent work of Harvard economist Dani Rodrik. In
In Search of Prosperity (2003b), Rodrik and a team of eminent scholars conduct "analytic narratives" of eight countries to identify what
made their quest for growth successful or not, thereby taking seriously
Robert Bates's reminder that development is inherently a dynamic process within a single country which is easily missed when we focus
only on explaining varying levels of growth across countries (2001),
a theme further developed in Rodrik's latest book *One Economics,
Many Recipes* (2007).[10]

A second explanation for the relative lack of success of our theorizing is the centrality of the state in our explanations. Governments
utilizing the state's power are thought to be the main force behind economic growth. Their success or failure in enacting the correct set of
policies therefore becomes the primary explanation for good or bad
growth. We have long recognized the power of the market to unleash
or deter the productive energies of private actors, yet private actors are
marginalized in recent theories, which is a lost opportunity. Our comparative advantage as political scientists is politics, and I certainly do
not intend to develop a theory of private entrepreneurial activity. But

[10] It's perhaps no coincidence that Bates was one of the early advocates of "analytic
narratives" or that he is a contributor to Rodrik's volume.

an inescapable fact is that governments and businesses are intimately connected in the quest for growth. One way of thinking of this is to see business as the *object* of the pro-growth policies recommended by international financial institutions and economists, and enacted or not by governments. As such, a pro-growth policy is one that encourages and enables private actors to invest in the economy, make profits, and plough returns back into the economy in a search for further profit. Considered from this perspective, the question thus becomes what sort of political institutions are most likely to create pro-business economic policies.

Surprisingly, we do not have much of an answer to this question with respect to the developing world. Consider one example: Dani Rodrik and Arvind Subramanian explain India's rapid growth over the past twenty years as the result of a shift in then-Prime Minister Rajiv Gandhi's perspective in the late 1980s, in the years immediately preceding his assassination. Rajiv Gandhi, they maintain, increasingly came to adopt a pro-business mentality and therefore to push for policies favorable to private economic activity (Rodrik and Subramanian 2004).

But here is the question: why did private economic actors believe this sudden change of heart? Given the fragmentation of the Indian political system, ruling governments in Delhi have rarely enjoyed anything resembling a coherent majority, let alone a permanent majority of the kind that would predict long-term stability of a painful economic reform strategy. Indeed, in our emphasis on the content of policy (i.e., whether it is pro-growth or not), we too often ignore the fact that policy uncertainty is often as important – if not more so – to private business. Fatas and Mihov (2005) demonstrate this fairly conclusively in a recent paper, finding that while policies themselves have little impact on economic development once institutions are accounted for, policy volatility "exerts a strong and direct negative impact on growth." Michael Bechtel and Roland Füss (2008) use stock-market data from Germany to demonstrate investors' preferences for lower policy uncertainty, and Witold Henisz has demonstrated conclusively that constraints against policy change encourage investment and economic growth (Henisz 2000, 2002). Nathan Jensen's (2006) research on the determinants of foreign direct investment to developing countries finds that democratic governments are better able to attract FDI, which he interprets as the result of the greater checks and balances in democracies that reduce policy uncertainty by making policy change less likely.

Thinking about investors' preferences for long-term policy stability (certainty) as theoretically separable from the content of that policy provides additional analytic leverage on the question of why some countries succeed in their economic development goals while others fail: even if governments promise the most pro-growth policies possible (assuming again that we know and agree on what these are), investors might stay away if the policy promises are considered incredible. This insight – that governments face an inescapable credible commitment problem in dealing with private economic actors – is well-established in the political economy literature.[11] The problem stems from a core feature of the government – business interaction: asymmetric information in the bargaining process. That is, investors do not, and cannot, know if governments are sincere in their promises. Prior to making their investments, businesses possess the upper-hand in bargaining with governments as the latter seek to attract their investments. But once the investments have been made, the advantage shifts to the government who can renegotiate the basic terms of the original bargain knowing that businesses have incurred sunk costs that are at least partly irreversible and which make them unlikely to want to leave.[12] Recognizing this, investors avoid making the investments they might otherwise have chosen.[13] Of course, governments do not renege on commitments lightly and businesses know that. A government with a long time horizon would hesitate to develop a reputation for expropriating private investments because it would make it near-impossible to attract future investment.

The risk of outright expropriation, while still real, is nevertheless a reasonably rare occurrence in today's world. More insidious are

[11] Readers interested in a more technical treatment of these issues should begin with the seminal work of Finn Kydland and Edward Prescott (1977).

[12] Raymond Vernon (1980) referred to this as the "obsolescing bargain." Joshua Aizenman has written extensively about irreversible investment (Aizenman and Marion 1993, 1999). See also Lucas and Prescott (1971).

[13] Note that this is not the same as saying that investors will *not* invest. In a risk-return trade-off, investors will still enter if the expected returns outweigh the risks. But for increased risk the desired rate of return to make the investment worthwhile also increases, thereby crowding out all the investments below that return-rate but that would have been viable had the risk been lower. I develop this insight more fully below. See Wong (2010).

the more normal changes to policies – a "creeping" appropriation – governing aspects of doing business such as tax rates and policies, labor laws, environmental regulations, tariff rates, infrastructure development, and the host of other business-relevant issues that form the daily work of government. These after all are what we mean when we discuss pro-growth policy.[14] Yet governments have an incentive to change their minds on policies, even if they were quite sincere at the time of their original promises. As conditions change, leaders might need to reoptimize (or recalibrate) their policies to adjust to new realities. Thus, a presidential candidate who promises "No new taxes" might nevertheless raise taxes once in office in an attempt to pull out of a recession. Or leaders might reconsider the political wisdom of free trade policies if a visible and organized group in society is hurt by increased import competition. Or an anti-regulation government might nevertheless feel compelled to introduce new regulations in the aftermath of a high-profile environmental disaster or the near-meltdown of the financial system due to a mortgage crisis brought on by banking practices. In all these cases, the key is that the government could have been perfectly sincere in its original statements, but the changing political climate necessitated new policy directions that are deviations from the original conditions promised to and anticipated by business. This too forms a real risk to business and a principal argument of this book is that businesses consider the risk of large policy shifts in deciding whether and how to invest.

These two perspectives on the sources of credible commitment difficulties – the obsolescing bargain of Raymond Vernon or the time-consistency or reoptimization problem of Finn Kydland and Edward Prescott, or Guillermo Calvo – have clear implications for our expectations of how different political institutions might affect economic activity. A focus on expropriation risks might imply that authoritarian governments are a large risk because of a relative absence of audience costs or checks and balances on their behavior. But, if we consider the possibility of changes in policy in response to changing political conditions, then it appears democracies might have a harder time keeping their promises given their greater sensitivity to shifts in public preferences. Additionally, democracies are characterized by the presence of

---

[14] The World Bank issues an annual *Doing Business* report in which it ranks countries on the basis of how easy it is to do business there.

institutionalized mechanisms of alternation of parties and leaders in office. Parties compete on the basis of their differences in economic policy (among other differences, of course), but this means that part of doing business in democracies is accepting the possibility of the next election bringing a suspected less business-friendly government to power (think Hugo Chávez in Venezuela or Evo Morales in Bolivia, both of whom were popularly elected in democratic elections and have since adopted arguably anti-business policy stances). Again, as in the earlier discussion of regime type and economic growth, a facile distinction between democracies and non-democracies does not seem sufficient. The principal goal of this book, therefore, is to complicate our understanding of how political institutions might facilitate governments' ability to make credible commitments to long-term policy stability, allowing them to attract and sustain stable patterns of economic activity that in turn generate stable and high economic growth.

Credible constraints: an institutional theory of national economic performance

The preceding discussion yields two main insights. The politics of growth, I argue, involves two things: (1) making pro-investor and pro-growth policies, and (2) convincing investors that such policy commitments are credible. Both are important, but, if anything, recent research might suggest our earlier emphasis on the content of policy has been overstated and the importance of policy uncertainty has been comparatively underemphasized. To some extent, I am content to treat the debate over the relative importance of content versus uncertainty as an empirical matter, but the key point I wish to stress is that thinking of credibility of policy commitments suggests that explanations that simply focus on "political will," "strong leaders," "ideas," and the like are simply insufficient unless they are accompanied by a theory of why economic actors deem the promises made by strong, politically willful leaders credible. Likewise, distinctions between democracies and non-democracies also do not suffice as explanations of credibility because both regime types face unique challenges to their ability to maintain commitments (an absence of checks and balances in non-democracies versus party alternation and re-election-induced defection in democracies).

One way institutions matter for national economic performance, I argue, is by enabling governments to signal to economic actors about the content and direction (i.e., the likelihood of change, as well as the content of that change) of future policy. In particular, institutional configurations that enable governments to commit credibly to future policy stability help them attract investment and therefore to generate improved economic performance. In this framework, policy content might matter, but only if investors believe that the "good" policies will continue into the future.

For improved economic performance, one wants governments with the incentives and ability to initiate pro-growth policies while being moderated and checked by institutions that provide credible constraints against arbitrary and drastic policy change. Specifically, I argue, governments in which policymaking authority is dispersed across multiple actors, each accountable to different societal constituencies, are better able to commit credibly to long-term policy stability, which, in turn, increases certainty for economic actors, leading them to choose higher and more stable forms of investment, leading to stable economic growth. Explaining the institutional sources of such constraints is the goal of this section.

Why are some governments considered more credible than others? Rather than rely on subjective evaluations of credibility, I prefer instead to try to identify the institutional bases of credibility. Further, since I am interested in policy certainty perceived by economic actors, I have argued that institutions that constrain policy change are most likely to bolster credibility. What sorts of institutions might serve this function? Due to the obvious importance of questions of credibility to understanding investor behavior, scholars have expended some time and energy formulating answers.[15] The basic conclusions of such research are as follows.

First, since governments' promises not to change direction are inherently incredible, one possibility is to delegate authority for policymaking to "independent" bureaucracies with well-defined preferences for particular types of policies. Consider two common examples of how this strategy is employed in practice:

1. Governments wish to convince investors of their commitment to maintaining low levels of inflation. Therefore, they delegate the

---

[15] See Borner *et al.* (1995) and Brunetti (1998) for a thorough introduction to the policy credibility literature.

making of monetary policy to independent central banks governed by bankers with well-known anti-inflationary bona fides (Cukierman *et al.* 1992).

2. To convince business that their property rights will be maintained, governments create judiciaries that are independent of political interference (by giving judges life tenure, for example) and invested with the ability to exercise judicial review of legislative decisions (Jorgensen 2006).

Second, and building on the delegation-to-independent-agent logic, a government might impose discipline on itself by entering into conditional-lending agreements with international financial institutions such as the International Monetary Fund or the World Bank. Here again the idea is to take policymaking discretion out of the hands of self-interested governments by publicly agreeing to follow a set of conservative economic policies. To borrow the title of an important recent book on this topic, here the IFIs "lend credibility" to the governments with whom they enter Structural Adjustment Programs (Stone 2002).[16]

Third, returning to the domestic arena, governments might enhance their credibility by making themselves accountable to another party for their performance in office. This is an argument we have seen before, and suggests that democratically elected leaders can appeal to the fact that they would be punished for defecting from earlier publicly made promises. In this formulation, elections are a source of credibility as they impose "audience costs" on leaders. Kenneth Schultz and Barry Weingast refer to this as the "democratic advantage" and argue that it allows democratic states to raise more international capital and therefore to enjoy a financial edge over their non-democratic counterparts who have a harder time convincing potential lenders of their intent to honor their debts (because they face fewer audience costs for reneging) (see Schultz and Weingast 2003).

Finally, building on the seminal work of George Tsebelis, scholars now point to the role separation-of-powers institutions (or

---

[16] Jensen (2004), however, finds that "countries that sign IMF agreements, ceteris paribus, attract 25% less FDI inflows than countries not under IMF agreements." See Vreeland (2003) and Nooruddin and Simmons (2006) for similarly pessimistic conclusions about the IMF's effects in developing countries.

veto players) might play in bolstering the credibility of government promises. Barry Weingast and Douglass North develop an early version of this argument in their explanation of England's Glorious Revolution of 1688 in which the English sovereign, James II, was able to convince the nobility to contribute to his war coffers only after agreeing to grant Parliament the ability to check his arbitrary power. A more modern articulation of this idea can be found in the *Federalist Papers*, wherein the Federalists argue for the creation of a system of checks and balances against the executive. There are two sources of these checks and balances arising from separation of powers.

In a purely institutional version of the separation-of-powers story, the checks and balances work because the actors in the different parts of government represent different geographic constituencies and therefore have different preferences over policy. Thus, to use the United States as an example, the President represents a national constituency; Senators represent their states' interests; and members of Congress represent the even more narrowly defined interests of their district. Thus, even if all chambers of the US system are controlled by the same political party, the separation-of-powers system is thought to work on account of this separation of geographic constituencies.

Another instance of such a geographic veto player is the creation of a federal structure of government where powers are delegated from the center to local governments. Here again the fact that all levels of government might be controlled by the same political party is less relevant than the fact that leaders at different levels represent different geographic constituencies. Jensen and McGillivray (2005) exploit this fact to examine the effect of federal governments on multinational investors, finding that federal structures have an especially large effect on FDI inflows in non-democratic countries, where credibility is in short supply otherwise.

An alternative to the purely geographic or institutional veto players just discussed is the partisan veto player, which emerges as the result of the political process. Voters choose political parties to represent them, and parties compete on the basis of different agendas. When different parties capture different parts of the policymaking process, the fact that their preferences over policy diverge provides a "partisan" check and balance on policy creation. In presidential systems, this occurs when a candidate of one party captures the presidency (executive office), a condition typically called "divided government." In parliamentary systems, where the executive and legislative branches are fused, a parallel situation arises when no single party captures a pure majority of the seats in parliament. Then the party winning a plurality of the seats is typically invited by the head of state to try to form a government, which it can do by inviting smaller parties to join a ruling coalition or by forming a minority government whose survival is conditional on the goodwill and support of some of the opposition. Regardless of the specifics, what divided presidential and coalition or minority governments have in common is that no single actor can unilaterally make public policy. In divided presidential systems, the typical consequence is "gridlock" as the executive and legislature find it difficult to reach agreement on a policy (M. Jones 1995; Lijphart 2004; Linz 1994; Linz and Stepan 1996; Shugart and Carey 1992; Shugart and Haggard 2001). An unintended consequence of this is that investors' concerns of large policy swings are allayed (Bechtel and Füss 2008), even if their desires for radical reform might be stymied by the gridlock (Howell *et al.* 2000; Krehbiel 1996, 1998; Lohmann and O'Halloran 1994; Milner and Rosendorff 1996).[17]

The expectations for coalition and minority governments are similar, yet different in an important way. In these settings, since the survival of the government is intimately linked to the survival of parliament, incentives to overcome gridlock are greater (Mainwaring and Scully 1995; Stepan and Skach 1993; Valenzuela 1994). Rather the expectation here would be that policy moderation would dominate the status quo alternative of no policy change (M. Jones 1995). Thus, the resulting policy is the result of negotiations between different parties in the government. Additionally, since extreme parties are unlikely to form viable coalitions or minority governments, the core of such governments is typically a party located fairly centrally in the ideological space (Müller and Strøm 2000; Strøm 1990). Therefore, as in the case of divided presidentialism, minority and coalition governments in parliamentary democracy can credibly claim their hands are tied, and assure investors that policies are unlikely to change rapidly during their tenure. The existence of a strong institutionalized opposition thus

---

[17] Gehlbach and Malesky (2009) have an interesting working paper that suggests this pessimism about the prospects for reform might be misplaced, which accords nicely with my analysis here.

checks policy excesses by the government, and has two distinct effects on policy production:[18]

1. policies *initiated* are more incremental in nature and closer to the ideological center; and
2. there exists a status quo bias making policy *reversal* harder.

The distinction drawn above between presidential and parliamentary systems reflects the dominant perspectives in comparative politics, but recent scholarship on Latin America has begun to push back in important ways. In an important recent contribution to the debate, Cheibub (2007) counters what he calls the Linzian – named for the preeminent exponent of this position, Juan J. Linz – pessimism expressed by many Latin Americanists about the prospects of presidentialism in that region (Linz 1978, 1990a, 1990b, 1994; Linz and Stepan 1996). In a compelling analysis, Cheibub shows that coalitions do form in presidential systems, at rates far higher than might be expected from any reading of Linz and his collaborators. And, relevantly, Figueiredo and Limongi (2000) show that the logic of such coalitions, at least in Brazil, are similar to coalitions elsewhere: parties support the president in achieving his policy agenda subject to reaching acceptable bargains. Further, Cheibub shows that the breakdown of democratic regimes in Latin America has had less to do with pathologies of "policy gridlock" inherent to presidential systems, and far more to do with that region's toxic history of military interventionism in civilian politics. But, Cheibub's corrective notwithstanding, the basic claim that parliamentarism does better at policy moderation in the face of diffused policymaking authority still has merit. Cheibub's own data make clear that coalition formation is most common in parliamentary democracies (2007: 77–80), and it is important to recall that the debate to which he is contributing seeks to understand regime "survival" rather than policymaking on which point the evidence of divided government's effects is more unequivocal. A fair reading of these arguments, I think, supports the two main empirical implications of the argument: parliamentary systems with coalition governments should do better than divided presidential systems; and both types of democratic systems will

[18] Research in American politics supports this claim: Coleman 1999; Edwards *et al.* 1997; Howell *et al.* 2000; Mayhew 1991a, 1991b).

do better than their non-democratic counterparts.[19] I turn to the latter point below.

The institutions of credible constraints thus far are typically associated with democratic governance and, indeed, an implicit assumption of most studies on credibility is that the more complex institutional architecture of democracy – a system intended after all to promote the contestation and sharing of power – makes credible commitments easier. This has not stopped scholars from trying to identify possible sources of credibility in authoritarian states too. Two recent studies deserve particular attention. First, Wright (2008) has argued that dictators take a page out of the *Federalist Papers* and create legislative bodies to bolster their credibility (see also Gandhi 2008a). Even though such institutions are hardly equal to the executive's power, their existence does add another layer of government that can debate policy, resulting possibly in more moderate policy choices. Second, Scott Gehlbach and Philip Keefer (n.d.) point to well-institutionalized ruling parties (like the Chinese Communist Party) as a potential source of credibility for authoritarian states. Institutionalized ruling parties will have longer time horizons, they argue, which will make them loathe to incur reputation costs from reneging in the present because it hurts their ability to attract investors in the future.[20] The longer the time horizons governments possess, Gehlbach and Keefer suggest, the more heavily weighs the shadow of the future on present decisions, a fact that bolsters present credibility.

Are all the suggested "solutions" to governments' credibility problems equally theoretically satisfying? I will argue that they are not, and further that they imply different causal paths to increased credibility. Considering all of them simultaneously has the additional benefit of allowing me to discriminate between their utility on empirical grounds.

---

[19] Others have documented the policy advantages of parliamentary systems over their presidential counterparts. For instance, Andersen and Aslaksen (2008: 227) find that the "resource curse" exists in democratic presidential systems but not in parliamentary countries, and, in fact, that being parliamentary or presidential matters more for the growth effects of resources than does regime type. More provocatively, Persson (2005) shows that reforming a country from non-democracy or presidential democracy to a parliamentary arrangement leads to more growth-promoting trade and regulation policies.

[20] Simmons (2008) applies a similar logic to explain cross-national variation in innovation policy in democratic systems.

Before we get to data, however, what are the different causal paths implied?

The preceding discussion implies four basic strategies for bolstering credibility, onto which, at the risk of some repetition, it is worth mapping the institutional mechanisms surveyed thus far:[21]

1. credibility by *signaling type*
2. credibility via *accountability*
3. credibility through *gridlock*
4. credibility through *forced compromise*.

The first strategy is for a government to signal its "type." Market actors are unsure whether a government is to be believed with respect to its policy promises. Government protestations that they are in fact credible are dismissed because talk is cheap. All governments – insincere or not – have an incentive to insist they should be believed. If anything, the only government which could be taken at its word is one that promises to violate its commitments, since the only reason it would say this is if it meant it! Therefore, governments must find other ways to demonstrate their true "type," and one way to do this is by engaging in a costly action that they would not favor unless they were serious about getting results. Examples of such actions would include delegating monetary policy authority to independent central banks, subjecting their legislation to review by independent judiciaries, and entering agreements to enact painful economic reforms or lose aid and loans that are conditional on successful implementation of the reform package. This way of thinking about how central banks, judiciaries, and IMF programs influence government credibility – as a signal of type – makes more sense to me than thinking of them as "checks" or "balances" on government actions. Theoretically it remains unclear to me why we should expect a priori central banks and judiciaries to remain impartial and unbiased in their dealings with economic policy. The fact is that governments can and do pressure central banks to make

---

[21] Some other suggestions scholars have made to states seeking to enhance the credibility of their commitments in the eyes of private economic actors include (1) reducing political instability (Alesina *et al.* 1992; Barro 1991); (2) increasing the transparency of decision-making and lowering information costs (Krueger 1990: 20); (3) pegging exchange rates to developed states (Bleaney and Fielding 2002).

favorable policy decisions, and uncooperative central bankers can and are removed from their posts. Likewise the arbitrary removal and even imprisonment of "difficult" judges remains common in many developing countries (the recent episode in Pakistan pitting ex-President General Musharraf against the Chief Justice is a good example). And, to the extent that governments endogenously select themselves into IMF programs, it's unclear just how constraining the latter actually are (Vreeland 2003). Similarly, central bankers and judges are chosen by the same governments they allegedly constrain, and they are chosen despite, or indeed because of, well-articulated policy preferences that tend to align with those appointing them. No, rather than a check, the real purpose of such institutions is to increase the predictability of policy outcomes for market actors who can use the fact that they know how bankers will react, judges will rule, and IFIs will advise, to condition their expectations of future policy, and therefore adjust their behavior accordingly.

Signaling type also provides a way of understanding recent arguments about why certain authoritarian states are able to convince economic actors of their credibility relative to others. For instance, Wright (2008) has argued that some dictators create "binding" legislatures that serve as a check on behavior. Gehlbach and Keefer (n.d.) argue that dictatorships ruled by well-institutionalized ruling parties also enjoy a credibility boost because of longer time horizons and internal party checks. I remain skeptical that there exist truly binding legislatures in dictatorships or that ruling parties cannot change their minds when or if they so desire. As Barry Weingast put it, governments strong enough to create property rights are also strong enough to violate them. Rather, to the extent that such authoritarian institutions yield any credibility boost, it's more likely because they signal that dictators with binding legislatures or ruling from within institutionalized ruling parties are "different" from those who did not create such legislatures or who rule in more personalistic fashions.

The second source of credibility is an institutionalized mechanism for holding governments accountable for their actions, and, in particular, for violating their commitments. This is a pro-democracy argument in that it suggests that elections are a source of greater credibility if voters punish governments that break promises, i.e., impose "audience costs." Here, as above, I am skeptical of this mechanism (see Przeworski *et al.* 1999). While the basic claim that voters might punish a government that does not deliver good economic performance is plausible, it is a stretch to suggest that voters recall – or even know of – all the other policy choices governments make that business might not approve. Further it is just as plausible that electoral concerns push leaders to engage in anti-business populist appeals that scare market actors. Finally, elections bring with them the possibility of change, which investors fear (Brooks and Mosley 2008).

Compared to these first two mechanisms, I think the last two credibility devices are much more plausible. The "gridlock" and "compromise or policy moderation" perspectives are closely related, but have important differences worth pointing out for these help generate different expectations for different institutional configurations by which policymaking authority might be dispersed. In the "gridlock" model, policymaking authority is dispersed to two or more actors whose policy preferences diverge. Since both, or all, actors must agree for the policy to be enacted, policy change is less likely, especially if the actors' preferences are far apart. Gridlock is most common in separation-of-powers systems when different parties capture control of the executive and legislative branches of government ("divided" government). Research on the consequences of divided government is relatively new, and then too mainly focused on the US experience though recent work has begun to study divided government elsewhere (Bechtel and Füss 2008; Elgie 2001). The standard finding is that divided government generates a strong status quo bias. Poterba (1994) finds that divided government at the US state level makes deficit reduction harder; Roubini and Sachs (1989) argue unified governments react to income shocks more quickly; Milner and Rosendorff (1996) suggest that trade agreements are harder to ratify under divided government; and Fowler (2006) shows that inflation risk is reduced under divided government. More directly, numerous scholars have demonstrated that, while the level of law production is more or less the same under unified and divided government (Mayhew 1991b), "important" or landmark bills are less likely to pass under the latter (Coleman 1999; Edwards *et al.* 1997; Howell *et al.* 2000). The up-side of such policy gridlock is that leaders can credibly claim to have their hands tied and investors can have increased confidence that policies will not change dramatically.

In the context of the developing world, where much needs to be done by governments, however, one might understandably be less sanguine about the virtues of such gridlock. More preferable might be institutions that promote policy moderation while still generating incentives for governments to agree and enact necessary legislation. To my mind, the archetypical such institutional configuration is coalition or minority parliamentary democracy. In this setting, the largest party in the legislature cannot enact its ideal policies because it does not possess a majority of the seats. Rather it must compromise with members of its governing coalition or with key supporters outside the coalition to enact policy. A simple claim in this setting is that the resulting policy will be some weighted average of the positions of the parties in the coalition. Policy change in this setting – as under gridlock – is unlikely to be drastic, but rather to tend to the status quo, a tendency bolstered by the fact that the core party in the coalition forming the minority government will likely fall near the ideological center of the policy space (Müller and Strøm 2000; Strøm 1990). This is an important point, because it implies that even if the composition of the coalition changes, its center will remain relatively stable, and so the status quo bias will be preserved. Importantly, however, unlike in divided presidential government, the survival of the key players in this situation is jointly determined, which should generate a real incentive to compromise and make policy when required, or to risk dissolution of parliament and face new polls. This analysis of coalition and minority governments thus takes seriously arguments that social-compromise institutions are an important part of democracy (for example, see Rodrik 2000), on which more will be said later), and adds to that insight by identifying one scenario by which such compromise is mandated. Compromise from my perspective is not inherent to democratic governance but rather arises because of the diffusion of policymaking authority to multiple actors accountable to different social constituencies, which is more likely to happen in democracies than in non-democracies.

In summary, then, the main theoretical expectation is that countries in which such "credible constraints" against unilateral and arbitrary policy change exist are more likely to generate more stable patterns of savings and investment, and of national economic performance.

The importance of credibility and policy stability for national economic performance

I have argued thus far that existing theories of economic growth have overemphasized the importance of "strong" governments capable of making the "right" policy, and ignored comparatively the importance of establishing the credibility of policy promises and especially of policy stability. In this section, I flesh out in more detail the causal argument about why credibility and policy stability matter for national economic performance by focusing explicitly on the private economic actors that are the object and audience of government policy.

Governments influence national economic performance directly through their choice of economic policy and indirectly through the effects these policy choices have on the behavior of private economic actors. High inflation, bloated government sectors, and budget deficits all make growth less stable (Caballero 2000a, 2000b, 2000c; Quinn and Woolley 2001). Frequent reversals of policy programs also hurt economic performance (Yago and Morgan 2008). Economists William Easterly, Roumeen Islam, and Joseph Stiglitz find that "policy variability, whether it relates to fiscal or to monetary policy, is associated with higher volatility" (Easterly *et al.* 2001: 10). To the extent that the institutional checks and balances discussed in the previous section reduce policy volatility (and the evidence suggests that they do; see Henisz 2004), they should also provide for more stable growth outcomes. But governments affect national economic performance also through their impact on private economic behavior by creating conditions and incentives conducive or hostile to private savings and investment. While this fact is the central insight motivating analyses that focus on the importance of property rights and the rule of law, much less has been said about what it tells us about the importance of political structures that promote the diffusion of policymaking authority. Doing so is the goal of this section.

Private economic actors make decisions each day that affect all aspects of the economy, including whether the economy grows in a stable manner over time. Of principal interest here, as the 1997 Asian Financial Flu highlighted, are the decisions of investors to withdraw their capital and move it elsewhere – whether abroad or under their mattresses – since such capital flight hinders economic growth by denying the economy of capital-generating economic production (MacIntyre 2003). Governments compete for long-term investment from private actors over so-called "hot money" because the former generates more stable economic performance.

While the international political economy literature has focused mainly on the importance of large multinational or investment banks as

Table 2.1 *Game of "common interests"*

		Private economic actors'	
		investment options	
		Irreversible (II)	*Reversible (RI)*
Government	*Stable Policies (SP)*	(3,4)	(1,5)
Preferences	*Flexible Policies (FP)*	(4,1)	(2,2)

shaping capital movements, the decision to invest and consume is made at all levels of the economy. Indeed, foreign capital forms only a small share of the economies of most developing countries (Bosworth and Collins 1999), and developed countries remain the largest recipients of foreign direct investment (the United States is the largest). Rather most of the savings and investment required to foster economic growth in the developing world must come from within (Bates 2001). What drives the decision to save or invest scarce resources?

To understand the complex and continuous interaction between governments and investors, simplifying the interaction is useful. This interaction has the form of a repeated-play stage game of "common interests" with two players, whom I label the government and economic investors.[22] The game is illustrated in Table 2.1. The payoff structure reflects two assumptions of how preferences are ordered for each actor: first, it assumes that governments prefer to retain flexibility in their policymaking rather than ceding their autonomy to adjust policies as needed, but that this preference is contingent on investor behavior: governments care about output levels; if investors choose irreversible investments, output is more stable and governments benefit from a steady income stream and are willing to make more stable policy choices. Second, the game assumes risk-averse investors in uncertain environments prefer to make short-term (reversible) investments rather than long-term (irreversible) investments since the risk associated with short-term investments is much lower. However, if investors

---

[22] Huff *et al.* (2001) use a repeated play prisoner's dilemma game to model the investment decision; see Diermeier *et al.* (1997) for a similar analysis in the context of privatization in centrally planned economies. My analysis reveals the same intuition as theirs.

can be certain of future government policy stability, then they benefit from being able to make longer-term investments since the associated risk is lower. Thus, governments recognize that they can gain more from committing to stable policies if and only if private actors commit to long-term investments, but not otherwise. Similarly, private actors know that they have much to gain from long-term investments if and only if government actors reduce future uncertainty by committing to maintaining a stable macroeconomic environment.

Table 2.1 presents a form of prisoner's dilemma in that although both actors would prefer the stable policies and irreversible investment (SP,II) equilibrium with payoff (3,4), the Nash equilibrium is that governments retain flexibility in policymaking and investors choose investments with easier abandonment options (FP,RI with payoff (2,2)) (Wong 2010). The reason for this suboptimal outcome is the government's inability to commit to future policy stability once the private investors have made irreversible investments, a form of the time-consistency problem first noted in the context of optimal planning (Kydland and Prescott 1977). Or, as Michael Bruno puts it, "The most important – and *hardest* – service for a government to deliver is the irreversibility of a new policy environment" (1995: 15, emphasis mine).[23] The reason is once private investors make irreversible investments, governments are free to change the policies that attracted the original investment. Since investors know this risk exists, they resist making irreversible investments and the suboptimal equilibrium results.

Suppose the government is able to meet the private investors and assure them of their intention to maintain a stable policy environment in the future.[24] The question is why should the investors take the government's assurances at face value? Regardless of the government's true intentions, the government gains if investors make irreversible investments; therefore, no matter how the government intends to behave in the future, it stands to gain by promising investors a stable policy environment. In other words, neither player should expect its assurances to convince the other and the Nash equilibrium (FP,RI) results even

[23] Bruno's concern is the credibility of the economic reform process. Mehlum (2002) makes a similar argument about the importance of reform credibility for investment.
[24] Interested readers can find a more technical discussion in Fudenberg and Tirole (1991: 20–2, and Chapter 5, esp. pp. 385–1).

Table 2.2 *Policy quality and stability both matter for investment*

		Expected policy stability	
		Volatile	*Stable*
Policy	*Bad for investors*	None	Low but stable
Content	*Good for investors*	Low-to-moderate; volatile	High

though it was dominated by (SP,II). Therefore, the key to obtaining the (SP,II) equilibrium is the government's ability to commit credibly to future policy stability.[25]

In some senses, the importance of policy stability is independent of the content of the policy. If policies are good, where good is defined as benefiting private investors (e.g., low taxes), then we would expect the level of investment to be high; but if policies are stable, regardless of whether or not they are good or bad for investors (e.g., low or high taxes), investors enjoy lower uncertainty about the future and can form strategies accordingly, reducing the volatility of their behavior Henisz (2002), for instance, describes direct ownership and joint-ventures as solutions to different levels of uncertainty and political risk).[26] Thus, putting these two arguments together, we might expect the following relationship (see Table 2.2) when bad policy is accompanied by unpredictability, no investment occurs, but if the policy environment is "predictably bad," then investors can find ways to hedge their risk and will invest even as they bemoan the policy content. In good policy environments, policy instability will yield lower investment than where policy stability is high (Roberts 2006), and investors should be expected to choose more liquid forms of investment so that they can move should the policy environment change.

The formula for reducing growth-rate volatility then appears simple: governments must commit to maintaining macroeconomic stability, which then leads to a virtuous circle of stable long-term investments

[25] Henisz and Zelner (2002) concur: "The relevant political variable of interest to investors is not democracy or instability per se, but rather the ability of the government to craft a credible commitment to an existing policy regime."

[26] This argument follows Hamori and Hamori's (2000: 15) call to "pay more attention to the *expectations formation* process [of economic agents] to better understand volatility" (emphasis added).

and lower overall growth-rate volatility (Cerra *et al.* 2008). Bleaney (1996: 464–5) summarizes this policy prescription well:

> Poor macroeconomic management creates needless uncertainty in the economic environment, which increases the risk associated with investment. Lack of credibility of government policy may be regarded as a tax on investment, because of the possibility that the policy will not be sustained ... The issue [therefore] is the ability of the government to minimize the destabilizing impact of [exogenous] shocks and to avoid creating unnecessary macroeconomic uncertainty by its own policy decisions.

If arbitrary policy reversals (changes) by the government and private investment decisions contingent upon (endogenous to) such policies are the source of growth-rate volatility, the crucial question is what determines why some countries are more susceptible to such reversals and the consequent capital inflow/outflow volatility. The answer I have posited is that political institutions matter and that the probability government leaders make stable policy and private economic actors withdraw their capital is endogenous to the country's framework of formal political institutions. These institutions affect the probability of both whether a country has a volatile (unstable) macroeconomic policy environment and whether private economic actors invest in long-term projects, and whether they withdraw their capital in anticipation of crises. Private economic actors base their long-term investment decisions on cues given by the environment in which government actors make policy decisions, but government commitments mean little unless accompanied by costly signals or produced in an environment that otherwise renders reversal difficult.

The constraints from potentially arbitrary policy and from policy variability provided by the diffusion of policymaking authority bolsters confidence among private economic actors. The investor confidence engendered by these institutions, in turn, both fosters longer-term, more stable investment and helps those countries withstand temporary shocks, preventing them from creating full-blown crises. Thus, the diffusion of policymaking authority to multiple actors with accountability to different constituencies lowers the average level of growth-rate volatility a country experiences.[27]

---

[27] My emphasis on multiple policymakers is similar to the notion of veto players, which Tsebelis defines as "an individual or collective actor whose agreement is

The diffusion of policymaking authority improves the stability of national economic performance through two channels. In the first, the diffusion of policymaking authority to multiple actors with account-ability to different constituencies increases policy stability. Second, where policymaking is diffused in a transparent manner, private investors expect policy stability to be more likely and that temporary shocks are unlikely to result in dramatic changes to the policy envi-ronment within which their investments are located. That is, credible constraints on policymakers created by the diffusion of policymaking authority to multiple policymakers with accountabilities to different constituencies bolsters confidence among investors leading to savings and investment stability and therefore to lower growth-rate volatility.

The discussion above suggests a complex and continuous interac-tion between the existence of credible constraints on governments and growth-rate volatility. On the one hand, credible constraints should lessen policy volatility, thereby reducing growth-rate volatil-ity directly. Further, such constraints should increase the terms and durability of investment, which also dampens growth-rate volatility. But, on the other hand, as MacIntyre (2003) argues, such constraints might reduce governments' responsiveness to crises, thereby increas-ing growth-rate volatility, but whether or not this occurs will turn on whether the institutional structure creates any incentives for compro-mise and collective action as opposed simply to generating deadlock (Franzese 2007). A perfect illustration of this point is the fact that India's major economic reforms in 1991 occurred on the heels of a significant balance-of-payments crisis and were initiated and enacted by a minority government (Chapter 5 discusses the Indian experience in greater detail).[28]

Conclusion

Why do some countries experience better national economic perfor-mance than others? I have argued that the answer lies in the political-institutional framework of a country and, in particular, whether the

necessary for a change of the status quo" (Tsebelis 1999: 593). See also Franzese (2007).

[28] See Keeler (1993) and the contributions to MacIntyre *et al.* (2008) for explana-tions about how governments can utilize crises to push through reforms.

combination of political institutions and partisan politics align to enable governments to commit credibly to policy stability. Rather than decry the policy stasis that arises when governments must form coalitions in order to gain a majority in parliament, or even rule as minority governments with outside support, the theoretical argument developed here suggests that such institutional configurations can be to the country's benefit because they assuage concerns of policy uncertainty among economic agents and encourage these actors to keep their money within the country and to invest it productively. Where political institutions do not constrain governments adequately, the risk of policy change, or even outright reversal, remains high, and investors respond by seeking other opportunities outside the country for their capital or by choosing short-term, less risky forms of investment. Thus, consistent with recent research in economics, I expect policy uncertainty to hurt investment flows and therefore economic growth, and, consequently, that political institutions that encourage policy compromise and restrict policy change to generate superior national economic performance. The theoretical framework thus yields clear empirical implications that can be tested against data, to which task I turn over the next four chapters.

3 | Coalition politics and economic development
Empirics

The previous chapter provided a new theoretical framework to explain cross-national variation in national economic performance. Unlike previous explanations that emphasize the importance of getting policies "right," having leaders with strong "political will," or protecting leaders from special interests, my argument takes an almost opposite tack. Rather than powerful governments capable of imposing the right policies, what the developing world needs, I argue, are institutions that promote policy moderation by dispersing policymaking authority to multiple actors, each accountable to different constituencies. In this sense, what I am calling for is "more democracy," even "too much democracy" (if such a thing can be even said to exist). The more voices that have to be heard before policy can be made, the harder it is for governments to make unilateral and arbitrary policy shifts, which in turn bolsters investors' confidence about the content and stability of future policy. This counter-intuitive argument comes with one condition: it is important that the actors to whom policy is dispersed have an incentive to cooperate with each other when absolutely necessary (e.g., in response to crisis). Therefore, I argued above that coalition or minority parliamentary democracies should fare best, but that the oppositional framework of divided presidential systems might lead to "gridlock" rather than "moderation" and therefore to less desirable outcomes.

This chapter is the first of four empirical chapters in which I shall try to convince the reader of the empirical utility of this explanatory framework. Specifically, here I will analyze the main outcome-of-interest – national economic performance – by disaggregating the concept into its components: the volatility of growth and the long-term mean around which it fluctuates. I will use a variety of statistical techniques to analyze a data set of all countries for which data are available between 1960 and 2004. The results are extremely supportive of the principal arguments made in this book: states whose leaders are credibly constrained from policy change experience higher and more stable economic growth over this time period.

The chapter is organized in five main sections. Given the dominant focus in the existing literature on average growth, the first section makes a case for focusing instead on growth-rate volatility as an important dependent variable in its own right, including for the simple reason that volatility itself is bad for long-term economic growth in the developing world. Then the bulk of the chapter is spent describing and explaining cross-national variation in growth-rate volatility. I then apply my argument to explaining average growth rates, both cross-nationally and within Africa. The final empirical section tackles the question of endogeneity, and utilizes matching techniques to bolster confidence in the core findings reported in this chapter. The conclusion considers the implications of my results for our understanding of economic development, and sets the stage for the second cross-national empirical chapter.

Why growth-rate volatility matters

The economic history of the world is replete with recessions and depressions. From the bursting of the British South Sea Bubble and the French Mississippi Bubble in 1720 ... to the industrial depressions of the 1870s and the 1930s, to the Latin American middle income debt crisis, African low income debt crisis, ex-Communist output collapse, and East Asian financial crisis, crises have been a constant of market capitalism. Add to that the collapses that have accompanied non-economic shocks like wars, hurricanes, earthquakes, volcanoes, fires, pests, droughts, and floods, and it is a wonder that anyone in the world has economic security. (Easterly *et al.* 2001: 1)

The history of economic development around the world is not a steady march towards ever increasing economic efficiency and production. The quote from Easterly *et al.* above makes that abundantly clear. Indeed, if it were, things undoubtedly would be better for the majority of the world's population. Instead, a more accurate characterization of long-term growth patterns cross-nationally presents them as volatile and unstable. For reasons as yet poorly understood, most countries do not maintain their economic growth rates over an extended period of time. Periods of steady, even outstanding, growth are followed by stagnation and disasters from one decade to the next. While most countries fortunately never experience crises on the scale experienced by the East Asian states in 1997 or by Argentina in 2002, most countries go through recessions and slight crises at some points in their history. Growth-rate volatility, of which crises are the most dramatic instances, is understudied in political science, but as the cases of Argentina and East Asia demonstrate, the human effects of extreme volatility make understanding the political determinants of growth-rate volatility a central question for comparative and international political economy.

The decision to focus on the volatility of growth rates rather than their mean does not alter the overarching question of what impact politics has on economic development. Traditional research strategies with their focus on long-term mean growth rates have yielded little partly because, as I argued in the introduction, averages of growth rates often mask as much as they reveal. World Bank economist Lant Pritchett underscores this point emphatically:

[the] fixation on differences in long-run (even possibly steady-state) differences in growth in the theoretical and empirical research explaining growth has led to an underestimation of the importance of the *instability* and *volatility* in growth rates ... Is explaining Brazil's "growth" explaining the 4.2 percent growth from 1965 to 1980 or explaining the stagnation from 1980 to 1992 (actually a fall of −0.2 percent) or explaining Brazil's average growth percent from 1960–1992 of 3.14. (Pritchett 2000: 3)

It is a fair question; most countries oscillate between good and bad periods of growth, but some do so much more frequently and more intensely (i.e., have bigger swings). Understanding the determinants of such volatility is important in its own right, since growth-rate volatility extracts large human costs as Argentina's 2002 experience demonstrates, but increasing evidence suggests that the volatility of growth is intimately linked to its long-term average too. In other words, it is not as simple as suggesting that high volatility is simply the price of high rewards (i.e., high average growth), but rather, in the developing world, that high volatility drags countries into a low *and* unstable growth equilibrium from which it is difficult to escape.

This idea – that volatility is something to be avoided even if one is solely interested in maximizing long-term average growth – is central to my thinking about national economic performance, and shortly I will provide some evidence to buttress this view. But before that it is worth considering the alternative view that volatility, while painful in the short term, might be beneficial in the long term. Growth-rate volatility could enhance future growth prospects in two distinct ways: (1) "positive" volatility could encourage technological progress while (2) "negative" volatility "cleanses" the economy of inefficient firms through a process of "creative destruction."[1]

Traditionally the business-cycle literature maintained that aggregate demand shocks had no permanent effects on technology or growth and that monetary shocks had no long-term impact on technological progress. By the late 1980s, however, endogenous growth theorists had begun to embed temporary shocks into the economy's long-run growth trajectory (King *et al.* 1988; Stadler 1990). In particular, temporary increases in the quantity of money in the economy were found to stimulate higher levels of economic activity in the short run, which in turn generated an otherwise unlikely increase in technological growth, either because firms experienced more rapid "learning-by-doing" or because they increased their research and development to maximize returns from increased profit opportunities. And, importantly, these effects prove not transitory, but stick around with real income ending up at "'a permanently higher level" (Aghion and Howitt 1998: 236).

A second tradition in business-cycle theory is based in the Schumpeterian "creative destruction" view that recessions (negative growth shocks) serve a cleansing or purging function for the economy, and reduce inefficiencies in firm organization and resource allocation (e.g., labor input utilization). Consider four separate mechanisms through which negative volatility might aid future productivity: (1) the "cleaning-up" effect, (2) the "opportunity cost" effect, (3) the "disciplinary" effect, and (4) the "externality" effect.[2]

First, the "clean-up" (also known as the "lame duck") effect states that recessions serve the purpose of eliminating inefficient and less productive firms, thereby increasing average productivity. The extent to which this effect might hold is limited by the severity of the recession since recessions also lower the rate of entry of new firms that push out the older inefficient firms. Second, the "opportunity cost"

---

[1] The discussion below borrows heavily from Chapter 8, section 8.3 of Aghion and Howitt (1998).

[2] Interested readers can find a more detailed and technical exposition in (Aghion and Howitt 1998: 240–2). See also the Clarendon Lectures in Economics by Aghion and Banerjee (2005).

(or the "cross-temporal substitution" argument) explanation suggests
that firms might be more inclined to invest in reorganization or retrain-
ing programs when business is slow since the opportunity costs of
doing so then are lower than when business is booming. This argument is most relevant for investments that are profitable in the long
term such as training, machine replacement, and labor reorganization
since such expenditures are likely to be counter-cyclical.[3] Third, recessions might aid growth by imposing a "disciplinary" effect, whereby
firms that do not make the necessary commitment to improving productive efficiency through investments in reorganization are more likely
to face bankruptcy. The fourth and final argument builds on the logic
of the previous three. The "externality effect" argument speaks to the
selection of which firms are more likely to be phased out of business
during recession. It posits that if the difference in performance between
good and bad firms (or labor) widens more than proportionally with
the degree of adversity, then good firms are more likely to survive
than "bad" firms, and this "Darwinian" selection process benefits the
economy as a whole.

Economic theory thus suggests that growth-rate volatility should
have positive effects for average levels of productivity and therefore for
long-run economic growth because (1) temporary increases in money
supply can generate rapid technological growth and (2) even recession-
ary periods can improve average productivity by weeding out inefficient
actors in the market. More volatile states should enjoy more of both
mechanisms and therefore have higher long-term growth.

The accumulated evidence, however, is much less sanguine, especially in the developing world, where volatility is more extreme. Indeed,
after summarizing the reasons that volatility might be good for the
economy, Aghion and Howitt offer this caveat: "these [positive] effects
should not be overemphasized ... [rather] *the idea that excessive
macroeconomic volatility is an obstacle to growth appears to be largely
supported by recent empirical evidence*" (1998: 243, emphasis in original). This evidence is mounting rapidly, staring with an influential

---

[3] While the "opportunity cost" argument suggests that recessions might generate
investment in physical infrastructure and reorganization activities, the same does
not necessarily hold for investment in technological R&D since those expenditures are more likely to be procyclical because of cash constraints (Stiglitz
1993).

piece by Ramey and Ramey in the *American Economic Review* in 1995, which used a panel of ninety-two developing states to show that "countries with higher volatility have lower mean growth, even after controlling for other country-specific growth correlates" (Ramey and Ramey 1995: 1139). Dennis Quinn and John Woolley replicate this finding in their 2001 paper which used data from 109 countries from 1974 to 1989 (Acemoglu *et al.* 2003b; Imbs 2007; Mobarak 2005).

What explains this conflict between theory and evidence? We do not know for sure yet, but the most promising explanation suggests that macroeconomic instability in the developing world discourages investment. High growth-rate volatility creates greater uncertainty that future growth will be stable, thereby making investment riskier (Aizenman and Marion 1993; Lucas and Prescott 1971; Ramey and Ramey 1991). Agenor and Montiel write that "uncertainty has been an important factor in the macroeconomics of development, in many instances triggering currency substitution, capital flight, exchange-rate crises, and the collapse of private investment" (1999: 37). This negative effect on investment is particularly pronounced if irreversibilities in investment exist since investors who cannot withdraw their investment without losing significant sunk costs, such as the costs of physical plant construction, tend to be more risk-averse. Aghion and Howitt (1998) summarize this argument well: "Large swings in output increase uncertainty, which may be a major factor in delaying or stopping investment and R&D." Similarly, Ramey and Ramey show "if firms must commit to their technology in advance, then volatility can lead to lower mean output because firms find themselves producing at suboptimal levels *ex post*" (1991). As plausible as this sounds, one might wonder nevertheless, if higher volatility implies higher equilibrium average return, why might volatility not encourage investment, even if of a riskier sort. Possibly. To compensate for the higher risk, though, a project must have a higher expected (average) return to attract investment, which means that higher volatility probably deters investments in projects that might have occurred at lower levels of volatility, something developing countries cannot afford.

Figure 3.1 uses data from 1960 to 2004 to shed some light on the question of whether volatility is good or bad for economic growth. Since previous research has found that volatility appears to have different effects depending on the level of development in the economy, I separate the developed OECD states (those in Europe and

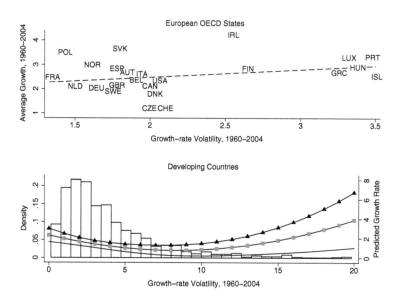

Figure 3.1 Volatility and growth (source: author's calculations from World Bank 2006).

North America) from the developing world (defined here simply as non-members of the OECD group). Efficient high-growth economies might in fact benefit from Schumpeterian "creative destruction," while less efficient economies might be hurt if the uncertainty introduced by economic volatility deters business activity, thereby lowering future growth (Quinn and Woolley 2001). The top graph in Figure 3.1 is for the OECD states only, and indicates a positive relationship between volatility and average growth, which is in line with economic theory. But the relationship is the opposite in the developing world, where volatility hurts growth except at very high levels. The developing world graph plots the predicted growth rate for different levels of growth-rate volatility, along with a 95 percent confidence interval, *ceteris paribus*.[4] Nor is this negative relationship for over 90 percent of the developing world sample (note the distribution of growth-rate volatility in the

[4] There's no clear theoretical justification for the quadratic relationship between volatility and growth but the data demand one. A closer look at the data suggests that this is because there are many fuel and mineral exporting countries with higher levels of growth even though they are quite volatile too. It remains an interesting question for future research.

background of the lower panel of Figure 3.1) spurious; in fact, the plot reflects the predicted growth rate from a model of 123 developing countries that included controls for previous levels of economic growth, regime type, political instability, population size, level of economic development, trade openness, the share of agriculture in the economy, the share of government consumption in the economy, and levels of foreign direct investment (see Appendix B for full results). The effect of volatility on growth is also quite sizable: for the bulk of the distribution with growth-rate volatility under ten, a one-point increase in volatility leads to one-third of a percent lower growth!

A model of growth-rate volatility

The results above indicate the existence of a vicious trap where states are stuck with low-and-volatile economic performance, which should move identifying the political determinants of growth-rate volatility squarely and firmly onto the central policy agendas of developing countries. In this section, I develop an empirical model of growth-rate volatility designed to test the theoretical framework of national economic performance offered in the last chapter. Since this forms the main empirical assessment of my argument, I proceed carefully, and organize the section as follows. I will first discuss how I measure growth-rate volatility, and describe some basic empirical trends in the data so that it is clear to the reader just what we are seeking to understand. I then discuss three alternative political explanations for growth-rate volatility offered by scholars in recent years, and contrast my explanation with theirs, pointing out similarities and points of divergence. A discussion of the specific indicators used to assess my argument versus the existing explanations follows, as does a consideration of the economic control variables to be included in the model. After presenting the results and discussing a robustness check using an alternative dependent variable, I turn to the growth model.

The dependent variable: measuring and describing growth-rate volatility

Economic data on economic growth come primarily from the World Bank (World Bank 2006). Data were collected for all developing countries for the years 1960 to 2004, but missing data in the included variables mean that the regression results reported below are based on fewer than that many cases at times (the fewest number of developing countries represented in any of the models reported below is 105).[5]

The dependent variable of interest in this section is *growth-rate volatility*, where the growth rate is measured by the annual percentage growth rate of real GDP per capita. Conceptually volatility contains two closely related but importantly distinct aspects: stability and predictability. Applied to economic growth, stability refers to a country's ability to return to its normal performance levels following a shock to the system. Predictability, on the other hand, has less of a long-run equilibrium feeling to it, but rather speaks to how well one can forecast future performance based on the past. Therefore, predictable states have future growth rates that are accurately foretold by their current growth rate and macroeconomic conditions.

The most commonly used strategy for measuring growth-rate volatility is to calculate the standard deviation of the growth rate of a country for the period of interest.[6] Using the standard deviation as a measure of volatility captures the concept of stability perfectly. Here the unconditional mean growth rate serves as a measure of the long-run (or steady-state) equilibrium and deviations from this mean are treated as shocks to the system. The larger the deviation, the larger is the shock. Thus, if the growth rate for a particular state is stable, the standard deviation should be low, since the stable growth trajectory will be well-represented by the trend.

While the standard deviation accurately measures a country's long-term growth-rate stability, it ignores the dynamics of the growth trajectory that aggregate to form the long-term stability. The core concern is that the standard deviation would be unable to distinguish

---

[5] Summary statistics and a list of countries included in the analysis are reported in Appendix B. By comparison, the largest sample size used for any of the regressions reported by Quinn and Woolley in their 2001 *American Journal of Political Science* article is 105. Rodrik's sample, as reported in his 2000 *American Economic Review* article, covers ninety-six countries. Therefore, while I certainly wish I had more data for more countries, the results reported in this chapter are based on approximately the same number of cases as in previously published studies.

[6] Easterly and Kraay (2000); Easterly *et al.* (2001); Quinn and Woolley (2001); Ramey and Ramey (1995); Rodrik (2000); Wu and Rapallo (1997) all use this measure.

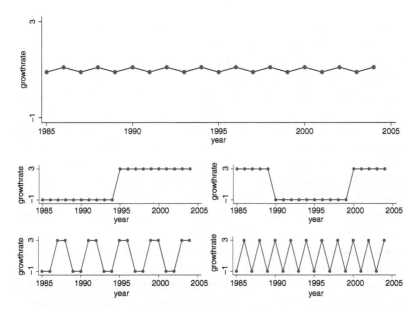

Figure 3.2 Measuring growth-rate volatility.

between two countries, one of which had volatile growth about a stable trend and another that had stable growth but around two very different trends (for instance, if there's a structural break in the time series). But distinguishing between such cases is very important if we are to understand the determinants of volatility. Therefore, I use an alternative to the standard deviation of growth rates: the standard deviation of the residuals from the autoregressive process for growth in GDP per capita, estimated for each country in the sample. The mechanics are simple (*i* indexes countries of which there are *n* in total; *t* indexes time which runs from year 1 to year *T*; and Trend is a year variable):

$$y_{i,t} = \beta_0 + \beta_1 y_{i,t-1} + \beta_2 \text{Trend}_t + \varepsilon_{i,t}$$
$$\varepsilon_{i,t} = \widehat{y_{i,t}} - y_{i,t}$$
$$\text{Volatility}_i = \sqrt{\frac{\sum_{t=1}^{T}(\varepsilon_{i,t} - \bar{\varepsilon}_i)^2}{n}} \tag{3.1}$$

Figure 3.2 illustrates the advantages of this alternative approach over the conventional technique quite vividly. In it, I plot the growth rates of five hypothetical countries. Just looking at the figures, it should be fairly clear that the top graph is the most stable growth trajectory, and that the the bottom-right graph is the least stable or most volatile. The second row shows growth trajectories of countries that are fairly stable but around different means in different sub-periods of their history, while the bottom-left graph shows a slightly less volatile version of the bottom-right. The two ways of measuring volatility provide the same answer in the first most-stable case, but they diverge with the more interesting cases illustrated in the lower four graphs. There the standard deviation of growth is exactly the same in all four cases (2.05), which means that the conventional method for measuring volatility is unable to distinguish between these very different cases. The alternative method, fortunately, does distinguish between them, and in a way that accords with our intuition: the top-left graph is least volatile of the four (1.72) and the bottom-right graph is most volatile (2.43), with the top-right and bottom-left graphs coming in between (1.77 and 2.07 respectively).

Having decided on a measure of growth-rate volatility, the second decision to be made is the appropriate length of time over which to measure volatility. How long a period is long enough? There's no clear theoretically prior answer to this question, and different choices come with different trade-offs. On the one hand, one could calculate the volatility over the entire time period for which data are available, thereby producing one observation per country under study, but this reduces the number of cases available for analysis. An alternative would be to create shorter panels from the larger time series, collapsing five- or ten-year time periods at a time, a tactic common in studies of long-run correlates of economic growth (see Barro 1997). The problem here is that it is not any clearer that five or ten years is the right length of time.[7] Therefore, I err on the side of caution and estimate the regression models using three different dynamic specifications: a pure cross-section in which volatility is measured over the entire period available; ten-year panels; and five-year panels. To the extent that the results are robust across all three choices, we should have more confidence that they are not being driven by research design choices.

Figure 3.3 compares the growth-rate volatility of the OECD states to that of the developing world, and also over time. Regardless of the

---

[7] For instance, Rose and Spiegel (2009) justify using eleven years as the length of the panel in their study since they have fifty-five years of data and this allows them to create five panels of equal length.

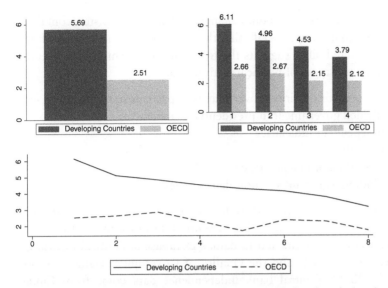

Figure 3.3 Volatility is higher in developing countries, but has declined over time (source: author's calculations from World Bank 2006).

length of time used to calculate volatility, the OECD states have much lower volatility than the developing world, less than half in fact (Prasad *et al.* 2006).[8] However, while the gap between the developed and developing world in terms of volatility persists, the good news is that volatility appears to be declining in recent years (note the downward trend in volatility in both the ten-year and five-year panels (top-right and bottom graphs respectively)).

Political determinants of growth-rate volatility

Credible constraints
What explains the variation in growth-rate volatility cross-nationally?[9] In the previous chapter, I developed a theoretical framework that emphasized the diffusion of policymaking authority to different actors,

---

[8] Between 1960 and 2004, OECD states had an average growth rate of 2.60 percent while the developing world averaged 1.62 percent. Given that we know from previous research as well as Table B.2 that volatility hurts growth, it is quite plausible that much of the difference in growth between developing and OECD countries may be due to volatility.

[9] Appendix A of Klomp and de Haan (2009) provides an extremely useful summary of previous research on the determinants of economic volatility.

which checks arbitrary policy change, and therefore bolsters confidence of economic actors. Specifically, the discussion of the sources of government credibility suggests the following set of empirical indicators for different types of political institutions:

1. minority or coalition governments in parliamentary democracies
2. divided government in presidential democracies
3. independent judiciaries
4. federalism
5. central bank independence
6. binding legislatures in non-democracies.

I construct binary indicators for the existence of these institutions from various cross-national data sources. Data for the first four indicators come from the World Bank's Database of Political Institutions (Beck *et al.* 2001) and the Quality of Government Dataset (Teorell *et al.* 2009). Central bank independence data come from Cukierman *et al.* (1992) and Stürm and de Haan (2001a). Finally, Wright (2008) provides the data on the existence of binding legislatures in non-democracies. Details on the construction of each indicator can be found in Appendix B.

Because volatility is measured over time (either all years, ten-year or five-year panels), the independent variables are measured similarly. Given the binary nature of these indicators, taking their average over time yields a pleasing measure of the percentage of years during which the particular institution was present. That is, if a country never had minority or coalition government, then its average will be 0, whereas if these were present throughout the period, the average would be 1. If minority/coalition government was in effect for only half the period, the average will be 0.5, and so on. The expectation quite obviously is that the longer these credible constraints were in place for a given time period, the lower should be the growth-rate volatility in that time period. Table 3.1 provides preliminary evidence to support this claim. The pairwise correlations between the prevalence of the credible constraint indicators and the level of growth-rate volatility in a given period indicate that coalition/minority governments in parliamentary democracies are correlated with lower volatility (recall that the sample for that correlation is developing country parliamentary democracies only). Similarly, among presidential democracies in the

Table 3.1 *Pairwise correlations between growth-rate volatility and credible constraint indicators*

	Length of panel		
	All years	Ten years	Five years
Minority and coalition governments	−0.31	−0.21	−0.18
Parliamentary democracies only			
Divided government	−0.12	−0.13	−0.14
Presidential democracies only			
Independent judiciaries	−0.19	−0.04	−0.07
Democracies only			
Federalism	−0.07	−0.03	0.03
Democracies only			
Central bank independence	−0.25	−0.09	−0.04
Democracies only			
Binding legislatures	**−0.29**	−0.13	−0.08
Non-democracies only			

Note: Cell-entries are pair-wise correlation coefficients. Correlations that are statistically significant at the 0.05 level or better are reported in **bold**.

developing world, greater frequency of divided government is also correlated with lower volatility, though this correlation is lower than in the parliamentary case. None of the other institutions has a robustly statistically significant correlation with growth-rate volatility, which suggests that partisan checks exert greater influence than more formal institutional structures that might have less credibility in the eyes of investors.

Of course, countries do not necessarily have coalition or minority governments for the entire period (whether all years, ten years, or five years) that constitutes the unit of observation in Table 3.1. This raises the very real concern that the good years within a period might in fact be those in which the credible constraint institutions are absent! The correlations above suggest that this is not the case, but additional confirmation would be useful. Therefore, I utilize annual data to compare years in which, for instance, a minority or coalition government was in charge in a parliamentary democracy to those in which a unified government held power. Unified governments in this sample have a growth-rate volatility score of 5.69; their coalition and minority government counterparts have a score of 3.76, almost two full points lower. This is very encouraging and suggests that the pairwise correlations discussed above are not spurious to the construction of the institutional indicators.

Do these initial results hold up to controlling for alternative political and economic explanations? The main political alternative is that democracy itself is what matters, rather than the particular configuration the government takes. In fact, arguments that focus on democracy have become increasingly common in the literature.

Democracy
Prior to 2000 there were no generalizable explanations of growth-rate volatility in the political economy literature. Since then, however, economists and political scientists have recognized the importance of growth-rate volatility and a few competing explanations have been tendered. Three in particular merit consideration, each of which argues democracies should have lower growth-rate volatility than non-democracies, albeit for different reasons. Harvard economist Dani Rodrik argues that democracies deal with social conflict through compromise rather than through volatility-inducing divisive policymaking. Dennis Quinn and John Woolley argue that democracies have lower growth-rate volatility because leaders are constrained by risk-averse citizens through elections in democracies but face no such constraints in non-democracies. Finally, Siddharth Chandra and Nita Rudra attribute lower growth-rate volatility in democracies to the diversity of institutions found in democracies relative to non-democracies.

In a series of papers, several of which focus exclusively on the Latin American context, Dani Rodrik discusses the fact that democracies have lower growth-rate volatility than non-democracies. Rodrik argues that democracies experience lower volatility because they "induce greater willingness to cooperate and compromise in the political sphere, generating greater stability as a result" (Rodrik 2000: 3). He offers three causal mechanisms through which democracy might facilitate such social cooperation. First, the process of deliberation inherent to democracies can alter original preferences of diverse actors and make them "less selfish and more public spirited" (Ibid.). Second, democracies have more restrictions on the sorts of redistribution possible through policy due to "constitutional rules [that] curtail the power of the majority to expropriate the minority" (Rodrik 2003: 3), which makes contending groups more likely to compromise with each other *ex ante*. Third, democracies induce cooperation by providing a forum for repeated interaction among political groups. So long as political groups in power know that they will not be in power forever, but are likely to return to power at some point in the future, they have an incentive to cooperate with their competitors for fear of retribution when their turn to be out of power arrives.

This cooperation-inducing effect of democratic governance is the reason democracies are better at dealing with negative external shocks than non-democracies (Rodrik 1998a). In the face of negative economic shocks, competing political actors must decide how to behave and, more specifically, how much of the economic pie to demand. The worst-case scenario for a country would be if these political groups were not able to put aside their narrow preferences to attempt to formulate the best policies possible for the nation as a whole. Good institutions, by which Rodrik means institutions that facilitate conflict management and social cooperation, make distributional outcomes less vulnerable to any group's opportunistic behavior aimed at obtaining a disproportionate share of the available resources (Rodrik 1998a: 10). Additionally, adjustment to shocks is worse in states with deep latent social conflicts, which presumably make cooperation that much more difficult by raising the stakes of any agreement (Rodrik 1997a: 8).

Unlike Rodrik's cooperation-based argument, Quinn and Woolley offer a preference-based explanation rooted in the notion of electoral accountability. The key to the Quinn–Woolley story is an assumption that national leaders are systematically different in their propensity to take risks from the populations they govern. Leaders are assumed to be more risk-acceptant than mass publics regardless of the country in which one resides. A second assumption is that "volatility is the result, among other things, of unpredictable, arbitrary, or poor government policies" (Quinn and Woolley 2001: 642). A final assumption is that democracies and elections are better able to hold leaders to avoid risk than non-democracies and threat of overthrow.

If risky or bad policy is the source of growth-rate volatility and leaders are risk-acceptant then countries will have different levels of growth-rate volatility depending on how effectively their leaders are

restrained from taking risks. Societies in which leaders face no consequences for poor policymaking should, by this logic, have higher
levels of growth-rate volatility than those that punish their leaders
for poor performance. Quinn and Woolley argue that the presence
of elections as an institutional means of selecting a nation's leaders is
critical to constraining leaders and preventing them from making risky
choices. Since leaders know that their publics are risk-averse and that
they will be punished for volatile national economic performance, in
countries where leaders are accountable to their publics for re-election
(i.e., democracies) leaders should be less likely to make poor choices.
Quinn and Woolley replicate three published studies of economic voting, including in these replications a measure for growth-rate volatility.
They find that increased growth-rate volatility hurts the vote share
of the incumbent, which they take as evidence that (1) voters punish
volatility and (2) that, therefore, leaders in democracies should avoid
volatility-inducing policy.

Siddharth Chandra and Nita Rudra draw on finance theory to model
a country's set of formal national institutions as a portfolio, where a
formal national institution "is an institution that has effective authority
over aspects of policy making and implementation" (Chandra 1998:
5). The more institutions a country has, the more diversified its institutional portfolio. And, institutional diversity should lead both to less
growth-rate volatility cross-sectionally (meaning that more institutionally diverse countries should have lower volatility as a group than
less institutionally diverse countries) as well as lower volatility over
time.

In the Chandra–Rudra model, each institution (i) takes a policy
action (j), the realization of which is a random variable (R_j). Of course,
not all formal national institutions are created equal and Chandra's
model allows for different institutions to have different powers (η_i)
relative to each other as well as to make different contributions (ϕ_{ij}) to
the implementation of any action j. Finally, institutional independence
is defined as the correlation $\rho(\phi_{ij}, \phi_{i'j})$, such that two institutions are
independent if the correlation is 0 and completely dependent if it's 1.
The relationship between the institutions matters too and policy variability is reduced if institutions are independent of each other since
their initial outputs are therefore not dependent on each other. The
overall output (O) of the economy is the expectation of a weighted

sum of these policy outputs from each institution:

$$E[O_j] = \sum_{i=1}^{n} E[\phi_{ij}\eta_i R_j] \qquad (3.2)$$

Given this set-up, "if the distribution of ϕ_{ij} is identical for all countries, it follows directly that the greater is the diversification of institutional authority among institutions, the smaller is the variance of outcomes in a sample of countries with that level of diversification" (Chandra 1998: 10). In other words,

In systems in which there is a relative absence of checks and balances, formal national institutions have the power to maintain an economic milieu which can have extreme implications for economic outcomes. In comparison, in economies that have strong systems of checks and balances, particular institutions are more constrained in the extent to which they can mold the economic environment, with the result that there is less room for formal national institutions to steer the economy toward any extreme. (Chandra 1998: 17)

We thus have three alternative political explanations for cross-national variations in growth-rate volatility, which I summarize in Figure 3.4. Each theory makes an important contribution to our understanding of the political sources of growth-rate volatility, specifically offering insights on some of the different roles democracy may play in mitigating volatility. However, each lacks precision and concreteness regarding the specific democratic institutions, economic policies, and mechanisms through which democracy and policy in the abstract reduce volatility. Empirically, all three studies use the same index of political and civil liberties to measure democracy, preventing one from distinguishing among these three possible mechanisms by which regime type could relate to volatility and from exploring what specific aspects of regime type produce that relationship.

For example, Chandra and Rudra's argument hinges on the diversification of formal national institutions (i.e., the institutional milieu), but they never specify which institutions should matter for growth-rate volatility and how. Formal national institutions, in their classification, include the press, judiciary, trade unions, religious organizations, businesses and business organizations (Chandra and Rudra 2008: 17). The only caveat they add is that each of these institutions should

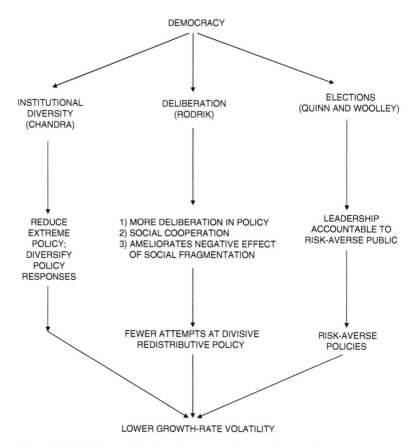

Figure 3.4 Existing political explanations of growth-rate volatility.

be "free," presumably so that each can have an independent effect on the policy outputs of the government, but there is no operational definition of "free," making it hard to know how to apply this framework to the real world. Furthermore, at this level of abstractness, it is impossible to know which institutions within a democracy are more important than others or to identify the precise causal mechanisms by which these institutions affect growth-rate volatility. (How, for example, do religious organizations or the press affect growth rates or their volatility?) Similarly, Rodrik's argument emphasizes the compromise-inducing effects of democracy but without identifying what aspects or types of democracy best produce this effect. Is compromise simply the result of democratic leaders being elected or is it a product of the legislative process? As such, should we expect parliamentary and presidential democracies to behave the same or differently?

A second area for extension is the role played by non-governmental actors. The arguments tendered by Rodrik, Quinn and Woolley, and Chandra focus on the role played by governments such that the only causal mechanism explored is that between government policy and subsequent growth-rate volatility. Missing from such formulations is any account of what private (non-governmental) economic actors are doing, how they are responding to (expected) government policy, or how these actions and decisions might generate or reduce growth-rate volatility.

The argument I presented in the previous chapter addresses these shortcomings of the existing literature. I identify a specific configuration of state institutions – diffusion of policymaking authority to multiple actors with accountability to different constituencies – that lowers the average level of growth-rate volatility a country experiences. Specifically, the diffusion of policymaking authority across different policymakers with different accountabilities provides a set of *credible constraints* on an executive's ability to change policy autonomously (and potentially arbitrarily). Such constraints from potentially arbitrary policy and from policy variability bolsters confidence among private economic actors. The investor confidence engendered in countries with such institutions, in turn, both fosters longer-term, more stable investment and helps those countries withstand temporary shocks, preventing them from creating the full-blown crises that are more likely to emerge in countries lacking such institutions as panicked investors flee the likely unstable and/or poor policy-environment in the aftermath of shocks. Thus, the inability of governments lacking the credible constraints of diffuse policymaking authority and accountability to commit credibly to present and future policies induces savings and investment volatility and, thereby, growth-rate volatility. Thus, my argument can incorporate the institutional diversification argument of Chandra as well as the social compromise thesis put forth by Rodrik and, since separation of powers is more likely in democracies than non-democracies, my framework accounts for Quinn and Woolley's explanation as well. However, unlike the extant theories, which focus exclusively on "risky" government policy as the source of volatility, I also focus on the role private investors play and introduce the importance of savings and investment volatility for growth-rate volatility.

An additional advantage of the framework I present is that it can be used to explain cross-temporal variation in growth-rate volatility within countries, as well as cross-sectional variation across states at a given point in time (or over some period of time). Consider the case of India, for instance. As I noted earlier, and as Kapur (2005) documents as well, India's economic growth trajectory displays significant variation in growth-rate volatility over time, with a definite trend towards lower volatility over time, and with clear breakpoints between periods of higher and lower volatility (I will return to the Indian case in Chapter 5). What explains such cross-temporal variation in growth-rate volatility? An explanation that simply emphasizes democracy is less useful for answering such a question since India has been a reasonably robust democracy since its independence in 1947. Yet, this difficult question of explaining dynamic variation in countries that do not experience regime transitions is answered fruitfully by using my framework of credible constraints, which directs our theoretical attention beyond questions of regime to more sophisticated considerations of the particular networks of institutions that comprise the "state."

This critique aside, I control for democracy in the models to get at other aspects of democracy not captured by my credible constraints indicators (for instance, accountability-by-elections, civil society, and free press). I use a binary indicator from José Cheibub and Jennifer Gandhi for the existence of democracy (Cheibub and Gandhi 2004).

Political instability
The final "political" factors included in the model concern political instability. Including these variables allows me to distinguish the effects of "political" instability from "policy" instability, which is what the credible constraint institutions help prevent. I use two different indicators of political instability. The first is the widely used political instability index compiled by Arthur Banks, which includes the following forms of domestic conflict: assassinations, general strikes, guerilla warfare, government crises, purges, riots, revolutions, and anti-government demonstrations. The second focuses on the incidence of violent political conflict that exceeds a minimum threshold of people killed in the conflict; this variable comes from the Uppsala Conflict Data Project. Both indicators of political instability are expected to

scare economic actors, hurt growth, and generate economic instability (Alesina *et al.* 1992).

Economic factors

While my interest in growth-rate volatility lies in its capacity to illuminate how politics influences economic outcomes, the fact is that much of what causes some countries to be more volatile than others lies in the realm of economics rather than politics. Economists' explanations for growth-rate volatility can be divided into two categories: those arguing output fluctuations are due to exogenous shocks to the economic system and those suggesting the causes of such fluctuations are endogenous to the economic system. Exogenous factors are typically terms-of-trade shocks caused by natural disasters in either the home state or a trading partner. The endogenous factors identified are generally the strength of the financial sector and investment patterns, as well as the stability of government policies thought to affect growth.

Trade

Openness to trade has long been considered an important aspect of a country's growth strategy. The arguments on behalf of trade-led growth are widely documented and I will not repeat them here.[10] The effect of trade openness on growth-rate volatility is less definitely known. Two relationships suggest themselves. First, countries with large trade sectors are more vulnerable to instabilities in foreign markets, which might flow across borders through the interdependent trade relationships that have been created, affecting sources of imports or markets for exports. Second, terms-of-trade shocks[11] can cause growth-rate volatility because sharp changes in the relative prices of exports to imports have dramatic effects on the trading portfolio of

[10] See Bhagwati (2004) for a recent discussion, but see Rodrik (1997b, 1998a) or Rodriguez and Rodrik (1999) for a more skeptical view.
[11] A terms-of-trade shock is defined as "the growth in the local currency price of exports times the share of exports in GDP less the growth in the local currency price of imports times the share of imports in GDP, which captures both the magnitude of price fluctuations (changes in export and import prices) and their importance for the domestic economy (weighted by the shares of exports and imports in GDP)" (Easterly and Kraay 2000: 2021). Terms-of-trade shocks are typically treated as exogenous to the economy (Barro 1997: 30).

the states in question. This is especially true if the state is largely dependent on a few exports or imports, such as minerals or natural resources (Auty 2001; Sachs and Warner 1995).

The empirical support for these hypotheses has been mixed. Wu and Rapallo (1997) test the first of the above hypotheses and find no relationship. This is not really surprising since the simplistic hypothesis that states where trade comprises a larger share of gross domestic product (GDP) are more volatile is probably incorrect. The relationship between trade and growth-rate volatility is far more complex, involving the interaction of various factors. For instance, whether trade exposure dampens or heightens volatility should depend on whether domestic or foreign shock variance dominates and the diversification of the domestic economy, especially the state's export portfolio.

These interactive effects are supported by Easterly and Kraay (2000) who, in their study of why small states, such as island nations in the Caribbean or Pacific, have more volatile growth rates than their larger counterparts, argue small states are more sensitive to terms of trade shocks because international trade comprises a relatively higher proportion of their national economy and because smaller states have more specialized export portfolios "both in terms of products exported and in terms of export markets" (Easterly and Kraay 2000: 2022). Adverse trade shocks therefore reverberate through the small economy quickly and often devastatingly since the domestic economy is too small to balance the foreign shock. Extending this argument beyond small island states, Easterly *et al.* (2000: 10) find that terms-of-trade volatility and openness to trade are associated with increased growth-rate volatility across their sample.

To account for these effects of trade, I include in the model four independent variables, each designed to capture a different part of the overall relationship trade has with volatility. First, I measure total "trade openness," which is simply the proportion of a country's gross domestic product comprised by exports and imports. Just which way this relationship works is unclear, and depends on just what is being traded and with how many countries, i.e., how diversified the country's trading portfolio is.[12] What we are particularly interested in is

---

[12] Malik and Temple (2009) find that geographically remote countries have less diversified export portfolios and greater volatility in output growth. Rose and Spiegel (2009), discussed below, report a similar finding for financial remoteness.

the degree to which a country's trading patterns make it vulnerable to external shocks. Therefore, I control for whether a state is a primary commodity exporter. Oxford University's Paul Collier summarizes the concern with respect to African countries, which comprise the bulk of the world's primary commodity exporters:

The world prices of primary commodities are highly volatile, producing both booms and crashes. Most African countries are dependent upon a very narrow range of commodities and this exposes them to severe macroeconomic shocks. For other developing regions such shocks are largely a thing of the past due to export diversification. Globally these large shocks are problematic for exporting countries. Typically, booms do not translate into sustained increases in income – they are missed opportunities – whereas crashes produce devastating and long-lasting declines. (Collier 2002: 2–3)

Put another way, high concentration of exports on a few primary commodities is a major source of terms-of-trade and growth-rate volatility. I therefore create an indicator for whether over 75 percent of a country's exports are comprised of primary commodities, excluding fuels.[13] Third, I control for the size of the agricultural sector in the economy. Finally, I calculate whether a country experienced a terms-of-trade shock using World Bank data on the country's export and import values.

Financial sector and capital flows

In a report to the Annual Bank Conference on Development Economics, Easterly *et al.* (2001) point their collective finger at the financial sector as the principal culprit for growth-rate volatility. Neoclassical economic theory, in their opinion, fails to anticipate wealth and cash flow constraints arising in imperfect markets. As a result, previous macroeconomic analyses have underestimated how the behavior of firms facing cash and wealth flow constraints results in output fluctuations. This relationship is mediated by financial market institutions (such as banks and security markets), which affect how firms handle

---

[13] Data come from UNCTAD (2002). By this definition, primary commodity exporters are Belize, Botswana, Burundi, Chad, Chile, Côte d'Ivoire, Cuba, Ethiopia, Guinea-Bissau, Jamaica, Kiribati, Malawi, Mali, Mauritius, Mozambique, Myanmar, Nicaragua, Niger, Paraguay, Solomon Islands, Sudan, Suriname, Tajikistan, Tanzania, Tonga, Uganda, Zaire, and Zimbabwe.

shocks to their cash flows (Easterly *et al.* 2001: 191). The most important role of such financial institutions is to deter the occurrence of
bankruptcy chains, which could be triggered by the bankruptcy of a
single firm in conjunction with the complex credit interrelationships
among firms characterizing modern economies.

Initial empirical investigations by Easterly *et al.* (2001: 193) on a
sample of "60 to 74 countries in a panel created by aggregating over the
periods 1960–78 and 1979–97" support the hypothesis that financial
depth, as measured by the ratio of private credit to GDP, dampens
growth-rate volatility. Therefore, I control for the financial liquidity of
the country by including a measure of the level of credit available in
the economy, operationalized as the level of money and quasi-money
(M2) as a percentage of GDP.

An alternative claim is that capital-account openness might give
states access to international capital, thereby easing credit constraints,
or that capital-account openness actually induces volatility. Since the
behavior of capital-holders is a consequence of the political institutions
that are the focus of the analysis, I prefer not to control for capital-
account openness in the model. However, when I use the Chinn and Ito
(2006) measure of capital-account openness, that variable is not statistically significant in the models reported below.[14] Another alternative
financial factor has been identified recently by economists Andrew Rose
and Mark Spiegel (2009), who find that international financial remoteness – a country's proximity to major international financial centers – is
positively correlated with macroeconomic volatility. Yet, as the authors
themselves note, the effect of financial remoteness "does not matter
as consistently or robustly as political institutions" and their results
are sensitive to model-specification details. Nevertheless, their analysis
makes clear that future research must pay greater attention to the role
of financial integration in affecting output volatility.

Macroeconomic conditions and policy

The final set of economic factors concern the macroeconomic conditions present and policy choices of governments. Quinn and Woolley
state that "volatility is the result, among other things, of unpredictable,
arbitrary, or poor governmental policies" (Quinn and Woolley 2001:
642). In this view, macroeconomic crises are the result of unsustained

---

[14] Results available from author.

or unsustainable government policies, such as large government sectors, budget deficits, and high inflation. These particular policies are also associated with poor economic performance in general and have been roundly condemned by international development agencies. For instance, the World Bank states that "high inflation increases uncertainty, discourages investment and technological change, [and] distorts relative prices" (World Bank 1987: 14), while Ricardo Caballero, in his work for the Inter-American Development Bank, argues that inflation and inefficient government budgets are the primary cause of Latin American economic crises (Caballero 2000b, 2000c). Acemoglu *et al.* (2003b) investigate the relationship between macroeconomic policies and volatility empirically using cross-national data from 1970 to 1997. They find that "average size of government (measured by government consumption to GDP ratio) [and] (log) average rate of inflation" have a robust positive effect on growth-rate volatility and the likelihood of severe crisis. Therefore, I include a measure of government consumption as a share of GDP and the level of inflation in the model.

I also control for basic macroeconomic conditions that form the backdrop for the country. I control for overall growth in the economy, population growth, and the overall level of economic development in the economy. Joined with the political variables and other economic variables discussed above, this gives me a theoretically motivated model of growth-rate volatility, suitable for empirical testing. While I have tested variants of this model to ensure the robustness of the results reported below, I focus in the text on this base model to ease presentation.

Results

I combine the set of economic and political factors suggested by theory in a single model of growth-rate volatility. Because the credible constraint variables are only coded as present if the country is a democracy, the baseline political category is non-democracy. Some might protest the lack of differentiation in my treatment of non-democratic governments, but to the extent that non-democratic governments can form credible commitments and reduce the volatility they experience, this should make it harder to find any effect in the credible constraint indicators, and therefore this constitutes a more rigorous test of the argument.

As a robustness check, I have checked to see if Wright's conception of binding legislatures in authoritarian regimes gives us any purchase on growth-rate volatility, but it does not. Since that variable is more limited than the rest of the data set (it only exists from 1991 to 2002), including it here is very costly in terms of missing data. However, given the fascinating scholarly work being done on dictatorial institutions by scholars such as Jennifer Gandhi and Joseph Wright, among others, future scholars should definitely add to the models described below once we have more comprehensive indicators for these regimes.

Table 3.2 presents the results of four regression models explaining growth-rate volatility. The results broadly confirm the expectation that states in which credible constraints against policy change exist experience lower levels of growth-rate volatility, but with important exceptions. Minority and coalition governments in parliamentary democracies emerge as the most consistent dampener of volatility, with independent central banks a close second. Neither federalism nor judicial independence appear very important for volatility. Interestingly, however, while the divided presidential government indicator is largely insignificant, when one considers the shortest-length panel of five years, that indicator is correlated with *higher* levels of growth-rate volatility ($p = 0.06$), *ceteris paribus*. To some extent, this could be seen as confirmation of the intuitions of scholars who have bemoaned the gridlock it has created in Latin America (Ames 2001; Mainwaring 1993). The dynamics of divided government differ fundamentally from those of minority/coalition governments: while the latter encourage policy moderation, the former generates policy gridlock, making it nearly impossible for states to make the policies they require in order to attract savings and investment or stimulate economic growth.

Interestingly these results are robust to controlling for democracy more generally, which also proves a robust determinant of lower growth-rate volatility. Clearly the channels through which democracy dampens volatility are multifarious, and may include any or all of those suggested by scholars like Rodrik, Quinn and Woolley, or Chandra and Rudra.[15] Given that democracy co-exists with the credible constraint institutions, finding an effect for the latter while controlling for the former provides strong evidence that the effects of credible constraints are

[15] See also Mobarak (2005); Klomp and de Haan (2009).

Table 3.2 Regression results: credible constraints and growth-rate volatility

DV: growth-rate volatility

Sample:	All years, all LDCs	All years, democracies	Decade, all LDCs	Five-year, all LDCs
Minority/coalition govts	-2.34 $(1.61)^{0.15}$	-4.03 $(1.09)^{0.00}$	-1.59 $(0.96)^{0.10}$	-1.35 $(0.71)^{0.06}$
Divided presidential govts	3.64 $(3.05)^{0.24}$	1.51 $(1.29)^{0.27}$	2.11 $(1.33)^{0.12}$	2.03 $(1.07)^{0.06}$
Independent judiciaries	-0.93 $(1.14)^{0.42}$	0.54 $(1.03)^{0.61}$	-0.52 $(0.60)^{0.39}$	-0.45 $(0.53)^{0.40}$
Federalism	-0.08 $(1.14)^{0.95}$	2.77 $(0.97)^{0.02}$	0.35 $(1.04)^{0.74}$	0.23 $(1.01)^{0.82}$
Central bank indep.	-1.73 $(0.75)^{0.02}$	-0.71 $(0.92)^{0.46}$	-1.28 $(0.56)^{0.02}$	-0.81 $(0.49)^{0.11}$
Democracy	-2.89 $(0.92)^{0.00}$		-1.70 $(0.66)^{0.01}$	-1.28 $(0.66)^{0.05}$
Political instability	0.25 $(0.14)^{0.09}$	0.04 $(0.24)^{0.87}$	0.07 $(0.07)^{0.32}$	-0.03 $(0.07)^{0.72}$
Civil wars	0.09 $(0.61)^{0.88}$	-1.29 $(0.73)^{0.10}$	1.09 $(0.64)^{0.09}$	0.62 $(0.66)^{0.35}$
GDP growth	-0.08 $(0.20)^{0.69}$	-0.39 $(0.18)^{0.06}$	0.06 $(0.09)^{0.51}$	-0.05 $(0.11)^{0.65}$
Population growth	-0.49 $(0.24)^{0.04}$	-0.72 $(0.27)^{0.02}$	-0.19 $(0.18)^{0.29}$	-0.24 $(0.19)^{0.23}$
GDP per capita (Log)	1.79 $(0.45)^{0.00}$	0.29 $(0.74)^{0.69}$	1.25 $(0.42)^{0.00}$	1.05 $(0.34)^{0.00}$
Inflation (Log)	0.26 $(0.24)^{0.28}$	-0.18 $(0.29)^{0.54}$	0.39 $(0.25)^{0.12}$	0.33 $(0.29)^{0.25}$
Trade openness (% GDP)	0.01 $(0.01)^{0.36}$	0.04 $(0.01)^{0.01}$	0.02 $(0.01)^{0.05}$	0.01 $(0.01)^{0.39}$
Agriculture (% GDP)	0.16 $(0.04)^{0.00}$	0.13 $(0.13)^{0.12}$	0.13 $(0.04)^{0.00}$	0.13 $(0.03)^{0.00}$
Primary commodity exporter	0.12 $(0.66)^{0.86}$	1.46 $(0.81)^{0.10}$	-0.06 $(0.63)^{0.92}$	-0.16 $(0.64)^{0.81}$
Terms-of-trade shock	0.02 $(0.04)^{0.63}$	0.20 $(0.10)^{0.07}$	-0.004 $(0.01)^{0.77}$	0.01 $(0.01)^{0.41}$
Government consumption	0.17 $(0.06)^{0.01}$	-0.04 $(0.07)^{0.58}$	0.07 $(0.04)^{0.07}$	0.05 $(0.04)^{0.13}$
Financial liquidity (M2)	0.02 $(0.02)^{0.36}$	-0.09 $(0.03)^{0.01}$	0.01 $(0.01)^{0.63}$	0.03 $(0.01)^{0.07}$

Table 3.2 *(cont.)*

| DV: growth-rate volatility | | | | |
Sample:	All years, all LDCs	All years, democracies	Decade, all LDCs	Five-year, all LDCs
Time trend			-0.57 $(0.25)^{0.03}$	-0.21 $(0.16)^{0.19}$
Constant	-14.21 $(4.55)^{0.00}$	3.04 $(8.50)^{0.73}$	-8.34 $(4.29)^{0.05}$	-6.22 $(3.81)^{0.11}$
No. of countries	108	30	105	105
No. of observations	108	30	260	349
Root mean square error	2.44	1.09	2.94	3.49

Note: Cell entries are OLS coefficients with standard errors corrected for clustering by country reported in parentheses and two-sided p-values superscripted.

not just those of democracy, but represent a distinct channel: increased confidence that policy will remain intact or change only incrementally. I will provide more direct evidence of this channel in the next chapter, but more discussion of these results is called for before I get to that.

What other factors influence volatility? As expected, political instability (as distinguished from expected policy instability due to political institutions) increases volatility, though this result is not very robust to using different lengths of time over which to measure volatility. The more consistent predictors of growth-rate volatility tend to be variables such as level of economic development, which in the developing world has the opposite relationship to volatility than we might have expected. Richer countries have higher levels of volatility in this analysis, which makes sense when we recall that the volatility measure is sensitive to changes in the mean trend in the data. That is, as these high-performing states transition from low levels of growth early on to higher levels of growth later, the volatility measure picks this up. This might raise a concern that the volatility-dampening effects of coalition governments reported above are coming at the expense of overall growth, but I will provide some additional data later in this chapter to show that the opposite is in fact true.

Another consistent factor is the size of the agricultural sector in the economy. Agriculture is a volatile sector of the economy, subject to the vagaries of the weather and to price shocks. As expected, my analysis confirms that states that are more dependent on agriculture in the economy experience higher levels of volatility. The same is not true for primary commodity exporters or terms of trade shocks, neither of which is revealed to have any effect on growth-rate volatility (though both variables are statistically significant in the democracy sub-sample model reported in column 2 of Table 3.2). Likewise, financial liquidity only appears to matter in democratic settings (column 2) but not overall. One explanation might be that democratic states have a considerable financial advantage over non-democratic states; the mean value for M2 as a share of GDP for democracies is 44 percent, while it is just 32 percent for non-democracies, a difference that is highly statistically significant. Controlling for democracy masks the effect of financial liquidity, which becomes more apparent when we only focus on democracies. The same is likely true for why terms-of-trade – a factor that has consistently emerged in the economic literature – is not significant in the pooled sample. Non-democratic states experience much larger terms-of-trade shocks on average (2.84 percent in these data) than democracies (-0.61 percent), and this difference is also statistically significant.

The final economic factor that affects growth-rate volatility is the size of government consumption as a share of the economy. Economists have long bemoaned the dangers of large states for the economy, and this concern is borne out by these results. High levels of government consumption are not sustainable and make states prone to fiscal crises.

The preceding analysis focused on the developing world's experience, and some readers might wonder if the argument fits the OECD experience in the least. The literature on the increased macroeconomic stability in the OECD focuses almost exclusively on economic variables and the improvement of demand management strategies by governments and central banks. While not disputing any of these claims, I would argue that the OECD experience is nevertheless consistent with its central argument. For most of the 1945–present period, the United States has had divided presidential government, and this coincides with the most stable period of US growth in its history, a point documented by Douglas Hibbs in his seminal work on the American political economy (Hibbs 1987). Further, many of the OECD states in Europe have the types of centrist coalition parliamentary governments that I argue should be most likely to enjoy high credibility.

This point aside, decreases in macroeconomic volatility in the OECD have much to do with increased technical expertise in smoothing the business cycle, and the delegation of authority over monetary policy to independent central banks. This is a point anticipated by my argument which makes clear that delegation to independent central banks is one method of achieving credibility, but it does highlight the puzzle of why such institutions have been less effective in the developing world. That is a question beyond the scope of this book, though I will return to it tangentially in later chapters, and deserves more attention by future researchers.

Robustness check: extreme volatility

The results reported in the previous section support the argument that credible constraints that promote policy moderation reduce the volatility of growth rates experienced by developing countries. And this result is robust to controlling for democracy and a host of economic and other political factors. But how confident can we be in the results? To assess their robustness, I use another dependent variable. I create an indicator for "extreme volatility," which I define as volatility greater than the world average volatility in a given year. That is, a state is coded as having experienced extreme volatility if in a given year its deviation from average growth is greater than the world average deviation from average growth in that year. All states experience year-to-year fluctuations in growth, of course; what the extreme volatility indicators seek to highlight are those states whose deviations from the normal are exceptional relative to their counterparts. This comparison also takes into account common international shocks that affect all states in the international system in a given year (for instance, the oil crisis of 1973). I calculate the percentage of years over the entire period that a state experienced extreme volatility. Table 3.3 reports the pairwise correlations for the frequency of years of extreme volatility with the credible constraint indicators.

As in the main analysis, only the *partisan* constraints emerge as significant correlates of volatility. Both coalition/minority parliamentary governments and divided presidential governments are correlated with fewer years of extreme volatility. The first of these findings is consistent with the prior analysis, but the divided government finding appears to contradict the earlier result that this institutional configuration increases growth-rate volatility. This is not true though.

Table 3.3 *Pairwise correlations between extreme volatility and credible constraint indicators*

	Length of panel		
	All years	Ten years	Five years
Minority and coalition governments	−0.12	**−0.21**	−0.15
Parliamentary democracies only			
Divided government	**−0.14**	−0.12	−0.13
Presidential democracies only			
Independent judiciaries	0.11	0.03	0.05
Democracies only			
Federalism	**−0.14**	−0.02	−0.03
Democracies only			
Central bank independence	**−0.25**	−0.11	−0.07
Democracies only			
Binding legislatures	−0.11	−0.09	0.08
Non-democracies only			

Note: Cell-entries are pairwise correlation coefficients. Correlations that are statistically significant at the 0.05 level or better are reported in **bold**.

Presidential democracies in which the executive and legislature are controlled by different parties experience fewer years of *extreme* volatility but it remains true that they do experience higher levels of growth-rate volatility than their unified counterparts. Since democracies overall are far less likely than non-democracies to suffer extreme volatility, it is not a surprise that divided presidential democracies are also less likely to have extreme fluctuations in growth relative to the rest of the world. But once one accounts for democracy, as I did in the previous analysis, the gridlock inherent in divided presidentialism is seen to lead to less stable growth rates.

Using the same set of variables as in the regression analysis of growth-rate volatility above, I estimate a pair of models using this "extreme volatility" variable as a dependent variable. Since extreme volatility, by definition, is an unusual event, I utilize the entire period as the unit of observation. The results are therefore based on a cross-section of countries for which data are available, and the dependent variable is thus the proportion of years under study during which a country had extreme volatility. Table 3.4 reports the results of this analysis.

Table 3.4 *Regression results: credible constraints and extreme volatility*

Sample:	DV: extreme volatility	
	All states	*LDCs only*
Minority/coalition govts	−0.21	−0.18
	$(0.11)^{0.05}$	$(0.13)^{0.15}$
Divided presidential govts	−0.05	0.004
	$(0.15)^{0.77}$	$(0.18)^{0.98}$
Independent judiciaries	−0.04	−0.01
	$(0.05)^{0.45}$	$(0.05)^{0.89}$
Federalism	−0.03	−0.01
	$(0.05)^{0.59}$	$(0.08)^{0.90}$
Central bank indep.	−0.09	−0.06
	$(0.04)^{0.02}$	$(0.05)^{0.18}$
Democracy	−0.15	−0.18
	$(0.06)^{0.02}$	$(0.07)^{0.01}$
Political instability	0.01	0.01
	$(0.01)^{0.25}$	$(0.01)^{0.16}$
Civil wars	0.03	0.02
	$(0.04)^{0.48}$	$(0.04)^{0.55}$
GDP growth	−0.01	−0.01
	$(0.01)^{0.17}$	$(0.01)^{0.14}$
Population growth	−0.03	−0.05
	$(0.02)^{0.05}$	$(0.02)^{0.02}$
GDP per capita (Log)	0.08	0.10
	$(0.02)^{0.00}$	$(0.03)^{0.00}$
Inflation (Log)	0.03	0.02
	$(0.02)^{0.05}$	$(0.02)^{0.23}$
Trade openness (% GDP)	0.001	0.001
	$(0.001)^{0.03}$	$(0.001)^{0.21}$
Agriculture (% GDP)	0.01	0.01
	$(0.002)^{0.01}$	$(0.002)^{0.00}$
Primary commodity exporter	−0.002	0.003
	$(0.03)^{0.95}$	$(0.93)^{0.91}$
Terms-of-trade shock	0.002	0.002
	$(0.003)^{0.54}$	$(0.002)^{0.49}$
Government consumption	0.01	0.01
	$(0.003)^{0.04}$	$(0.003)^{0.01}$

Table 3.4 *(cont.)*

Sample:	DV: extreme volatility	
	All states	*LDCs only*
Financial liquidity (M2)	0.004 $(0.001)^{0.49}$	−0.001 $(0.001)^{0.3}$
Constant	−0.64 $(0.27)^{0.02}$	−0.76 $(0.27)^{0.01}$
No. of countries	123	108
Root mean square error	0.14	0.14

Note: Cell entries are OLS coefficients with robust standard errors in parentheses and two-sided p-values superscripted.

The results of the extreme volatility analysis confirm the major results of the chapter thus far. Controlling for whether the country is a democracy, countries with parliamentary coalition or minority governments experienced lower rates of extreme volatility. Admittedly, this effect is strongest when one includes all countries in the analysis, and falls beyond conventional thresholds for statistical significance when one limits the sample to developing countries only. Yet, even in the developing country sample, the estimated effect is negative and the estimated effect is quite stable. Rather the "loss" of significance is due to a slightly larger standard error and fewer degrees of freedom. Thus, for all intents and purposes, the volatility-dampening effect of coalition governments is substantiated by this robustness analysis.

Are both stability and higher growth possible?

Unlike the majority of studies on national economic performance published in political science or economics, I have focused thus far on explaining variation in the volatility of growth rather than its mean. This focus is justified for volatility as it has important consequences for people's lives, as well as for a country's ability to attract future investment and foster longer-term economic development. To the extent that volatility does hurt future growth, as the analysis earlier in this chapter suggests it does, political institutional configurations, such as coalition governments in parliamentary democracies or independent central banks, have at least an indirect effect on future economic growth. But critics might well argue that the focus on future growth underestimates the costs of potentially sacrificing growth in the present. That is, if institutions like coalition governments make policymaking harder and therefore prevent necessary economic reform, they might hurt economic growth. What good is more stable growth if the stability is around a low average level of growth? Would not poor countries prefer higher average growth even if it comes at the price of increased volatility? At one level, it is unclear that this trade-off is so simple or at any rate that its distributional implications are straightforward, and suggests that future research might want to consider the consequences of such a trade-off explicitly. At what point, for instance, do human development outcomes become impervious to increased volatility and sensitive to the level of economic growth, or vice versa? But, at another level, even without answers to such interesting and policy-relevant debates, the question of whether stability and growth are both attainable is empirical. This section seeks to answer it.

Studying economic growth has a rich heritage. Growth is not the only outcome worthy of attention, but it might certainly be one of the more important because of its importance for other things citizens desire such as increased nutrition, better health, and longer lives. The dominant strategy among growth theorists is to focus on getting economic policies correct. To this framework, I have added the necessity of convincing private economic actors that policy commitments are credible and that they can plan economic activity with the understanding that policy changes will be infrequent and incremental. When scholars have studied the impact of politics on economic growth, they have emphasized the importance of democracy in the main, even though empirical evidence for the value of democracy for promoting economic growth is sorely lacking (Przeworski *et al.* 2000). But even democratic governments vary in how they distribute policymaking authority, and different institutional configurations that produce policy stability do so for different reasons. While coalition and minority governments in parliamentary democracies generate incentives for policy moderation, divided governments in presidential systems create policy gridlock. The former, I've argued, is far more desirable for developing countries that need their governments to govern, but that seek to moderate their behavior by requiring them to consider the diversity of views that abound in the society-at-large. The latter, on the other hand, by allowing different branches of government to exist independently of each other, reduces the likelihood of reform – even when it's sorely needed – and encourages a more divisive policy stasis. This argument was borne out by my analysis of growth-rate volatility; does it apply equally well to economic growth?

To find out, I apply the empirical model developed above to explain cross-national variation in economic growth. For consistency, I use the same set of independent variables as above, switching only the dependent variable, which makes sense since average growth and the volatility of that growth are two moments of the same time-series (data-generating process). I use averages of growth and the other independent variables over two different periods – ten-year panels and five-year panels – for the sake of robustness. And, as above, I use both the full sample and a sub-sample of countries that were democratic for at least half the period of study. Table 3.5 reports the results of this analysis.

The results from the growth model support the theoretical framework developed in this book: the most robust political determinant of economic growth is the presence of coalition or minority parliamentary governments. The more years in the period that a country was governed by a coalition or minority parliamentary government, the higher the country's average economic growth. Nor is the size of this effect small. According to the estimates for Model 1 (the first column) in Table 3.5, a country that had coalition government throughout the ten-year period had 1.33 percent higher growth per year in that period than its counterparts. If we limit the sample only to countries that were mostly democratic throughout the period, that effect increases by a full percentage point to 2.36 percent higher economic growth, all else held equal. Given that the average growth rate for developing countries over the time period being studied here is 1.6 percent, the potential gains from this political-institutional structure are significant. And it's worth emphasizing that this positive effect of coalition governments is found even when controlling for democracy, which is not significant itself. This accords with the pessimistic conclusions about democracy's growth-enhancing prospects in the existing literature, though I would hasten to remind readers that democracy had a robust negative effect

Table 3.5 *Regression results: credible constraints and economic growth*

| | DV: economic growth | | | |
| | Ten-year panels | | Five-year panels | |
Sample:	All LDCs	Democracies	All LDCs	Democracies
Minority/coalition govts	1.33	2.36	0.91	1.73
	$(0.79)^{0.10}$	$(0.79)^{0.01}$	$(0.68)^{0.19}$	$(0.67)^{0.01}$
Divided presidential govts	−0.24	−0.44	−1.90	−1.81
	$(1.25)^{0.85}$	$(1.24)^{0.72}$	$(1.09)^{0.09}$	$(1.25)^{0.15}$
Independent judiciaries	0.76	0.57	0.47	−0.02
	$(0.59)^{0.21}$	$(0.45)^{0.21}$	$(0.68)^{0.50}$	$(0.67)^{0.98}$
Federalism	0.84	−0.49	1.59	2.26
	$(0.98)^{0.39}$	$(1.15)^{0.67}$	$(1.07)^{0.14}$	$(1.34)^{0.10}$
Central bank indep.	0.12	−0.29	0.15	−0.88
	$(0.55)^{0.83}$	$(0.55)^{0.73}$	$(0.51)^{0.77}$	$(0.57)^{0.13}$
Democracy	0.41		0.75	
	$(0.47)^{0.39}$		$(0.56)^{0.19}$	
Political instability	−0.20	−0.19	−0.11	−0.25
	$(0.06)^{0.00}$	$(0.09)^{0.03}$	$(0.06)^{0.06}$	$(0.13)^{0.06}$
Civil wars	0.76	1.32	0.35	1.92
	$(0.45)^{0.09}$	$(0.57)^{0.02}$	$(0.54)^{0.52}$	$(0.72)^{0.01}$
GDP per capita (Log)	−0.38	−0.0002	−0.69	0.31
	$(0.39)^{0.33}$	$(0.39)^{1.00}$	$(0.48)^{0.15}$	$(0.53)^{0.56}$
Population (Log)	0.35	0.06	0.20	−0.31
	$(0.28)^{0.20}$	$(0.24)^{0.79}$	$(0.31)^{0.52}$	$(0.32)^{0.34}$
Inflation (Log)	−0.47	0.11	−1.19	−1.29
	$(0.22)^{0.03}$	$(0.22)^{0.60}$	$(0.27)^{0.00}$	$(0.27)^{0.00}$
Trade openness (% GDP)	0.03	0.01	0.02	0.003
	$(0.01)^{0.02}$	$(0.01)^{0.41}$	$(0.01)^{0.11}$	$(0.01)^{0.78}$
Agriculture (% GDP)	−0.01	−0.02	−0.05	−0.01
	$(0.03)^{0.65}$	$(0.04)^{0.59}$	$(0.04)^{0.22}$	$(0.05)^{0.83}$
Primary commodity exporter	−0.17	0.07	0.26	0.70
	$(0.56)^{0.76}$	$(0.43)^{0.87}$	$(0.71)^{0.71}$	$(0.64)^{0.28}$
Terms-of-trade shock	0.02	0.07	−0.002	−0.03
	$(0.01)^{0.03}$	$(0.04)^{0.08}$	$(0.02)^{0.87}$	$(0.04)^{0.49}$
Government consumption	−0.09	−0.16	−0.12	−0.14
	$(0.04)^{0.02}$	$(0.05)^{0.00}$	$(0.04)^{0.00}$	$(0.06)^{0.03}$
Financial liquidity (M2)	0.01	0.01	0.01	−0.02
	$(0.01)^{0.33}$	$(0.02)^{0.62}$	$(0.02)^{0.44}$	$(0.02)^{0.52}$
Time trend	−0.01	0.44	0.14	0.46
	$(0.25)^{0.97}$	$(0.27)^{0.11}$	$(0.17)^{0.42}$	$(0.23)^{0.05}$

Table 3.5 *(cont.)*

Sample:	DV: economic growth			
	Ten-year panels		Five-year panels	
	All LDCs	*Democracies*	*All LDCs*	*Democracies*
No. of countries	105	53	105	58
No. of observations	262	87	352	135
Root mean square error	2.59	1.71	3.68	2.84

Note: Cell entries are OLS coefficients with standard errors corrected for clustering by country reported in parentheses and two-sided p-values superscripted.

on volatility. Democracy per se might lead governments to "muddle through" as Chandra and Rudra put it, i.e., achieve more stable but not higher economic growth than non-democracies, but the credible constraints framework highlights that certain types of democratic structures might allow governments to achieve both higher economic growth and greater stability.

The flip side, however, is also true. While not as consistently as in the growth-rate volatility analysis, divided presidential government is again associated with worse national economic performance. Above, I found that such governments have more volatile growth; here divided presidential governments are found to have a negative effect on economic growth, though this negative effect is only statistically significant when we use five-year panels as the unit of analysis. So, at best, we would conclude that divided presidentialism leads to only higher volatility, but, at worst, this increased volatility is accompanied by lower growth overall too. The "perils of presidentialism" are real indeed!

None of the other credible constraint indicators are statistically significant correlates of economic growth, though political federalism comes closest to boosting economic performance at statistically significant levels. This is consistent with the volatility analysis, and suggests that non-partisan formal credible constraint institutions have less direct bearing on national economic performance than their partisan counterparts, though it is quite possible that these institutions matter more indirectly through their effects on investor behavior. A second possibility is that such institutions might work in specific contexts, but on average – which after all is what a regression coefficient is estimating – do not have an effect in the developing world. I will address the first possibility in the next chapter, and consider the effects of these non-partisan institutions in the India case study in Chapter 5, but for now return to the other variables that affect economic growth.

Political instability is one of these, though the direction of the effect depends on the source of the instability. Greater domestic strife in the form of riots and anti-government demonstrations reduces economic growth, but more violent internal conflict (such as civil wars) has a positive effect on economic growth overall. The first half of this finding is consistent with existing literature and with our intuitions, but the second half is very counter-intuitive at first glance. Why would violent civil conflict be "good" for economic growth? Actually this finding is not all that at odds with existing research. In work with Thomas Edward Flores on post-civil-conflict reconstruction, I found that half of the conflicts in the developing world from 1960 to present were accompanied by economic expansion over the years of the conflict; the other half resulted in economic decline (Flores and Nooruddin 2009). The causal mechanisms that lead some countries to the growth outcome and others to the decline outcome are as yet unclear, though it remains a topic of current research for us. What we do know, especially from research by A.F.K. Organski and Jacek Kugler (1980), is that conflict often generates economic opportunities for entrepreneurs who must supply the fighters, and later to help rebuild the society. In fact, as the cases of Germany and Japan in the aftermath of World War II prominently attest, economic growth is often facilitated by the devastation of war, a phenomenon Organski dubbed the "Phoenix Effect."

The economic control variables behave as expected. High levels of inflation hurt economic growth, and countries with large government sectors grow more slowly as well. Trade appears to have a positive effect on economic growth overall, though this effect is only statistically significant over the longer ten-year period (it is slightly less precisely estimated in the shorter five-year-period analysis). Finally, I should note that I do not include a variable commonly used in growth regression models – human capital – because of a severe lack of data availability. But when I do control for the share of the labor force with a tertiary education, that variable is statistically significant and positively signed as expected (five-year periods: $\beta = 0.08$; *s.e.* $= 0.04$; $p = 0.04$; $n =$ seventy-two observations and forty-nine countries). Including this variable does not change the sign of the main effects reported above, though cutting the sample by 80 percent, from 352 observations to seventy-two, reduces the statistical precision of the estimates somewhat.

As a final piece of evidence for the utility of the credible constraints framework, consider the variation in national economic performance among African countries. While most countries in Africa remain among the world's poorest, and the problems of poverty rank as the most intractable there, one must be careful not to treat this very diverse continent as a monolith. African countries display considerable variation in reality in their national economic performance, and some governments are rightly hailed as examples of success (for example, Botswana; see Acemoglu *et al.* (2003a) and Chapter 6). Following a World Bank analysis of the growth patterns of thirty-five African states (World Bank 2008), I distinguish between two basic African growth types: bad and good. The average growth rate of the "bad" growth-type countries was a mere 0.2 percent during the period studied here; the "good" growth types had average growth rates of 1.5 percent during the same time period (the difference is statistically significant at $p< 0.05$). Likewise, while both types had higher-than-world-average levels of growth-rate volatility, the good types experienced more stable growth rates than the bad types (4.6 versus 5.6 respectively; $p = 0.11$). Can the credible constraints framework provide any explanatory leverage over why some states fall in the good category of higher and more stable growth, while others experience more volatile and lower growth? While the sample size of thirty-five is too small for a complete statistical analysis, Table 3.6 suggests that it can.

Table 3.6 presents the results from a series of difference-of-means tests for the different indicators of credible constraints across the two African growth types. "Good" performers were more democratic than the "bad" performers, though neither category was particularly democratic overall. Similarly, good performers had more experience with coalition or divided government, though these effects are both quite small. Rather, the factor that emerges as most useful potentially is judicial independence, with good performers having on average more years

Table 3.6 *African growth types*

African growth type	Regime type		Credible constraints				
	democracy	polity	Coalition	Divided government	Judicial Independence	Cent. bank Independence	Auth. binding legislature
Bad	0.11	−4.19	0	0.001	0.06	0.25	0.59
Good	0.24	−0.85	0.03	0.02	0.16	0.24	0.65
p−value	0.07	0.001	0.17	0.15	0.09	0.57	0.33

List of countries in each growth type

Bad: Burundi, Central African Republic, Comoros, Eritrea, Guinea, Guinea-Bissau, Kenya, Lesotho, Madagascar, Malawi, Mauritania, Niger, Seychelles, Togo, Zaire, Zambia, Zimbabwe; *Good*: Benin, Botswana, Burkina Faso, Cameroon, Cape Verde, Ethiopia, Ghana, Gambia, Mali, Mauritius, Mozambique, Namibia, Rwanda, Sao Tome and Principe, Senegal, Sierra Leone, Tanzania, Uganda with strong courts than bad performers.[16] These results are hardly conclusive, but they certainly point in the direction hypothesized. Given the small sample size and the difficult test that explaining growth patterns in Africa presents, I am very encouraged.

Endogeneity?

A final point on the empirical evidence concerns the question of endogeneity. Specifically, given the work of Przeworski *et al.* (2000), one might wonder whether the results documented thus far are an artifact of some unexplored factor. For instance, might it be that coalition governments are more likely to survive only in good and stable economic conditions? If so, then any correlation between the existence of coalition governments and high economic growth might well be spurious. Addressing endogeneity concerns statistically has traditionally involved the identification and use of instrumental variables, but scholars are increasingly skeptical about whether such variables can be found (Bartels 1991; Bound *et al.* 1995). It is hard to imagine what factor might predict whether a country has a coalition government in a given year that is not also correlated with its economic conditions (potential candidates, for instance, might be constitutional rules, colonial legacy, or geographic region). Therefore, another strategy is called for. Increasingly scholars have turned to "matching" techniques as a means for addressing thorny endogeneity issues.[17]

As a robustness check against endogeneity, I conduct a basic matching analysis of the economic growth models.[18] I first limit the sample only to developing country parliamentary systems, and predict the likelihood a state had a coalition government in a given year on the basis of its Freedom House score of political and civil liberties, whether it

[16] Widner (2001) anticipates this finding in a fascinating account of how the rule of law is built from the perspective of the judicial actors at the center of the action.

[17] A full discussion of the potential virtues and limitations of matching is beyond the scope of this chapter, but interested readers would do well to consult the seminal works of eminent econometricians and statisticians such as James Heckman, Guido Imbens, Paul Rosenbaum, and Donald Rubin (Heckman *et al.* 1997, 1998; Imbens 2000; Rosenbaum and Rubin 1983, 1985; Rubin 1974, 1980, 2006).

[18] Matching was conducted using the PSMATCH2 routine in Stata (Leuven and Sianesi 2003).

was a democracy, its GDP per capita, urban population growth, trade openness, terms of trade, unemployment rate, population growth, and whether the country experienced an economic crisis that year. This model yields a "propensity score" which is used to create a matched sample of country-years that experienced a coalition government (the treated sample in the jargon of matching) and country-years that did not, but whose propensity score was very similar to those that did. This latter set of country-years is thus essentially identical in terms of the covariate profile used to create the match (and a balance test for the covariates verifies this proposition),[19] but different only in that it did not experience the treatment of interest. Stated more plainly, these years look very similar in all respects to the treated sample except that they did not actually have a coalition government in power. This then is the control sample, and any difference in economic growth between it and the treated sample is more validly attributed to whether there was a coalition government (the treatment). The results of this analysis are very encouraging: the average growth rate in the treated (coalition parliamentary government) sample was 3.16 percent, while the average growth rate in the control (unified parliamentary government) sample was 1.70 percent.

I next replicate this analysis but this time the treatment factor is divided presidential government. I limit the sample to developing-country presidential systems only, and utilize the same covariate profile as described above. A check reveals that satisfactory covariate balance is achieved, allowing one to turn to observed differences in economic growth between divided and unified presidential systems that have been matched on factors that might predict the existence of a divided government. The results confirm the negative finding reported above: divided presidential governments experienced lower economic growth (0.30 percent) than their unified counterparts (1.37 percent).[20]

---

[19] Balance is generally quite good across the covariate profile, but it is not perfect. The control sample after matching is slightly more democratic and richer, and less politically unstable, than the treated sample. If anything these differences should bias the findings against my argument, and so I consider this a conservative test.

[20] This result does not go away if one also matches on the country's region, specifically whether it is located in Latin America, though the difference is slightly muted with the control group's growth rate dropping to 1.17 percent as compared to 0.30 percent for the treated group.

A statistical analysis using matching techniques thus assuages concerns that the results reported in this chapter have been driven by endogeneity. In fact, if anything, these results make the benefits of parliamentarism relative to presidentialism even clearer, and provide strong evidence in favor of the credible constraints argument. Of course, as with any statistical analysis, this is hardly the last word on the question of endogeneity, and future research should strive to build a unified model of economic performance, government formation, and investor reactions.

A final point for now: statistics are but one way to tackle endogeneity. In the case-study chapters that follow the large-n empirical chapters, I will try consciously to utilize the country experiences to gain leverage on the question of endogeneity. The Indian case is especially useful in this regard since it is clear there that the party system fragmentation and growth of regional parties that have made coalition governments a fact of modern Indian political life had precious little to do with economic conditions, and are far more the unintended consequence of internal Congress Party politics. But more on that later.

Conclusion

The central argument of this chapter is that governments' inability to make credible commitments to future and current policies, i.e., of policy stability, to investors, foreign and domestic, induces those investors to avoid long-term commitments in and to their investment projects and makes them, because of the nature of their investments and because of their lack of confidence and/or certainty regarding future government policy, more likely to abandon the country at smaller signs of economic trouble. Thus, in addition to the direct effect of policy instability on output instability, governments' inability to commit credibly to present and future policies, induces savings and investment volatility and, thereby, growth volatility.

My theory advances our understanding of growth-rate volatility by specifying the institutions and economic policies that cause growth-rate volatility, thereby improving on the three existing political explanations of growth-rate volatility, each of which focuses on different roles democracy plays in mitigating volatility. First, Rodrik (1998a, 2000) argues that democracies exhibit higher levels of social cooperation and compromise in the face of exogenous shocks, which allows them to navigate and ameliorate the effects of these shocks. Next, Quinn and Woolley (2001) argue that risk-averse publics are able to constrain their more risk-acceptant leaders in democracies from making risky policies, which they argue are the cause of growth volatility. Finally, Chandra and Rudra (2008) argue that institutional diversification, which they associate with democracy, leads to less volatile policy outputs and therefore lower volatility.

Empirically, the credible constraints framework is shown to be quite powerful. In particular, the statistical analysis highlights coalition or minority parliamentary governments as a potent credible constraint that reduces growth volatility while increasing average growth overall. Divided presidential government, conversely, hurts national economic performance, presumably because policy gridlock hurts governments' ability to enact necessary economic reforms. Central bank independence lowers growth-rate volatility, though it has no discernible effect on average growth. Finally, judicial independence is found to explain variation in growth patterns in Africa, a finding that is particularly exciting given the severity of the challenges to good economic performance there.

While the evidence supports my argument, the causal mechanisms by which credible constraints reduce volatility and improve growth outcomes have thus far only been posited, rather than tested. The next chapter therefore provides direct tests of the causal mechanism implied by the theory, namely that, by reducing actual and expected policy instability, credible constraint institutions strengthen investor confidence, thereby encouraging new economic activity, promoting domestic saving, and reducing capital flight.

4 | Coalition politics and economic development
Mechanisms

Credible constraints improve national economic performance. Statistical analysis of cross-national data for over a hundred developing countries presented in the last chapter shows that constraints against policy change reduce the volatility of growth and increase its mean level. Thus, in the presence of such constraints, growth is both higher and more stable. And this result is robust to controlling for other factors that explain economic growth, as well as for democracy. Indeed, when we limit our investigation to those countries that have a deep experience with democratic rules for choosing leaders, the existence of coalition government still proves to be an important determinant of economic performance. But why?

The causal mechanism implied by the theoretical framework presented in Chapter 2 is that credible constraints against policy change encourage private economic actors to engage in increased investment activity because they do not have to worry that the government will change policies arbitrarily, unilaterally, or drastically. That is, the argument posits a strong status quo bias on the part of private economic actors, an assumption supported by previous research (Aizenman and Marion 1999; Bechtel and Füss 2008; Henisz 2002; Jensen 2006). The findings presented above are consistent with the major empirical implications of the theoretical framework: if investors fear policy uncertainty, and if the dispersion of policymaking authority across multiple actors reduces such policy uncertainty, then investors should invest more in the presence of such credible constraints against policy change, and national economic performance should improve. The basic hypothesis – that credible constraints improve national economic performance – is borne out by my statistical analysis. But thus far I have offered no evidence to support the implied causal mechanism. Even if it is true that credible constraints improve national economic performance as documented above, how can we be sure that the effect is because of their effect on economic actors' propensity to save capital rather than consume it, and to invest their savings in the economy rather than flee the state in search of better prospects?

This chapter tests the causal mechanisms of the theoretical framework. Two questions are at the center of its focus: does uncertainty reduce economic actors' proclivity for future economic activity? And do credible constraints against policy change reduce such uncertainty enough to encourage greater investment in the economy? I use two different types of data in this chapter in an effort to provide as convincing evidence as possible in favor of the argument. First, I use a new set of business enterprise surveys conducted by the EBRD and World Bank which allows me to get at firms' assessments of the business environment and the role uncertainty plays in shaping their behavior. Second, having established that firms do take policy uncertainty into consideration in deciding whether or not to increase their investment in the economy, I merge my data on credible constraints with the World Bank survey data, which allows me to show that certain credible constraint institutions reduce the type of uncertainty most damaging to investment activity. Finally, I return to the cross-national data set to demonstrate that credible constraints do in fact increase savings and investment across the developing world. Taken *in toto*, the results of the analyses presented in this chapter offer strong support for the causal mechanism posited by my theoretical framework.

Firm-level evidence on policy uncertainty and investment behavior

Is policy uncertainty as great an obstacle to economic activity as political economists typically posit? Theoretically the negative link between uncertainty and economic activity is well-understood. Economist Joshua Aizenman and his colleagues have investigated in considerable detail the consequences of irreversibilities in investment. Irreversibility refers to the fact that for any given investment there is some portion that cannot be retrieved if things go sour (sometimes called "sunk costs"). The greater the irreversibility of investment, the greater the premium on policy certainty – investors are understandably risk-averse and require strong assurances from governments that policies are unlikely to change and that their investments will be protected. In the absence of such assurances, or if such assurances are deemed incredible, investors will likely foreswear the opportunity unless the potential returns are so high as to make the higher risk worthwhile. What this means is that, for any given level of risk, there exist some potential investments that are not realized if the expected returns do not make the risk worth taking. For capital-scarce developing countries, such "wasted" investments can hardly be afforded.

While numerous scholars have argued thusly that policy uncertainty is bad for investment, evidence for such arguments has typically come from cross-national statistical analyses of the kind I presented in the previous chapter. The archetypical example of this type of research comes from Wharton economist Witold Henisz. Henisz constructs measures of policy uncertainty by taking the standard deviation over time for a series of government policy indicators. The greater the variance of a given policy over time, the higher the uncertainty of its future direction. He then correlates policy uncertainty thus measured with private investment, and finds robust support for the claim that private investors are deterred by greater policy uncertainty (Henisz 2002).

While such evidence is very useful (and indeed I will provide similar tests later in this chapter), one would ideally want to provide some evidence a little closer to the actual actor in such theories – the firm. National-level outcomes result from the aggregation of behavior by thousands upon thousands of individual firms. Studying these firms cross-nationally in sufficient numbers to provide a systematic test of the argument is virtually impossible for the individual scholar, but, fortunately, the desire for such firm-level information has led multinational financial institutions such as the World Bank to gather it in recent years and to make those data available to researchers. In this section, I analyse the 2002 and 2005 waves of the EBRD-World Bank's Business Enterprise Surveys to see if I can find firm-level evidence to support the causal mechanisms I have posited in my framework (EBRD-World Bank 2005).

Since 1999, the EBRD and World Bank have conducted a comprehensive survey of firms across over sixty developing countries. This endeavor built on earlier attempts in the late 1990s to survey firms in individual countries, but starting in 2002 the EBRD and World Bank made the important decision to have a common core of questions administered across countries, enabling researchers to engage in cross-national research. The countries in which such surveys are conducted are spread across all continents, though they tend to be concentrated among the larger and more important economies in their regions. Within each country, a random sample of firms is drawn from which survey responses are solicited.[1] The size of the firm sample from each country varies, from a low of seventy-nine in Eritrea in 2002 to a high of 1,827 in India in the same year, though most countries have between 250 and 1,000 firms surveyed. For each firm, the goal is to have the survey completed jointly by the managing directors, accountants, and human resource managers, and respondents are guaranteed confidentiality in exchange for their participation. Finally, the stated goal of the survey is to gather data on business perceptions of the business climate in their country with the object goal of offering the government policy advice about how to make the country more business-friendly.

My first goal is to use the surveys to shed light on how policy uncertainty affects business plans to increase their economic activity. The core questionnaire contains two questions about different types of policy uncertainty that are "investment climate constraints to the establishment." The first asks firms whether "economic and regulatory policy uncertainty" is an obstacle for the "operation and growth" of the respondent's business. The second asks firms if "macroeconomic instability (inflation, exchange rate)" is a problem.[2] Distinguishing between types of uncertainty is important for my purposes because it allows me to separate the types of uncertainty over which governments are more directly influential (economic and regulatory policy uncertainty) from macroeconomic uncertainty, which while governments can certainly affect is also a function of broader economic conditions at home and abroad. On both questions, about one-third of firms respond that uncertainty is a major or severe obstacle to their operations and growth

---

[1] Mostly the EBRD and World Bank draws a simple random sample of registered firms within each country, though they also use stratified random samples in some countries to ensure representativeness of the overall sample. There is a slight oversample of large firms since most countries have many more small and medium-sized establishments. However, since the costs of uncertainty should be most keenly felt by smaller firms, this slight sampling bias should militate against my hypothesis, if anything. For more details on the conduct of these surveys, see the Bank's online FAQ page (www.enterprisesurveys.org/Methodology/) or the EBRD website (www.ebrd.com/country/sector/econo/surveys/beeps.htm).

[2] The exact question wording is: "Please tell us if any of the following issues are a problem for the operation and growth of your business. If an issue poses a problem, please judge its severity as an obstacle on a four-point scale where: 0 = No obstacle; 1 = Minor obstacle; 2 = Moderate obstacle; 3 = Major obstacle; 4 = Very Severe Obstacle."

prospects, while a two-thirds majority characterize such uncertainty as either not a problem at all or as a moderate problem at worst.

Armed with these two questions to tap perceptions of uncertainty, I turn to the data, which I've pooled across multiple years of the survey, to construct a measure of firm decisions to invest in new capacity. In particular, I seek a question that captures business plans to grow their firms in the near future. Unfortunately, options are limited in this regard since the survey asks very few prospective questions, but there is a question about whether the firm has opened a new establishment within the past three years. Unfortunately even this question is not asked of all countries, but it is asked to over 5,000 firms across twelve countries, making it quite sufficient for an initial test of the claim that uncertainty reduces business incentives to take potentially productive risks.

Table 4.1 presents the results from a logit analysis in which the dependent variable is whether the firm opened a new establishment in the past one to three years. The main independent variables capture the two main types of uncertainty. I add to the model controls for the size of the firm in terms of its number of employees and also the share of the national market for its main product that it claims to control, whether it is an exporter (since such firms typically enjoy a privileged position in the economy and might be suspected to be insulated from policy uncertainty), the overall level of economic development in the country as measured by its GDP per capita, and its level of democracy as proxied by its Polity score. I include the country's democracy score not because of any *ex ante* expectation that democracies are more or less likely to encourage new business activity, but to ensure that the uncertainty variables do not spuriously pick up a "regime type" effect. Lastly, since this is a fairly sparse model, I include also a set of country fixed effects to capture any unobserved and unmeasured heterogeneity across countries.

The logit results support the contention that policy uncertainty makes firms less likely to invest in new capacity, even after control-ling for the firm's size and performance and for the country's level of economic development and democracy. Interestingly only policy uncer-tainty appears to matter for new business activity; macroeconomic uncertainty is not statistically significant in spite of the large sample size. As expected, larger firms are more likely to expand their capacity, as are exporters, which reflects the increased participation in the world

Table 4.1 *Uncertainty reduces economic activity*

DV: opened a new establishment in the past three years

	β	Std. Err	p-value
Regulatory uncertainty	−0.55	0.23	0.02
Macroeconomic uncertainty	0.12	0.19	0.53
Firm size	0.41	0.12	0.00
Firm national market share	−0.001	0.003	0.66
Firm is an exporter	0.30	0.14	0.03
Country GDP per capita (Log)	−0.21	0.04	0.00
Country polity score	−0.08	0.01	0.00
Country fixed effects		Yes	
No. of observations		3,454	
No. of countries		12	
% Correctly predicted		95	

Note: Logit model of whether a firm opened a new establishment within the past three years. Standard errors are corrected for clustering by country. Countries in estimation sample are Cambodia, Ecuador, El Salvador, Guatemala, Honduras, Mali, Nicaragua, Philippines, Syria, Tanzania, South Africa, and Zambia.

economy by developing countries over the past decade. Firms located in richer countries are less likely to have opened a new establishment recently, which likely attests to the fact that barriers to entry in more developed economies are going to be higher. Finally, firms in democracies are also less likely to have expanded capacity, though this effect is very small.

How large is the effect of uncertainty on the probability a firm will open a new establishment? To find out, I hold the other variables in the model at either their mean or modal values, but allow the regulatory uncertainty variable to take different values. When economic and regulatory policy uncertainty is low, the probability of a firm opening a new establishment is approximately 19%, but this drops to 12% when uncertainty is high, a decline of over 40%. Given how rare it is for firms in developing countries to consider even the possibility of opening new establishments (of the almost 3,500 firms in the estimation sample, only 169 had opened a new establishment in the past three years), reducing the probability that they would do so by almost half is a heavy price to pay for higher policy uncertainty!

Table 4.2 *Credible constraints reduce firm uncertainty*

	Sample: all developing countries			
	Regulatory uncertainty		Macroeconomic uncertainty	
Constraint	*Absent*	*Present*	*Absent*	*Present*
Coalition govt.	34.35%	29.57%	36.27%	25.62%
Divided govt.	33.94%	32.54%	35.47%	26.98%
Judicial indep.	32.38%	39.09%	34.77%	36.95%
CBI	40.69%	30.20%	45.44%	32.78%
	Sample: democratic developing countries			
	Regulatory uncertainty		Macroeconomic uncertainty	
Constraint	*Absent*	*Present*	*Absent*	*Present*
Coalition govt.	50.44%	30.31%	49.76%	26.34%
Divided govt.	45.08%	32.69%	43.66%	27.43%
Judicial indep.	49.94%	37.89%	50.52%	33.61%
CBI	48.57%	38.16%	46.45%	41.93%

The firm-survey evidence thus supports the first part of the causal mechanism: higher uncertainty does act as a deterrent to potential investors. What about the second part of the argument? Is policy uncertainty lower when there exist credible constraints against policy change? Table 4.2 suggests that it is.

Across a much broader set of countries than was available for the first analysis (a list of countries is provided in Appendix C), the dispersal of policymaking authority to multiple actors results in a reduction in uncertainty in both the economic/regulatory policy and macroeconomic realms. The effect of such credible constraints is markedly stronger when we limit the sample only to democratic countries. For instance, among democracies, only one-third of firms in countries governed by coalition and minority parliamentary governments claim policy uncertainty to be a major obstacle while half of their counterparts in countries with other forms of governments say it is a problem. The same holds for divided presidential government, judicial independence, and central bank independence: in all these situations, the

Table 4.3 *The effect of credible constraints on firm uncertainty*

DV: is regulatory uncertainty an obstacle?

	β	Std. Err	p-value
Macroeconomic uncertainty	2.70	0.14	0.00
Firm size	0.06	0.04	0.14
Firm national market share	−0.002	0.001	0.16
Firm is an exporter	−0.03	0.07	0.68
Country GDP per capita (Log)	0.57	0.02	0.00
Country polity score	0.004	0.001	0.00
Minority/coalition govt	−1.99	0.02	0.00
Divided govt.	−0.27	0.04	0.00
Judicial independence	−0.01	0.03	0.61
Country fixed effects		Yes	
Year fixed effects		Yes	
No. of observations		11,433	
No. of countries		38	
% Correctly predicted		81	

Note: Standard errors are corrected for clustering by country.

constraint against policy change succeeds in reducing the perceived risk of policy uncertainty.

Of course, these institutions are not mutually exclusive (other than minority/coalition parliamentary governments and divided presidential governments of course). That is, parliamentary governments, whether unified or coalition, could also benefit from having independent judiciaries or central banks that reduce policy uncertainty. To separate these effects, I include the credible constraints indicators together in a logit model where the dependent variable is whether the firm perceived policy uncertainty to be a major obstacle to its operations. Once more, I control for the firm's size and performance and for the country's overall level of economic development and democracy, as well as for the firm's response to the macroeconomic uncertainty question since the two types of uncertainty are likely to be heavily correlated. The full results from this model are reported in Table 4.3, but I focus my discussion on the effects of the credible constraint institutions on policy uncertainty.

Since I would expect non-exporting small firms in poor countries with hybrid regimes to be most prone to uncertainty (Kenyon and Naoi 2006), I give the other variables in the models values to generate such a country profile. Holding these constant, changing only the value of the credible constraint institutions is instructive. For instance, if such a country has a unified government and an independent judiciary, the probability of perceiving regulatory uncertainty to be a problem is 0.94. If we switch the profile so that the country is a divided presidential government instead, this predicted probability declines marginally to 0.92. But, when this hypothetical country is set to have a coalition or minority parliamentary government, the probability of perceived policy uncertainty drops to 0.68, a decline of twenty-four points. This provides clear support – at the firm-level across forty-three developing countries – for the main causal mechanism in my framework: credible constraints that prevent arbitrary policy change and encourage policy moderation instead reduce policy uncertainty for businesses, which in turn encourages them to engage in new economic activities that help grow the economy.

Credible constraints and domestic savings and investment behavior

The World Bank firm-level surveys provide micro-level evidence that credible constraints encourage entrepreneurial behavior by reducing expectations of regulatory policy uncertainty. In this section of the chapter, I analyze country-level data to see if macroeconomic indicators tell a corresponding story. Two indicators are of particular interest: the level of domestic savings in the economy and the extent of capital flight out of the economy. Together, domestic savings and capital flight tell us why some countries engender confidence in citizens to save and invest their income in the economy while others encourage them to hedge against risk by locating their funds abroad beyond the reach of their governments.

Domestic savings

The importance of a government's ability to attract capital that can be used for investment purposes is well-recognized in the growth literature (Barro and Sala-i-Martin 1995). This recognition motivates the considerable attention political scientists have paid to country's abilities to attract foreign direct investment (Ahlquist 2006; Biglaiser and DeRouen 2006; Jensen 2003, 2006; Li and Resnick 2003). The leading political science scholar of FDI, Nathan Jensen, demonstrates quite persuasively that democratic governments hold a definite advantage over their autocratic counterparts when it comes to attracting FDI. Jensen's explanation for this anticipates mine: he argues that democratic governments have more veto players in their structure, which allows them to commit more credibly to long-term policy stability and therefore to attract more foreign investment. His analysis thus supports my argument and I'll provide my own analysis of FDI data below, but first I focus on a comparatively neglected factor in capital generation for economic growth: domestic savings.

That political scientists have ignored domestic savings as an outcome-of-interest is perplexing given the prominent role it has played in theories of economic growth. For W.W. Rostow, the key determinants of a country's successful transition to the "take-off" stage of development was savings and investment's share of national income crossing the 10 percent threshold. More mature economies, he argued, were characterized by savings rates of 10–20 percent. Importantly, these savings should occur in the formal sector, via banks, so that the capital can be used for further productive endeavors. Thus, to borrow Rostow's evocative phrase, "Compound interest becomes built, as it were, into [a society's] habits and institutional structure" (Rostow 1971: 7).

Rostow's insight is conventional wisdom today; the World Bank, for instance, states that high domestic savings are "critical for economic growth and economic development." And the size of these savings in most developing societies dwarfs the size of FDI inflows. The median country in my data set saved 14.8% of its GDP, while the median level of FDI inflows was a mere 1.04% of GDP. The disparity is even greater at the high end: the 90th percentile for savings is 33.41% of GDP, while it is 5.89% for FDI. These facts are offered not to suggest that FDI is unimportant for developing country growth, but rather to make the point that domestic savings are at least equally, if not considerably more, so. Besides, to the extent that we are interested in identifying how domestic political institutions shape growth outcomes, one would expect that domestic savings should be relatively more responsive to local political considerations than are foreign capital investors.

To examine why some countries save a greater share of their national income than others, I examine two different indicators. The first is a measure of gross domestic saving compiled by the World Bank, which is the difference between total GDP and government and private consumption (World Bank 2006). The second is a measure developed by economists Mancur Olson, Philip Keefer, Steven Knack, and Christopher Clague, which they call contract-intensive money (Clague *et al.* 1999). The idea behind contract-intensive money is to see how much of the money in a country is held in the formal sector where it can be used for productive purposes. The original purpose of the measure was as an indicator for the strength of property rights, as Olson and his colleagues argued that states in which property rights were more secure would encourage citizens to put their money in the formal sector rather than hide it from public view. That purpose is consistent with the basic argument made here, but I use the contract-intensive money indicator as a signal of citizens' general confidence in the government, both in terms of property rights protections but also in terms of their confidence that future policy will not deviate dramatically from the present path.

I use the measures of gross domestic saving and contract-intensive money as dependent variables in regression models in which the primary independent variables are the credible constraint indicators described above. As in the analyses reported in the previous chapter, I estimate two versions of each model. In the first, I include all countries for which data are available and control for the country's overall level of democracy to ensure that the credible constraint indicators are not simply picking up a "democracy" effect. In the second version, I limit the sample only to those countries that were democratic for at least half the time period under investigation. The democracy variable itself has different expectations depending on the dependent variable being analyzed. Since forced savings and austerity programs are politically unpopular, one expects autocratic states to be more likely to "encourage" higher domestic savings rates, which is borne out by the high savings rates enjoyed by the less-than-democratic East Asian Newly Industrializing Countries in the 1960s and 1970s. Therefore, one expects a negative effect of democracy on domestic savings. In the contract-intensive money model, by contrast, democracy is expected to have a positive slope. Placing one's resources in the public sphere requires citizens to be confident that their money will be protected, an expectation that tends to be higher in democratic societies (Clague *et al.* 1996, 1999).

In addition to the credible constraint and democracy indicators, all the models discussed in this section include a set of control variables identified in the relevant literatures. First, to distinguish between the effects of policy versus political instability, I include Banks's political instability index, which measures the frequency of destabilizing events such as riots, anti-government demonstrations, coups, and the like. Second, I account for the state of the economy by controlling for the country's overall level of development (GDP per capita), as well as the growth rate and inflation rate of the economy. The expectations here are that richer developing countries have higher rates of saving and contract-intensive money as do faster-growing economies as there is more surplus capital to be accumulated. Higher inflation on the other hand should encourage consumption as citizens fear their savings will be devalued. Third, I control for the level of fixed capital formation in the economy, as a proxy for the economy's level of industrial development. I expect this variable to be more relevant for the FDI and capital flight models to be discussed later in the chapter. Fourth, one might expect citizens to be more willing to save their money and locate it in contract-intensive activities if they do not have to worry about getting the money out of the economy should conditions change or worsen. Therefore, I include two indicators of a country's openness to the international economy, both of which I expect will encourage saving. The first is the Chinn and Ito (2006) index of capital account openness; the second is the country's overall level of trade openness. Fifth, I include two indicators of the country's overall credit-worthiness. These are the level of financial liquidity in the economy, which I expect to be positively correlated with savings rates, and the level of debt service paid by the country, for which a similar expectation is held. Finally, the model includes a time trend to avoid any spurious correlations in the data. Table 4.4 reports the results of these regression models.

The results support the credible constraints argument, though the evidence is stronger with respect to the domestic savings models than it is in the contract-intensive money models. Consider the first two columns of Table 4.4 – the savings models – first. In both models, the effect of having a minority or coalition parliamentary government is large, positive, and statistically significant. Countries in which such

Table 4.4 *Regression results: credible constraints and domestic savings*

Dependent Variable	Gross domestic savings		Contract-intensive money	
	All LDCs	*Democracies*	*All LDCs*	*Democracies*
Minority/coalition govts	12.02 $(4.29)^{0.01}$	7.50 $(2.82)^{0.01}$	3.85 $(2.76)^{0.17}$	1.27 $(3.54)^{0.72}$
Divided presidential govts	0.77 $(3.07)^{0.80}$	3.87 $(2.33)^{0.11}$	−0.94 $(2.38)^{0.69}$	0.33 $(2.07)^{0.87}$
Independent judiciaries	1.22 $(2.57)^{0.64}$	2.42 $(2.07)^{0.25}$	5.39 $(1.67)^{0.00}$	3.71 $(1.63)^{0.03}$
Federalism	3.02 $(4.59)^{0.51}$	5.57 $(3.07)^{0.08}$	0.56 $(2.79)^{0.84}$	1.69 $(2.93)^{0.57}$
Central bank indep.	−1.25 $(1.90)^{0.51}$	0.23 $(1.83)^{0.89}$	2.84 $(1.61)^{0.08}$	−1.56 $(1.38)^{0.27}$
Democracy	−5.92 $(2.56)^{0.02}$		4.36 $(1.54)^{0.01}$	
Political instability	0.01 $(0.23)^{0.95}$	0.13 $(0.30)^{0.66}$	0.47 $(0.22)^{0.04}$	0.21 $(0.24)^{0.40}$
GDP per capita (Log)	8.28 $(2.73)^{0.00}$	4.43 $(1.22)^{0.00}$	3.85 $(1.02)^{0.00}$	3.79 $(0.83)^{0.00}$
Growth in GDP per capita	0.21 $(0.27)^{0.44}$	0.36 $(0.28)^{0.19}$	0.45 $(0.21)^{0.04}$	0.42 $(0.25)^{0.11}$
Inflation (Log)	−1.55 $(1.01)^{0.13}$	−0.30 $(0.86)^{0.73}$	0.10 $(0.84)^{0.90}$	−0.61 $(0.79)^{0.45}$
Fixed capital formation	0.27 $(0.39)^{0.49}$	−0.45 $(0.46)^{0.33}$	0.10 $(0.18)^{0.57}$	0.11 $(0.14)^{0.44}$
Capital account openness	0.32 $(0.77)^{0.68}$	0.10 $(0.77)^{0.89}$	1.03 $(0.79)^{0.19}$	0.15 $(0.69)^{0.83}$
Trade openness (% GDP)	−0.09 $(0.07)^{0.17}$	−0.02 $(0.05)^{0.71}$	.09 $(0.05)^{0.06}$	0.05 $(0.04)^{0.25}$
Financial liquidity (M2)	−0.08 $(0.10)^{0.47}$	0.17 $(0.12)^{0.18}$	0.02 $(0.07)^{0.84}$	0.16 $(0.09)^{0.09}$
Debt service (% exports)	0.07 $(0.08)^{0.35}$	0.01 $(0.07)^{0.86}$	0.09 $(0.08)^{0.32}$	0.06 $(0.06)^{0.40}$
Time trend	0.24 $(0.43)^{0.58}$	−1.38 $(0.63)^{0.03}$	0.30 $(0.46)^{0.52}$	0.32 $(0.57)^{0.59}$
Constant	−34.89 $(8.77)^{0.00}$	−6.58 $(8.06)^{0.42}$	32.29 $(8.83)^{0.00}$	40.56 $(7.55)^{0.00}$

Table 4.4 (*cont.*)

Dependent Variable	Gross domestic savings		Contract-intensive money	
	All LDCs	*Democracies*	*All LDCs*	*Democracies*
No. of countries	73	41	72	40
No. of observations	341	119	329	116
Root mean square error	12.29	8.01	10.04	0.06
R-squared	0.36	0.51	0.45	0.61

Note: Cell entries are OLS coefficients with standard errors corrected for clustering by country reported in parentheses and two-sided p-values superscripted.

governments are more common have greater expectations of long-term policy stability and therefore citizens have greater confidence to save their money for the future rather than consume it in the present. This effect holds regardless of whether we control for whether the country is a democracy, or limit the sample only to democracies. Indeed, as expected, the democracy variable is negatively signed and statistically significant. Overall, non-democracies are better able to encourage high rates of domestic savings, but the exception to this rule lies in coalition parliamentary governments! None of the other credible constraint indicators is found to have a statistically significant effect on domestic savings, and, of the control variables, just the level of GDP per capita matters.

The contract-intensive money model provides weaker support for a fine-grained version of the credible constraints story. As expected based on the prior research of Clague *et al.* (1999), the democracy variable is positively signed and statistically significant, which is consistent with the broader claim that democracies are in a stronger position to offer credible commitments to risk-averse agents. Of the other credible constraint indicators, only judicial independence emerges as a consistent and strong predictor of the level of contract-intensive money in the economy. Certainly this is consistent with my argument, since judicial independence does provide some check on arbitrary and radical policy change by governments, but it is also consistent with the Clague *et al.* argument that contract-intensive money responds to protections of property rights and the rule of law.

The basic argument made in this book is that certain political institutional configurations, by limiting governments' ability to make arbitrary and dramatic policy changes, bolster investors' confidence, leading to higher levels of savings and investment, and therefore to more stable and higher levels of economic growth. In this chapter, I have provided evidence that these institutions do affect the willingness of firms to undertake new productive endeavors and the overall savings rates in the society. Below I add the final piece of evidence to the picture.

Easy come, easy go? Capital flight and FDI inflows

Attracting capital that can be reinvested in the economy can occur from within the economy by encouraging higher savings domestically. But in capital-scarce economies it is little wonder that governments often devote a greater share of their effort to attracting foreign capital in the form of foreign direct investment. Such FDI has an additional advantage beyond providing capital; it can also provide technology as domestic firms initially learn from and later mimic their foreign competitors. Such growth-enhancing technology diffusion can happen through multiple channels, of which foreign direct investment by multinational corporations (MNCs) is one of the most important. Due to the high costs of doing business abroad, "MNCs are among the most technologically advanced firms, accounting for a substantial portion of the world's research and development (R and D) investment" (Borensztein *et al.* 1998: 116). Foreign direct investment thus increases the prospect for growth in the host country by enabling technological diffusion through imitation on the part of domestic firms of the MNCs' technology and management practices and by providing an infusion of capital into the economy (Findlay 1978; Jensen 2003, 2006).

The obvious benefits of FDI have made it an attractive topic of study for political economists in recent years. But it is only one half of the capital flows story, for while we are accustomed to thinking of developing countries as simply recipients of developed country capital, the facts are that many developing countries are in fact net exporters of capital (Boyce and Ndikumana 2000; Cerra *et al.* 2008; Ndikumana and Boyce 2003). Capital flight, a process by which developing country capital is moved abroad in ways that cannot be tracked easily, denies the originating country valuable productive capital for investment and economic growth. First, as has been long documented in numerous studies extolling the virtues of capital accumulation and productive investment for economic growth, high flight represents a "diversion of scarce resources away from domestic investment and other productive activities" (Boyce and Ndikumana 2000: 7). Second, capital flight has "pronounced regressive effects on the distribution of wealth" since political and economic elites are typically more able to acquire and stash monies abroad. However, "the negative effects of the resulting shortages of revenue and foreign exchange fall disproportionately on the shoulders of the less wealthy members of the society," a situation which is exacerbated when the result of the financial imbalances is devaluation, as in such cases, the rich are protected by their external assets while the poor are extremely vulnerable (Boyce and Ndikumana 2000: 7–8). Given the speed at which capital can move, this has potentially devastating consequences for economies as was evidenced by the East Asian financial crisis of the late 1990s (MacIntyre 2003). Yet relatively little work, especially compared to the now voluminous literature on FDI inflows, has been done to this point to understand why some countries are more prone to such detrimental capital flight than others.

FDI inflows and capital flight are thus two sides of the same coin – money flows in and out of economies, and whether these resources produce economic growth depends on whether more money stays in than leaves. Yet scholars of these topics have tended to treat each by itself, rather than seeking a common framework to understand both FDI inflows and capital flight. From the perspective of this book, the key factor common to the literatures explaining capital flight and foreign direct investment is the role of policy uncertainty in shaping the decisions of private economic actors. Writing about capital flight, Hermes and Lensink (2002: 3) state: "Capital flight is motivated by the fear of losing wealth due to, for example, expropriation of wealth by the government, sudden exchange rate depreciation, non-repayment of government debts, (changes in) capital controls and financial market regulations, and (changes in) tax policies." And Schineller (1997: 11) writes, "the *credibility and perceived sustainability of government policy* underpin the motive to engage in capital flight" (emphasis mine). Where future policy is unpredictable, risk-averse investors hedge their bets by choosing less irreversible forms of investment or by investing abroad in more stable environments. Similar arguments are made by scholars of foreign direct investment. Thus, Jensen (2003) documents a positive relationship between democracy and foreign direct investment specifically, and argues that the relationship is linked to the ability of democratic governments to make credible promises to maintain *ex post* policy stability of market-friendly policies. Jensen argues that democracies enjoy this "credibility advantage" because of their increased transparency, accountability to the masses who benefit from higher growth due to foreign direct investment (audience costs), and higher numbers of potential veto points. Henisz (2000) and Stasavage (2002) similarly argue that political institutions that serve as checks and balances on each other increase the credibility of pro-business policies and of future policy stability and therefore increase the level of foreign direct investment entering the country and levels of private investment in the country respectively.

The argument developed in this book has much in common with the recent work on foreign direct investment done by Jensen, Henisz, and Stasavage. Like them, I argue that the configuration of a state's political institutions enhances the credibility of future policy stability, which should make foreign investors more likely to invest there, *ceteris paribus*. Further, like these scholars, I argue that such credibility-enhancing institutions are more likely to be found in democratic states than in non-democratic states because of the potential for more checks and balances against arbitrary and unilateral policy change in such states. Unlike them, however, my argument also sheds light on why some countries experience less capital flight than others. Specifically, my framework suggests that credible constraints against policy change should reduce perceived risks for capital-holders and therefore lower capital flight.

To assess these arguments, I use data on FDI inflows from the World Bank, and construct a measure of capital flight. The latter requires some discussion since capital flight is notoriously difficult to measure, or even to define. The term has classically been used to describe widespread currency speculation that leads to cross-border movements of private funds of a large enough magnitude to affect national financial markets. More recently, scholars have argued that "capital flight should be distinguished from normal capital outflows" (Hermes and Lensink 2002: 3), and, because of the obvious difficulties involved in measuring furtive and sometimes illegal capital outflows, have devised the so-called "residual" method to measure capital flight.[3]

The residual method is an attempt to measure capital flight indirectly by comparing the sources of capital inflows with the documented uses of these inflows. The sources typically considered are (1) the net increases in external debt and (2) the net inflow of foreign investment. The uses considered are (1) the current account deficit and (2) additions to foreign reserves. If the sum of these sources exceeds the documented uses of the capital inflows, the difference is termed capital flight. Capital flight can thus be calculated as:

$$KF_{i,t} = (\Delta ED_{i,t} + FDI_{i,t}) - (CAD_{i,t} + \Delta FR_{i,t}) \qquad (4.1)$$

where, for country i in period t, KF is capital flight, Δ represents period-to-period change, ED is the stock of external debt, FDI is the stock of foreign investment inflows, CAD is the current account deficit, and FR is the stock of official foreign reserves.[4]

Armed with these measures of capital flight and foreign direct investment inflows, I proceed to specify regression models similar to those used above. As in the savings and contract-intensive money models, the main covariates are the credible constraint and democracy indicators, and I control for political instability, economic performance and macroeconomic instability, capital account and trade openness, financial liquidity and debt service burdens, the level of fixed capital formation in the economy, and a time trend. The first models for each dependent variable utilize data from all countries; the second models utilize data only from those countries that were democratic for more than half of the five-year period that forms the basic unit of observation. Table 4.5 reports the results of the analysis.

The results reported in Table 4.5 strongly support the credible constraints argument. Democracy is positively signed and statistically

---

[3] See Hermes and Lensink (2002) for a detailed survey of the measurement of capital flight.

[4] There are some alternative specifications of the residual method. For instance, the Morgan Guaranty method counts the change in the short-term foreign assets of the domestic banking system as an additional use of capital inflows. Boyce and Ndikumana (2000: 17–18) utilize another variation to account for (1) "the impact of exchange rate fluctuations on the U.S. dollar value of the stock of long-term debt" and (2) "trade misinvoicing." Lack of cross-national time-series data makes it impossible for me to calculate these variants.

Table 4.5 *Regression results: credible constraints and international capital movements*

DV:	Capital flight		Net FDI inflows	
	All LDCs	*Democracies*	*All LDCs*	*Democracies*
Minority/coalition govts	−3.59 $(1.45)^{0.02}$	−4.46 $(1.99)^{0.03}$	−0.84 $(0.84)^{0.32}$	−0.31 $(0.96)^{0.75}$
Divided presidential govts	−1.65 $(3.25)^{0.61}$	0.53 $(4.27)^{0.90}$	−0.51 $(0.44)^{0.24}$	−0.66 $(0.49)^{0.19}$
Independent judiciaries	−3.47 $(1.93)^{0.08}$	−0.26 $(1.61)^{0.87}$	0.58 $(0.38)^{0.13}$	0.94 $(0.58)^{0.11}$
Federalism	−4.34 $(2.39)^{0.07}$	−8.58 $(3.43)^{0.02}$	−0.21 $(0.44)^{0.63}$	−0.67 $(0.73)^{0.36}$
Central bank indep.	−0.86 $(1.17)^{0.46}$	−1.42 $(2.20)^{0.52}$	0.08 $(0.22)^{0.73}$	0.11 $(0.36)^{0.77}$
Democracy	2.63 $(1.55)^{0.09}$		0.76 $(0.44)^{0.09}$	
Political instability	−0.32 $(0.15)^{0.04}$	0.17 $(0.35)^{0.64}$	0.04 $(0.04)^{0.23}$	0.03 $(0.08)^{0.74}$
GDP per capita (Log)	−2.71 $(0.74)^{0.00}$	−2.42 $(1.10)^{0.03}$	−0.04 $(0.18)^{0.81}$	0.08 $(0.23)^{0.73}$
Growth in GDP per capita	−0.85 $(0.24)^{0.00}$	−1.19 $(0.47)^{0.02}$	0.05 $(0.05)^{0.28}$	0.02 $(0.07)^{0.78}$
Inflation (Log)	2.26 $(2.53)^{0.38}$	4.17 $(3.34)^{0.22}$	−0.04 $(0.13)^{0.75}$	−0.23 $(0.15)^{0.13}$
Fixed capital formation	0.32 $(0.11)^{0.01}$	0.35 $(0.18)^{0.06}$	0.07 $(0.05)^{0.17}$	0.15 $(0.07)^{0.03}$
Capital account openness	−0.04 $(0.51)^{0.93}$	−1.37 $(0.91)^{0.14}$	0.14 $(0.13)^{0.29}$	0.12 $(0.22)^{0.60}$
Trade openness (% GDP)	0.03 $(0.02)^{0.03}$	0.02 $(0.03)^{0.54}$	0.02 $(0.004)^{0.00}$	0.03 $(0.01)^{0.01}$
Financial liquidity (M2)	0.05 $(0.06)^{0.45}$	0.20 $(0.16)^{0.21}$	−0.01 $(0.01)^{0.43}$	−0.05 $(0.03)^{0.08}$
Debt service (% exports)	0.14 $(0.06)^{0.02}$	0.09 $(0.09)^{0.34}$	−0.001 $(0.01)^{0.94}$	0.02 $(0.02)^{0.24}$
Time trend	−1.11 $(0.38)^{0.01}$	−0.36 $(0.55)^{0.51}$	0.22 $(0.11)^{0.04}$	0.51 $(0.19)^{0.01}$
Constant	15.95 $(7.35)^{0.03}$	−1.94 $(9.86)^{0.85}$	−2.34 $(0.99)^{0.02}$	−4.74 $(1.99)^{0.02}$

Table 4.5 *(cont.)*

DV:	Capital flight		Net FDI inflows	
	All LDCs	*Democracies*	*All LDCs*	*Democracies*
No. of countries	73	41	73	41
No. of observations	332	119	341	119
Root mean square error	9.48	9.66	1.85	2.23
R-squared	0.25	0.42	0.34	0.43

Note: Cell entries are OLS coefficients with standard errors corrected for clustering by country reported in parentheses and two-sided p-values superscripted.

significant at the 0.10 level (2-sided test), which is consistent with previous research on capital flight and foreign investment (Cerra *et al.* 2008). But, strikingly, coalition parliamentary democracies experience much less capital flight than other political-institutional configurations. This result holds up even with the matching techniques discussed in the previous chapter. In a sample of developing country parliamentary systems, after matching, capital flight in the treatment group of coalition governments is 4.85 percent, while it is 7.47 percent in the control group. The opposite is true for the presidential systems where, after matching, divided governments have higher capital flight than unified governments. The key result thus holds in a series of models using different dependent variables and even sources of data: coalition governments in parliamentary democracies provide a credible constraint against policy change, leading to lower capital flight, higher domestic savings, and therefore better national economic performance.

Two other institutional indicators emerge as potentially relevant in the capital flight model, though with lower levels of statistical significance. Judicial independence and federalism are both statistically significant at the 0.10 level, and both are negatively signed. When we limit the sample only to democracies, the federalism effect increases and is more precisely estimated too. Clearly federal structures appear to reduce the risk perceived by citizens, thereby reducing the desire to diversify their portfolios by engaging in capital flight.

As mentioned above, the democracy indicator is weakly significant in the FDI model, which is consistent with previous research by Nathan Jensen and Witold Henisz, among others. Their interpretation of this effect is typically that democracies are better able to commit credibly to long-term policy stability, which I obviously think is quite plausible. But none of the other credible constraint indicators are statistically significant in the FDI model, which suggests either that the "credibility advantage" of democracies more likely resides in the electoral accountability mechanism, or that the democracy effect is spurious to the fact that these societies are likely to be wealthier and faster-growing in the developing world (Przeworski *et al.* 2000). At the very least, this analysis does suggest that the question of whether foreign direct investors are attracted by democracy is yet to be answered conclusively.

Conclusion

The goal of this chapter was to provide evidence for the causal mechanisms implied by the theoretical framework developed in this book. I argued earlier that poor national economic performance – characterized by low and volatile growth – is the result of governments' inability to make credible commitments to future policy stability. This inability has two main effects. First, it makes investors nervous and more likely to flee with their capital, especially in times of trouble or increased uncertainty. Second, because investors fear *ex post* policy change, they are less likely to choose longer-term investment projects, as typified by foreign direct investment. Together these two effects can deprive a developing economy of much needed capital, increasing growth-rate volatility and hurting long-term economic growth.

The core argument that diffusion of policymaking authority to multiple actors accountable to different societal constituencies increases economic growth while reducing growth-rate volatility received robust statistical support in Chapter 3. This chapter therefore delved deeper to see if the alleged causal mechanisms had any merit. Using World Bank firm-level business environment surveys, I showed that economic and regulatory policy uncertainty affects business decisions to engage in new investment projects, and, further, that credible constraints against policy change can assuage such uncertainty significantly. Further, using World Bank macroeconomic data, I presented statistical tests of the effect of such diffusion of authority on gross domestic savings, levels of contract-intensive money, capital flight and foreign direct investment, finding support for my argument across these indicators: the presence of coalition governments has a robust positive effect on domestic savings and a strong negative effect on capital flight while judicial independence increases levels of contract-intensive money in the economy, even controlling for whether the country is a democracy, political instability, and a host of economic control variables drawn from the relevant literatures on each dependent variable.

This chapter, together with Chapter 3, offers consistent statistical support for the argument using cross-national data. The next two chapters turn to country case studies to bolster confidence in these findings. In the next chapter, I apply the theoretical framework to India, a country that has grown rapidly in recent years, to see if the cross-national finding that coalition governments bolster economic performance can explain cross-state variation in that country.

5 | Coalition dharma and India shining

The Indian economy is one of the true success stories in the developing world. Over the past decade or so, a long-sluggish economy appears to have matured and, unshackled from restrictive government policies, is emerging as a global player. One indicator of this is the veritable cottage industry in books about India's economic growth with titles like *India: Emerging Power* (Cohen 2002), *India: The Emerging Giant* (Panagariya 2008), *India as an Emerging Power* (Ganguly 2003), and *India Unbound* (Das 2002). Alongside these and many other books on the topic, numerous articles have been penned on the Indian economy, each trying to understand why, after years of trudging along, the "elephant started to trot."[1]

My comparative advantage does not lie in adding to the now voluminous literature on the sources of growth in the Indian economy, or identifying the timing of structural breaks in India's growth trend. To those interested in those topics, I am content to recommend Panagariya's magisterial account of India's post-independence economic performance (2008). Rather my goal in this chapter is to tackle questions less well-answered by economists concerning the role political considerations play in this story. Specifically I apply the theoretical framework developed in this book to India to see if it can resolve the apparent paradox of India's rapid growth coinciding with a period of immense political fragmentation and instability.

The chapter is organized in two main sections. In the first section, I discuss India's national economic performance over time, and argue that coalition politics at the Center has aided, rather than hindered, economic growth in India.[2] In the second section, I test the argument

---

[1] "Why Did the Elephant Start to Trot?" is the title of a recent article on the Indian economy by Kunal Sen (2007).

[2] "Center" refers to the central government in New Delhi.

using variation in business attitudes across major Indian states. The results of this analysis provide strong evidence in favor of the credible constraints argument, and I discuss the implications of my findings in the final section.

Elephant for sale: the modern Indian economy

Immediately after its independence from British rule in 1947, India launched an ambitious program to build a self-sufficient economy. Using tenets of the planned economy learned from the Soviets, early Indian plans emphasized the building of an indigenous industrial sector that would be supported ably by a vibrant agricultural sector (Balakrishnan 2007). This first phase of economic development had its successes, and by the late 1960s and its successful Green revolution, the Indian economy appeared to be poised for "take-off" (Panagariya 2008). But the second phase belied these lofty expectations. Political machinations in New Delhi led to an allegedly leftward and populist turn in policy and an emphasis on poverty alleviation over economic growth. The economy ground to a virtual standstill as industrialists struggled to do business in a stifling environment best epitomized by India's "Permit Raj." A bloated and uncompetitive state sector, coupled with restrictions on foreign competition and high tariffs on trade, led to years of poor economic performance and stagnant growth.

The late 1970s witnessed considerable political turmoil in India. Prime Minister Indira Gandhi enacted the Emergency in 1975, and began India's fortunately short-lived flirtation with dictatorship. Popular discontent with this move led to her ceding power in 1977 to the first non-Congress-led government in the form of the Janata coalition. Indira returned to power in 1980 for what proved to be her final stint in office (she was assassinated by her own bodyguards in 1984). Her return ushered in a third phase of the Indian economy. Starting in the late 1970s, the dismal performance of the economy had led to a growing recognition that change was needed, and efforts to liberalize the economy began. The economy responded, and for the first time in some years began to show signs of life. A severe balance-of-payments crisis in 1991 provided Prime Minister Narasimha Rao and then-Finance Minister (now Prime Minister) Manmohan Singh with the ideal opportunity to push through a comprehensive reform package that consolidated and furthered the path begun in the previous decade. The Permit Raj was over, and Indian business was finally free to compete domestically and internationally (Jenkins 1999; World Bank 1996). The Bharatiya Janata Party (BJP)-led NDA (National Democratic Alliance) government that ushered in the twenty-first century continued this reform agenda, and while the current Congress-led UPA (United Progressive Alliance) government has been unable to enact any new reforms, it has done nothing to reverse the momentum either, confirming Ahluwalia and Williamson's piquant observation that India had a "strong consensus for weak reform" (2003).[3] Meanwhile India's economy is growing at hitherto unheard-of rates for a country that a generation earlier appeared content to pursue the "Hindu rate of growth," averaging 8 percent growth annually in the most recent years, and fueling speculation that it might soon be a worthy economic rival to China (Bardhan 2009).

Figure 5.1 compares India's economic performance to the rest of the world since 1960. The first graph displays India's average GDP growth rate by decade versus that of the rest of the world. While India clearly lagged behind the rest of the world in the initial decades after independence, by 1980 the tide had turned and India's growth performance has outstripped the world average growth rate ever since. This improved performance is robust. No longer is India's growth fragile; in fact, growth-rate volatility is also decreasing over time as the second graph in Figure 5.1 attests. Using the popular coefficient of variation to measure volatility, this graph plots the volatility of India's per capita growth rates compared again to the rest of the world. Yet again, while India experienced more volatility prior to 1980, it was more stable after that point.

What do we know about this increased economic performance? Economists now believe that the major structural break of India's post-independence era occurred in 1978–9, even though public commentators often point to the economic reforms of 1991 as the major

---

[3] Chhibber (1999: 184) makes a similar point: "In the end, however, there is consensus among the parties on the desirability of reform – the parties hold the same position on whether to cut government expenditures or not – namely, that there shall be no cuts." Krueger and Chinoy (2003) provide a good summary of the reforms that remained to be implemented circa 2003 towards the end of the NDA government's rule. The *Economist* explicitly blamed coalition politics for the lack of progress on this reform agenda (October 29, 2005). Jenkins (2005) provides a cogent analysis of the NDA government's economic reforms.

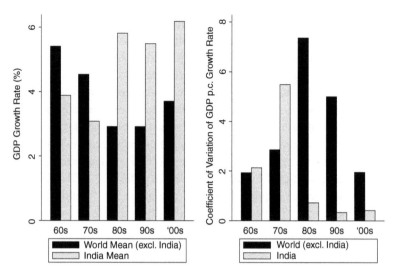

Figure 5.1 India's economic performance has improved in recent decades (source: author's calculations from World Bank 2006).

point of departure (Balakrishnan and Parameswaran 2007; Virmani 2006; Wallack 2003).[4] Further, the evidence suggests that rapid growth in the services sector, rather than in manufacturing or industrial growth, has been the engine for the Indian economy (Bosworth *et al.* 2006). Third, there exist real challenges to continued growth on account of limited infrastructure development and low levels of human capital formation, both of which hurt productivity. Finally, agriculture continues to be a volatile component of economic growth, with crop yields heavily dependent on rainfall (Virmani 2004).

The other thing we know is less easily understood. The rapid growth and increased stability of the Indian economy has coincided with a period of unprecedented political instability. The Indian party system has fragmented, shattering the stranglehold over power once exercised by the dominant and omnipresent Congress Party. Indeed, today, the Congress is but a faint shadow of its former self, unable to compete for power in many states around the country, and dependent on the

---

[4] A longer perspective reveals that 1950 provides the major structural break if one considers the entire twentieth century (Hatekar and Dongre 2005).

support of smaller regional parties in order to form a government in New Delhi. The Congress is not alone in this regard. Indeed, since 1984, when the Congress was swept to power riding a wave of sympathy after Indira Gandhi's assassination, no party has enjoyed a majority in the Central Government, and India has been ruled by a succession of minority and coalition governments for the past twenty years (see Table D.1 in Appendix D for a list of governments that have ruled India since independence).

India's experience with political fragmentation and increased propensity for minority or coalition governments provides important leverage on the question of whether the claims advanced here are spurious due to unexplored endogeneity. That is, are coalition governments *the result of* high and stable growth, rather than their cause, as I have argued here? More generally, did the form of India's political system and therefore the composition of national governments change because of economic factors? If so, then the relationship posited here might be spurious. Fortunately for my purposes, the India case unequivocally dismisses this as a possibility. In India, as Pradeep Chhibber and I have shown in previous research, the party system fragmented in the early 1980s (Chhibber and Nooruddin 2000), before the economic reforms of 1991 and the improved national economic performance since. Further, the reasons for this fragmentation had nothing to do with the economic performance of the period but rather with an Anti-Defection Law (ADL) enacted by then-Prime Minister Rajiv Gandhi (Nikolenyi 2009). The ADL changed incentives for politicians to remain with the catch-all Congress Party instead of branching off to form their own more regionally-focused parties from where they would wield greater influence over the government formation process and the flow of resources from the Center to the states. Ironically, Nikolenyi (2009) argues, Rajiv Gandhi pushed the Law through a reluctant Lok Sabha, (national parliament) hoping that it would improve party discipline within the Congress.

The political fragmentation of the Indian system is arguably accompanied by a social fragmentation too. Caste cleavages have become politically salient as parties try to win votes by offering reservations to different caste groups; the Hindu right continues to berate religious minorities; secessionist groups continue to fight the Indian government in Kashmir and the north-eastern states; and separatist groups, buoyed by the recent creation of three new states, are growing more vociferous in their demands for their own states.[5] If anything, India's "crisis of governability" (Kohli 1991) appears to be worsening, and yet, the economy continues to grow steadily, domestic savings continue to rise, and foreign capital continues to flow into the country at increasing rates. How can we explain this apparent contradiction?

This paradox – high stable growth at a time of social and political instability – poses problems for the two major alternative explanations discussed earlier in this book. Dani Rodrik, for instance, argued that growth-rate volatility is the result of government's inability to handle social conflict in a cooperative manner, but India has reduced its growth-rate volatility at the same time that social conflict has increased. Dennis Quinn and John Woolley, by contrast, emphasized the role of elections in allowing risk-averse citizens to hold accountable politicians who might be tempted to enact risk economic policy. India, of course, has had a long uninterrupted history of democratic elections stretching back to its founding as a republic in 1950, such that elections per se provide little analytic leverage for explaining cross-temporal variation in economic performance. Moreover, the Indian electorate appears to be anything but risk-averse if its anti-incumbency tendencies are anything to go by. If incumbency advantage in most countries suggests that voters prefer the "devil they know," in India the opposite is true. Incumbents are more likely to lose their seats than to retain them, and electoral volatility is extremely high leading to a regular turnover in office (Linden 2004; Nooruddin and Chhibber 2008). Such rapid turnover, and anti-incumbency, should shorten the time horizons of politicians rather than lengthen them, and make them more likely to enact risky policy than to exercise caution!

A more plausible explanation for what changed politically to enable better growth is a change in the attitudes of key politicians. Starting in the 1980s, Dani Rodrik and Arvind Subramanian argue, attitudes of the national government under Indira Gandhi towards the private sector changed from being anti-business to pro-business (2004). Atul Kohli argues that this was the result of the creation of a state-business alliance (2004; 2006a; 2006b; 2007). This new alliance, and the change in attitudes, went a long way towards assuring investors that

---

[5] At the time of this writing, a separatist crisis in Andhra Pradesh is in full swing, with no indication of how it will eventually be resolved.

the fundamental rules of the game had changed, thereby encouraging entrepreneurial activity and energizing business (De Long 2003).[6]

That government attitudes were pro-business by the second half of the 1970s is undeniable. But this was not the first time that this had been the case. As Kunal Sen points out, many of the pro-business features of the Indira government from 1980 to 1984 identified by Kohli were also evident during her earlier stint in power:

For example, in 1974, the national government declared the threatened strike by two million railway employees as illegal and arrested 20,000 workers and trade union leaders ... In the same year, the national government abandoned the nationalisation of the wholesale wheat trade, a pet project of the left at that time. There were also clear changes in the attitudes of the economic bureaucracy towards a more liberal view of economic planning ... While the changes in attitudes of the politicians and bureaucrats towards the private sector during this period were incremental, they were no less so than the ones pointed out by Kohli and [Rodrik and Subramanian] in the early-1980s. (Sen 2007: 39–40)

From my perspective, the question is not whether the changes documented by Kohli and others in attitudes of key political agents in the early 1980s were lesser or greater than those Sen alleges occurred in the mid-1970s, but rather why these changes had a more profound effect on the Indian economy in the latter period than in the former. The framework I have offered treats economic agents as inherently risk-averse, such that the major problem faced by politicians is to convince these agents of the credibility of their reform promises. This is where the answer must lie: the reforms enacted in the early 1980s must have been deemed more credible by economic agents than those in the mid-1970s. But why would this be the case? Indeed, to push Sen's point further, in both cases the reforms were announced by a Congress government led by the same individual, Indira Gandhi. So what had changed?

What had changed was the basic nature and structure of the Indian political system (McMillan 2005). The Congress had ruled India uninterrupted from independence until 1977, and this control had extended to the state level for the most part too. But by the early 1980s, the Congress's grip on power was inexorably and unmistakeably weakened. Most state governments had now

---

[6] Sengupta (2008) takes a different tack on this question.

experienced non-Congress governments, and the states were growing more assertive in their dealings with the Center. The growth of regional parties all over the country cemented this state of affairs (Chhibber and Nooruddin 2000), and turned these smaller parties into veritable king-makers in Parliament as it became increasingly impossible for any one party to command a clear majority of the seats in the Lok Sabha. Coalition politics had become the name of the political game in India, and twenty-plus years since the last true majority government, the situation evinces no sign of changing in the foreseeable future. If anything, analysis of public opinion data suggests that the Indian electorate has learned to live with the reality of coalition politics. Asked about what they thought of coalition governments, 15 percent of respondents to the National Election Survey in 2004 said that coalition governments were tolerable under special circumstances, and, strikingly, twice as many people (31 percent) stated that they saw no harm in coalition governments.[7]

The observation that the period of improved national economic performance in India coincides with the emergence of coalition politics is anticipated by the theoretical framework developed in this book, and owes much to an analysis of India's public institutions conducted by Devesh Kapur (2005). Kapur, anticipating a more recent argument by Siddharth Chandra and Nita Rudra, argues that "while economic reforms increased growth on the upside in India, the limited consequences of government instability are due to India's polymorphic institutions, which have provided a kind of institutional safety net that has limited the downside and given it a systemic resilience" (2005: 30). Like Chandra and Rudra, Kapur argues that democracies like India are more likely to create a "thick institutional web" of organizations that serve as informal checks and balances against each other. Thus, the weakening of one set of organizations is offset by the strength of another, and, importantly, vice versa, so that no one part

---

[7] Sixteen percent said that coalition governments were never good, and 32 percent expressed no opinion. The exact question wording is: "Now I would like to know your opinion about a coalition government. Some people believe that there is no harm in a coalition government. Others believe that in special circumstances there is no alternative to it. While, for others, a coalition government is not good in any circumstances. What is your opinion in this regard?" (Lokniti 2004). For a preliminary analysis of what explains variation in attitudes towards coalition governments, see Nooruddin (2009).

of the Indian political firmament can unilaterally alter policy direction without facing opposition from another.

The cornerstone of this complex institutional structure is coalition politics, which has had several noteworthy benign consequences. First, as a result of increasing anti-incumbency tendencies in the electorate, rapid governmental turnover has led to more political parties having a taste of power. This has bolstered norms of how to serve responsibly while in opposition (Bueno de Mesquita 1975; McMillan 2005). Second, coalition politics has bolstered India's federal structure and reduced the use of Article 356 powers (allowing the dismissal of state governments by the federal government). Third, and potentially most importantly over the long run, Kapur suggests that governmental instability has revitalized otherwise dormant "referee" institutions such as the Presidency, Election Commission, and the Courts that had previously been neglected. The lack of a dominant party, and the increasing churning of those in power, has led parties to turn to other public institutions in order to adjudicate policy debates (Kapur 2005; Rao and Singh 2005).

Of particular relevance to the question of national economic performance and the confidence of economic agents are signs that the Courts are becoming more assertive, and that the Reserve Bank of India is enjoying greater de facto independence (Khatkhate 2005; Mehta 2005). Courts in India have always been somewhat weak, but recent events suggest that they are waking up, and taking advantage of the relative weakness of the executive and legislative branches caused by coalition politics to assert their independence. The 1973 *Kesavananda Bharati* case is widely seen by scholars as a landmark judgment establishing the Court's right to judicial review and limiting Parliament's ability to amend basic features of the Constitution (Kapur 2005; Mehta 2005). The Indira Gandhi government did not take the Court's decision lying down. In 1976, during the Emergency, the Indian Parliament passed the 42nd amendment to the Indian Constitution, which limited the ability of India's Supreme and High Courts to decide if laws were constitutional or not. And, decisions by the Courts allowing the subsequent Central governments to use Article 356 provisions to dismiss uncooperative state governments had a deleterious effect on their perceived independence. In 1993, however, emboldened by a series of scandals that had significantly hurt the power of the executive and legislative branches, the Court reasserted itself, and assumed the power of appointment of judges, shutting out the executive branch from this role. In subsequent rulings, the judicial branch reduced the executive's role in appointing judges to lower courts as well as to many quasi-judicial bodies (Kapur 2005: 55). These decisions, and the inability of unstable coalition governments to challenge them effectively, have made Indian Courts more independent than most of their counterparts elsewhere, and the locus therefore of many important public policy decisions in recent years through their rulings on public-interest litigations. Of course, the problems and weaknesses of the court system arguably exceed its strengths: it's still slow, overburdened, and judges at all levels are essentially unaccountable. But, to echo Kapur's conclusion, "as long as succession procedures are institutionalized and it enjoys high external legitimacy, these weaknesses are not especially debilitating" (Kapur 2005: 55).

Another public institution to have gained power in recent years is the Reserve Bank of India (RBI). The RBI does not enjoy the statutory independence that characterizes the strong central banks of the United States and many OECD states, but economic liberalization and a relatively weaker Center have allowed it more leeway to act independently than in the past. The major problem historically was that the government's strong interventionist tendencies and ideological commitment to planning made the RBI a crucial instrument of government policy rather than allowing it to work independently. The liberalization of the financial sector of the economy in the 1990s has increased the room to operate for the RBI, and it responded well in its management of the debt crisis of the early 1990s, though it has done less well in terms of reining in the fiscal deficit run by the government or in providing price stability (Khatkhate 2005). The government is currently facing great pressure to bring inflation under control without sacrificing growth prospects, and one imagines that how the RBI responds will go a long way to shaping its future.

Returning then to the puzzle posed by India's recent economic growth, why did economic agents respond to the economic reforms of the last three decades vigorously ushering in a period of unprecedented growth rather than fearing that weak Central governments, the imperatives of coalition politics, and high electoral volatility would make any reform package short-lived and therefore any investment in response to such a package inherently risky? With the benefit of hindsight, the notion that India's leaders had seen the light and accepted the necessity and utility of liberalizing the economy is temptingly plausible, and indeed there's little doubt that having a new generation of leaders at the helm (such as Manmohan Singh and P. Chidambaram) was important for reassuring economic agents of the sincerity of the reforms. But this wasn't the first time that reforms had been enacted, and the mid-1970s had seen dramatic reversals of reforms, the nationalization of industries and banks, and overt hostility to foreign investors. Why was this time going to be different? The answer, I would argue, lies paradoxically in the fragmentation of the Indian political system that has made coalition politics a must, arguably strengthened other public institutions such as federalism, the judiciary, and the central bank, and made policy change predictable and gradual. Thus, even if many observers of the Indian economy are frustrated by the lack of progress in deepening the reforms of the 1990s, a longer-term perspective reminds us that little changes rapidly in India, and that from the point of view of economic policy, predictably slow trumps quick and uncertain.

The "credible constraints" argument appears to fit the Indian data, and to provide analytic leverage on why India's economic growth spurt has coincided with greater political instability. In particular, it bolsters our confidence in the finding that emerged in the cross-national analyses reported in the previous two chapters that coalition governments in parliamentary democracies are especially beneficial for encouraging domestic saving, reducing capital flight, and therefore providing stable and high economic growth. The problem, of course, is that it is not possible to use the national-level data for India to provide a conclusive test of this hypothesis, since the period of coalition governments of the past two decades is different in other ways too from the earlier period of slow and more volatile growth. For instance, the policy regime is clearly more pro-growth than ever before, the external sector is more open, India's terms-of-trade situation has improved, the working-age population has increased, and India benefited from the dramatic revolution in information technology that allowed it to take advantage of the business-processing revolution in the global economy (Kapur 2002, 2005). While the credible constraints argument is plausible enough, so are these alternatives, and while any fair-minded observer would understand that all (or none) of these arguments might be correct, we cannot tease them apart in the Indian context by remaining at the national level.

Fortunately for these purposes, India's states display tremendous variation in economic performance and political situations, allowing me to construct a state-level test of the theoretical framework. The next section describes this test and its results.

Explaining variation in state-level business environments

India has a federal structure with twenty-eight states and seven union territories governed by the Center. The bulk of the population resides in fourteen major states, and the economic lives of these citizens depend heavily on the state in which they live. Figure 5.2 plots the volatility and level of economic growth by state for the 1995 to 2004 period.[8] The data come from the annual bulletins of the Reserve Bank of India (Reserve Bank of India 1967–2004). I use the data through 2004 only to ensure that only revised estimates of state per capita domestic product are included, since the government updates the most recent years' figures up to two years after they are first published as budget estimates. The data represented in the figure thus represent the states' economic performance in the period after the major economic reforms of 1991.

The relative placement of the states in Figure 5.2 will not surprise anyone familiar with the Indian states (see Ramaswamy (2007) for a detailed analysis of regional trends in growth and employment in India). States in the Hindi heartland like Madhya Pradesh and Bihar perform least effectively with the lowest average growth rate and highest growth-rate volatility respectively. By contrast, states such as Kerala and West Bengal lead the pack over this time period, with the highest rates of growth and the lowest levels of volatility. The contrast between these two sets of states is striking in political terms. Madhya Pradesh, for instance, has experienced robust two-party competition with two effective parties contesting elections and has had single-party majority governments rule throughout the post-independence period. Kerala and West Bengal, by contrast, are coalition governments headed by Left or Communist parties. While West Bengal has been ruled by the

---

[8] Each of the fourteen largest Indian states, were they independent countries, would figure in the world's top fifty in terms of population, with the largest – Uttar Pradesh – placing in the top ten, just ahead of Japan. The comparisons that follow are therefore as significant in terms of the numbers of people affected as the comparisons of countries that underlay the last two chapters. I thank Jim Vreeland for reminding me of this point.

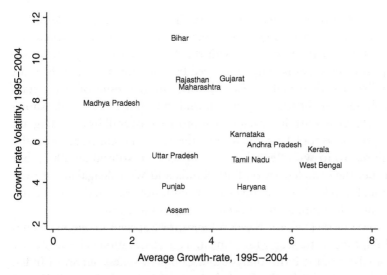

Figure 5.2 There exists considerable variation in economic performance across the Indian states (source: Reserve Bank of India, various issues).

Left Front throughout the period, Kerala has seen regular alternation in power, but has not had a single-party government since 1959. Since then, all ruling governments in Kerala have been coalitions led either by the Communist Party of India (Marxist) or the Indian National Congress (I), with only few exceptions (Kerala has almost seven effective parties that contest elections on a regular basis). Today there are two explicit pre-election coalitions that vie for power: the Congress-led United Democratic Front and the Communist-led Left Democratic Front. And yet, even though politics in Kerala is characterized by coalition in-fighting and incremental policy change, its economic growth has been both more rapid and more stable than its neighbors to the north that have had the supposed advantages of being governed by single-party governments capable of enacting good policy and of retaining office.

This contrast is replicated if we take a wider view and consider all fourteen major states for which data are available. If we compare states governed by single-party majority governments to those governed by coalition governments over the period of 1995 to 2004, the former have an average growth rate of 4 percent, while the latter grew a half-point faster each year (4.5 percent). The gap widens to almost a full point if we consider only the last five years of that time period.

One objection to this comparison should concern possible differences in the sources of growth in the two states, especially when one considers that the two states with the "best" economic performance appear to be states heavily influenced by Communist parties. Is it not possible that their high levels of growth are the result of heavy state involvement in the economy, which while boosting growth in the short-run is likely to hurt the development prospects overall by crowding out the private sector? To some degree, this is a valid concern, especially with regard to West Bengal (see Chhibber and Nooruddin 2007), but it is not the complete story. Both Kerala and West Bengal are attracting high levels of private investment, both domestic and foreign, and the latter has (infamously) been willing to buck trade unions within the state in its push for the development of Special Economic Zones (SEZs) for private sector investment. This observation is borne out by an analysis of the Firm Analysis and Competitiveness Survey of India, jointly conducted by the Confederation of Indian Industry (CII) and the World Bank in 2002.

In 2002, the CII and World Bank joined forces to survey 2,000 businesses in twelve major Indian states. The stated goal of the survey was to advise state governments on how they might change their policies to encourage the start-up and expansion of businesses in their states. The unit of observation therefore is an individual establishment of a firm, and the questionnaire posed a comprehensive battery of questions on the nature of the firm, its position in the Indian economy, and its perceptions about the major challenges facing it. These data thus provide a unique window into the business environments created by state governments, and allow a precise test of the hypothesis that coalition governments reduce fundamental uncertainties for economic agents, thereby encouraging them to engage in innovation and to take greater risks. The validity of this test is enhanced by the laboratory-like nature of India's states since one can control for national-level economic conditions and political institutions, and focus intensely on the key factor of interest, the presence of coalition governments.

Do coalition governments reduce uncertainty? The CII-World Bank survey asks firms about what issues are a problem for the operation and growth of their business. Specifically, the survey asks if "economic and regulatory policy uncertainty" is a problem. This question gets to the heart of my argument, and the data bear me out. In states governed by majority governments, 43.8 percent of firms said that economic and regulatory policy uncertainty constituted a "major" or "very severe" obstacle to their ability to conduct and grow their business. In states governed by coalition governments, the percentage drops to 38.4 percent; this difference is statistically significant at the 0.01 level. While a 5 percent difference might not strike some readers as particularly significant, I would argue that it deserves attention. This after all is a comparison of firm views within the same country, governed by the same national policies, and interviewed in the same year. That there should be any difference in views about policy uncertainty across states is itself puzzling, and the fact that this difference occurs in a theoretically predictable manner is encouraging.

The lower uncertainty associated with doing business in coalition-governed states extends beyond policy uncertainty. The survey also asks firms the degree to which macroeconomic instability (for example, inflation and exchange rate instability) is an obstacle to their business. In majority-government states, 40.3 percent of firms rate such macroeconomic uncertainty as a major to very severe problem; in coalition-government states, by contrast, 35.4 percent do, and again this difference is statistically significant ($p = 0.02$). State governments have little control over inflation and exchange rate policy; that there should be any difference in perceptions of uncertainty with regard to these policies is testament to the greater general confidence in policy stability firms in coalition governments enjoy.

These findings beg the obvious question: does the higher confidence in coalition government states result in different sorts of firm behavior? In particular, are firms in these states more likely to engage in innovation and to take risks to grow their business? This is an important question in general because innovation breeds productivity, competitiveness, and through them, higher growth (Dutz 2007).

Firm-level investment in innovation research and development (R&D) is on the rise in India, though it still lags behind the benchmarks of other economies of India's size. Further, since government spending on research and development is extremely low (less than 1 percent of GDP according to a recent World Bank (2007) survey), the onus for the development of new technologies, and for adopting existing technology to new commercial purposes, falls on private firms. Increasingly, the high level of competition in the formal sector is leading firms to have to innovate to stay ahead, and this process is being encouraged by pressures and technological spillovers from foreign multinational corporations that now operate within India. The continued growth and encouragement of such investment in innovation is vital for sustaining India's recent growth, and for broadening the bases of that growth. In particular, innovations that allow India's laggard industrial sector to catch up with the vibrant service sector will be crucial for providing a stable platform from which to grow the economy, and for creating broad-based inclusive growth through job creation (Chibber 2003; Dutz 2007).

The obvious benefits of investing in innovation notwithstanding, the risks of doing so have long appeared to dominate the thinking of Indian firms. Investment in research and development is future-oriented, and requires a willingness to take risks as there is a strong possibility that the investments will not pay off. Such irreversible investments – irreversible because the investment cannot be recouped once made, unless the innovation succeeds at some unknown future time – are less likely to be made under conditions of high uncertainty (Aizenman and Marion 1999). Therefore, other than the important tasks of enacting policies that create incentives for firms to invest in R&D, governments must also convince firms that the policies will persist well into the future. If, on the other hand, a firm is wary that a present reform-minded government will be replaced in the future by a less-innovation-friendly government that might roll back policies, it is likely to resist the incentives created in the present period and forego the investment opportunities. In India, where party system fragmentation and therefore electoral volatility are high, governmental instability will undermine firm confidence and make investments in innovation less likely.

The potential negative effects of increased party system fragmentation, I have argued, are counteracted by the stabilizing force of coalitional politics and the new status quo of coalition governments at the Center. To some extent, the increasing rates of innovation relative to the past offer basic evidence in favor of this claim, but as before it is impossible to rule out plausible alternative explanations by looking only at over-time national-level data. Fortunately, the 2002 CII-World Bank competitiveness survey asks firms explicitly about their investments in R&D. One such question is of particular interest for it asks firms whether they employed staff *exclusively* for the purpose of conducting R&D activities in the previous year. The hiring of staff exclusively for R&D represents a significant commitment

Figure 5.3 Investing in innovation is still uncommon among Indian firms (source: author's calculations using 2002 CII-World Bank survey).

of firm resources to innovation; so why are some firms more likely to incur these costs than others?

To begin, some basic trends in this variable are worth describing. First, as expected, most firms do not hire staff exclusively to conduct research and development; in fact, fewer than one-quarter of all firms surveyed in 2002 said that they had done so (see Figure 5.3). Second, there exists considerable variation across states in the degree to which firms located in them are willing to commit resources exclusively to research. Andhra Pradesh leads the way, with 45 percent of firms reporting that they employed staff exclusively for R&D activities. Gujarat (41%), West Bengal (30%), and Kerala (30%) follow as the most innovation-friendly states. The lowest level of innovation activity by this measure occurs in Madhya Pradesh, where just four out of 101 firms reported having staff exclusively to pursue innovation. Haryana (9%) and Punjab (10%) also bring up the rear. It's no surprise that these patterns mirror those of the overall state-level economic performance discussed above.

Does this state-level variation in firms' investments in R&D have anything to do with the political situation in the state? We would expect the bulk of the variation in innovation activity to be explained by firm-level characteristics, especially since all these firms operate under the same national-level policy regime. But, if my argument is correct, we should expect to see at least some evidence that firms in coalition-government states, whom we already know to perceive fewer obstacles due to policy uncertainty, to be more likely to invest resources to engage in research and development, *ceteris paribus*.

Using the 2002 Confederation of Indian Industries (CII) and World Bank Firm Analysis and Competitiveness Survey, I estimate a logit model of whether the firm employs staff exclusively for conducting research and development. The model controls for firm-level characteristics that are plausibly linked to innovation activity. These are: (1) whether the firm was a stand-alone establishment or part of a larger network of establishments; (2) the age of the firm; (3) whether the firm is publicly traded on India's stock exchanges; (4) the market share the firm commands for its primary product; and (5) whether the firm exports any of its products to international markets. Data for all these questions come from the 2002 CII-World Bank survey. The political variables included were whether the state was governed in 2002 by a coalition government, and the level of party system fragmentation in the legislature, which I measure as the effective number of parties holding seats in the Vidhan Sabha (state assembly). Data for the political variables were collected by Pradeep Chhibber and myself from the Election Commission of India website (Chhibber and Nooruddin 2004; Election Commission of India 1987–98; Nooruddin and Chhibber 2008). I also include a random effects term to account for unobserved state-level heterogeneity. The results from this analysis are reported in Table 5.1.

To ease the interpretation of the results, Figure 5.4 reports the predicted probabilities predicting whether a firm employed staff exclusively to conduct R&D for different state-level political situations.

Clearly the state's political environment matters for firms' decisions about whether to commit resources exclusively to conducting research and development. Both political factors – whether there was a coalition government and the level of party system fragmentation in the state legislature – are statistically significant at the 0.05 level, even when one controls for firm-level characteristics that drive innovation and when one accounts for unobserved state-level heterogeneity. Further, the political variables matter in ways that are theoretically plausible. Coalition governments, as argued in this book, foster an environment conducive to innovation, while legislative fragmentation in the absence of coalition

Table 5.1 *Firm-level investment in R&D across Indian states*

DV: staff exclusively for doing R&D?

	β	Std. Err	p-value
Firm-level characteristics			
Stand-alone establishment	0.66	0.16	0.00
Firm age	0.001	0.004	0.88
Firm is publicly traded	0.57	0.19	0.00
Firm's national market share	0.01	0.003	0.00
Firm is an exporter	0.99	0.15	0.00
State-level political variables			
Minority/coalition govt	1.35	0.69	0.05
Party system fragmentation	−0.74	0.37	0.05
Constant	−0.32	0.90	0.72
State-level random effects		Yes	
No. of observations		1,220	
% correctly predicted		77	

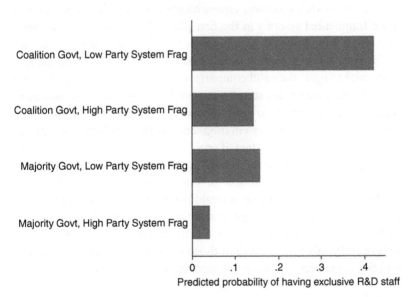

Figure 5.4 Firms in coalition government states with low party-system fragmentation are most likely to invest in R&D.

governments creates innovation-discouraging instability. To assess the counterfactual scenario of how much a firm's probability of hiring staff only to do research would change if one held all other factors constant but simply moved the firm from a state governed by a majority government to one governed by a coalition government, I generate predicted probabilities by setting all other variables at their modal or mean outcomes depending on whether they are dichotomous or continuous. The results are striking. *Ceteris paribus*, in a state with two effective parties in the Vidhan Sabha, changing only whether the state is governed by a majority versus coalition government, increases the probability the firm will emphasize innovation almost three-fold, from 0.16 to 0.42. In highly fragmented states, where at least four effective parties control seats in the state legislature, simply introducing a coalition government increases this probability from 0.04 to 0.14. Thus, even when one accounts for the dampening effect of legislative fragmentation, coalition governments encourage innovative behavior by firms.

While the use of such predicted probabilities is accepted practice for evaluating the effect of any one variable on the dependent variable in a multiple-regression setting, a valid objection to the above analysis might be that coalition governments are more likely to exist in more fragmented systems in the first place. When fewer parties compete effectively, the odds that one of them will secure a simple majority of the seats are higher than if many parties vie for power. As such, a critic might argue, the valid comparison is really whether firms located in coalition-government states are more likely to invest in innovation than their counterparts in majority-government states even when one allows the level of party system fragmentation to vary between the two. The answer is, they are. In fact, if one simply compares the average predicted probability for firms located in majority-government states to that of firms located in coalition-government states (a comparison that implicitly acknowledges that it might not make sense to "hold all else equal" since legislative fragmentation and coalition government are highly correlated with each other), firms in the latter are more likely to hire staff only for R&D than those in majority-government states, and this difference is statistically significant ($p = 0.048$).

Conclusion

India is growing, and with it the hopes and aspirations of its people. Conversations and newspaper editorials now debate questions with utmost earnestness that not too long ago would have been dismissed as fanciful. Can India surpass China? How long until India is recognized as an economic superpower? The heady success of some of India's leading companies, which now are in a position to purchase leading foreign companies, underscores this new confidence in India's economic potential.

The same conversations and editorials also bemoan the hindrance to this potential posed by India's increasingly fractious political system. In particular, the new normal of coalition politics is seen by many as a problem to be overcome, even if no solution is apparent, as economic reforms do not proceed as fast as some would like, and as some critical members of ruling coalitions indulge in what critics decry as populist politics. The emerging wisdom among the pundits is that India's growth, to use Edward Luce's wonderful phrase, is "In spite of the Gods." In this telling, the real question is how much more would India have grown, or could India grow, if, rather than having to deal with coalition governments that are held "hostage" by minor parties, India could be governed by strong majority governments committed to pushing through difficult economic reforms.

This book takes a provocatively different tack. Using a broadly comparative perspective, I have argued that rather than viewing its coalition politics as a problem, we might do better by recognizing its benefits. Coalition politics in a parliamentary democracy does make policy change more incremental in design, but it does not make it impossible. In fact, it's worth remembering that the major economic reforms of the past twenty years that are now lauded by economic entrepreneurs throughout India were enacted by minority and coalition governments. And in spite of the carousel-like nature of Indian elections, in which incumbents have a higher probability of losing their seats than of retaining them, the economic reforms passed have not been reversed even when the steadfast opponents of the previous government take their turn in power, or when the parties of the Left form the crucial support bloc for the government. This willingness to maintain the reform status quo certainly has much to do with a widespread recognition that the way forward for India requires increasing economic liberalization, but it owes as much, if not more, to the status-quo-preserving nature of coalition politics. If the *diktats* of coalition politics are to be blamed for slowing the reform process, they must also be praised for preventing its reversal (Gehlbach and Malesky 2009).

This argument is borne out both by a reinterpretation of India's recent economic growth in its light (see Kapur (2005) for a related effort), and by an original analysis of firm-level survey data, which shows that firms located in coalition-ruled Indian states are less likely to perceive economic and regulatory policy uncertainty, and macroeconomic instability, to be important obstacles to the growth and conduct of their business. This reduced uncertainty has the positive benefit of encouraging firms to commit resources to research and development, which should provide large future gains as the innovations bear fruit. The pervasive rhetoric calling for "stability" by India's captains of industry is striking in this regard. In fact, an analysis of the role of big business in Indian elections came to this startling conclusion a decade ago: "Big business in India today has set itself the goal of stability and this is an end that it sees as best served by the BJP or the Congress (I). *The ultimate ideal would of course be of a coalition that combines the two forces*, an Indian version of the 'historic compromise' that seemingly enshrines national interest above partisan political dissonances" (Muralidharan and Mahalingam 1999, emphasis added).

Nothing I have argued in this chapter should be read as denying the very real problems facing the Indian economy (Bardhan 2006, 2009). Sixty percent of all firms surveyed in 2002 said that corruption was a moderate or greater obstacle to their business; just over 50 percent said that basic infrastructure deficiencies, specifically in the provision of electricity, were a problem for their business. And almost as many identified high tax rates and inefficient tax administration as concerns. Others pointed the finger at poor skills and inadequate education of the workforce, which limited productivity gains. All of these problems must be attended to in short order if India's economy is to continue to grow at rates high enough to begin to lift the majority of its population out of poverty. The data analyzed here do not reveal any differences in perceptions of these problems across majority and coalition states, but future research on India would do well to investigate if either has a particular advantage in solving these problems. But, for now, the extant research suggests that coalition governments do at least as well, if not better, than their majority counterparts. In research with Pradeep Chhibber on the provision of public goods across the Indian states, I find that coalition governments in fact spend slightly less of their budgets on government wages and salaries than do majority governments, but that there is no statistically significant difference in spending on development expenditures (Chibber and Nooruddin 2004: Table 2). Joshi (2004) suggests that national-level coalition politics might have the unanticipated benefit of encouraging parties to focus on "essentially local problems like roads, water and electricity." If true, he continues, coalition politics "might actually come out to be more conducive to national progress and India's rise as a world power than all that done in the name of holistic planning in the days of single-party rules."

Whether this positive scenario comes to pass will depend largely on how India's political parties choose to deal with the seemingly inevitable reality of coalition governments at the Center. The signs are positive. As Kapur (2005) argues, one benefit has been that formerly moribund public institutions, of which the Courts are the most salient example, are being revived. Another is that parties are beginning to negotiate the terms of "coalition dharma," a set of rules by which to conduct politics within a coalition. The dharma stipulates that all coalition partners treat one another as equals and no major decisions are taken without evolving a consensus over it. If observed, the theory developed in this book would predict a positive economic future for India. But if violated, as some have accused the Congress of doing in its pursuit of a nuclear deal with the United States during the summer of 2008, governmental instability will increase and policy production will decrease. Yet, even in that less-than-ideal scenario, little else is likely to change as India's polycentric institutional structure will preserve its core stability.[9]

India is an incredibly diverse society, with a politics to match. In this, it is not much different from many other developing societies that are struggling to generate economic momentum, while allowing for vigorous political competition between diverse political perspectives. I will develop this theme more in the conclusion to the book, but simply offer for now the thought that one way to incorporate such political diversity within a democratic framework is to necessitate power-sharing agreements, of which coalition governments are the most common. The recent experience of India's one billion people suggests that it is an experiment worth considering.

---

[9] Kapur (2005) uses the idea of polycentric structures to describe a system with multiple centers of power.

6 Developing coalitions in Italy, Spain, Brazil, and Botswana

The credible constraints framework helps explain India's growth performance, and finds confirmation in cross-national statistical patterns as well. The principal claim is that constraints on arbitrary and capricious policymaking enhances policy stability which engenders greater confidence on the part of economic actors. In particular, coalition governments in parliamentary systems have been identified as especially useful for providing such "credible constraints." The central mechanisms in generating the status quo bias in policymaking that leads to favorable economic outcomes have been two: first, coalitions require compromise among members of the ruling coalition to obtain the support required for successful legislation, and, second, the process of government formation privileges centrist parties as potential government formateurs (Strøm 1990; Strøm and Müller 1999).

In this chapter, I analyze the growth experiences of four countries to illustrate better the logic of the theoretical argument. The emphasis in each – admittedly cursory – case study is to understand the within-country experience with the dynamics of coalition politics and their effects on national economic performance. Therefore, the purpose is not to compare across cases since more factors affecting volatility and growth exist than can be controlled. That after all was the purpose of the statistical analysis in Chapter 3 since regression is an ideal tool for providing just such control. But the limits of statistics are just as clear in their inability to illuminate the mechanisms at work in producing the varied outcomes that form our dependent variables. The case studies offered here, coupled with the more detailed analysis of India in the previous chapter, hopefully add more to our understanding.

I begin by considering the post-war Italian experience since both the volatility of its politics and rich experience with coalition governments

148

are well-documented. Next, I turn to Spain, a developed democracy but with memories of dictatorship in its not so distant past. The Spanish case is especially useful for illustrating the advantages of competitive democracy over dictatorship. Finally, I turn to the experiences of two developing countries – Brazil and Botswana. Brazil provides an example of a presidential system whose institutional structure is often criticized for the gridlock it creates, while Botswana is a Westminster system often hailed as an African success story. The four cases thus vary interestingly in their domestic political-institutional configurations. To the degree the argument travels across these four cases, our confidence in its generalizability and veracity is bolstered considerably.

Italy

Italian politics have always been characterized by relatively high political fragmentation and frequently changing coalition governments (Strøm 1990: Ch. 5). On the face of it the high levels of government instability in Italy would lead one to predict that Italy should have very high levels of growth-rate volatility. But such a prediction ignores the fact that Italy's party system has made coalition governments a constant feature of Italian politics, and that the ideologically central location of the Christian Democratic Party (DC) has allowed it to dominate the country's coalition governments for most of the post-World War II period. The influence of the DC began to wane in the early 1980s amid widespread corruption scandals. By the early 1990s, the DC no longer dominated Italian politics and the effective number of political parties has increased since that time. While any single case does not provide a conclusive test of any causal relationship, as in India, the trend towards an increasingly effective number of Italian parties in the 1990s is correlated with a decline in growth-rate volatility. In particular, the Italian case highlights an instance in which the exclusion of certain interests, notably those of the Left and Labor, may be responsible for producing policies that promoted more unstable growth.

Like Spain, which I will discuss next, Italy demonstrates the virtues of democratic rule. Prior to 1945, when Italy was ruled by dictators, growth rates were quite volatile. After 1945 and the transition to democracy, Italian growth rates became remarkably stable and

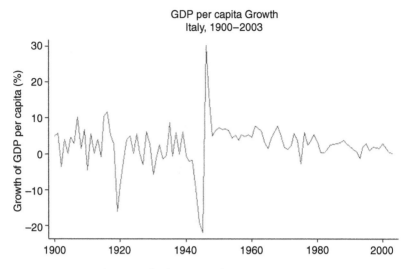

Figure 6.1 Growth-rate volatility in Italy, 1900–2003 (source: Maddison 2007).

remained so throughout the remainder of the twentieth century (see Figure 6.1).[1]

The persistence of low growth-rate volatility has occurred in spite of remarkable instability in governments in Italy. Indeed, for conventional theories linking politics to economic development, Italy's stable growth would appear a paradox. But the theoretical framework presented in this book provides a plausible solution to this paradox through its emphasis on coalition governments and their tendency to produce stable policies and to prevent drastic policy changes. In Italy's case, the key factor has been that the ideological center of Italy's myriad coalition governments has been stable, which has resulted in stability in economic policy too. The Christian Democratic Party deserves a large share of the credit for this stability. Indeed, despite the existence of a number of political parties, the DC dominated Italian coalition governments from 1948 until the early 1990s. From 1948 through the 1960s, the DC won a plurality of votes in every general election and

---

[1] Throughout this chapter data on GDP per capita are provided by Angus Maddison, and are in 1990 International Geary-Khamis dollars (Maddison 2007).

established a broad political base that included supporters from different classes and regions so that some scholars have referred to it as an "aggregative" political party (Zariski 1965). Until 1981, every prime minister had been selected by the DC. While governments never lasted more than a few years, there was great stability despite frequent alternations in power because the "cost" of forming a coalition was cheap in light of DC dominance (Mershon 1996, 2002).

The trends in growth-rate volatility apparent in Figure 6.1 roughly correspond to the three phases of Italian political life discussed in Morlino (2001). First, during the post-war period (1948–60) there were a large number of parties of which the DC and the Italian Communist Party (PCI) are the most influential. Second, the main consolidation phase occurred in the early 1960s and lasted until the early 1990s during which time the DC expanded its base in an "opening to the left." Third, electoral reforms passed in 1993 marked the beginning of a third phase of Italian politics. During this final stage, political fragmentation has increased as the dominance of the DC has waned.

From 1945 to 1977, the DC relied on patronage politics to maintain their influence throughout the country with corruption being pervasive enough to extend into the industry and commerce sectors. During the early post-war period, the De Gasperi government pursued a policy of fiscal austerity and stabilization intended to prevent inflation (the Einaudi plan). These policies are credited with promoting growth in the 1950s. Despite its center-right tendencies, in the 1950s the DC promoted the expansion of state-controlled industrial and commercial enterprises (Posner 1977).

Economic policymaking was highly centralized although different actors controlled policy depending on the sector. The DC governments relied on monetary policy whose course was determined by the Central Bank. By giving the Bank extensive control over monetary power, the intention was to depoliticize monetary policy. Likewise, industrial and commercial policy were largely determined by state-controlled enterprises and large, private corporations both of which were strongly tied to the DC (Posner 1977). Although power was highly centralized, Posner notes that the government's decision to defer to these groups on economic policy reflected the "passivity and lack of direction engendered by Italy's coalition politics" (1977: 828). Furthermore, the "macroeconomic-monetarist" approach of the Central Bank was incongruous with the "microinterventionist strategy" of the state enterprises ultimately creating an incoherent national economic policy (Locke 1995). As a result, Italy's economic policy during this period has been criticized for lacking coherence and direction.

A number of interests were excluded from 1947 to 1960. The direct involvement of businesses was limited. Private business interests were forced to try to negotiate with the DC, however, because the Italian Liberal Party (PLI) had been excluded from the coalition (Posner 1977). The DC excluded the PCI, labor, and business interests, but in the early 1960s these groups gained increasing influence. In 1956, the DC allowed for the establishment of a public enterprise employers' organization called Intersind. The early 1960s marked moves towards bargaining at the industry and firm level. This was part of a larger trend of an "Opening to the Left" in the 1960s (Posner 1977). During this period, the DC created a center-left coalition in which the PCI played a central role (Morlino 2001). Including the PCI was a strategic move to broaden the political bases of the DC and bring the PCI within its patronage system. In the 1990s, the influence of labor has continued to improve as there has been a trend towards more institutionalization of collective bargaining practices over labor and wage issues (Perez 2000).

The Italian political system has considerable problems that hinder the government's ability to rule efficiently. Widespread charges of corruption within political parties hurts the legitimacy of the political process, and for much of the post-1945 period, the government has been a revolving door for parties as coalition governments were extremely fragile and short-lived. However, as Strøm (1990: 138) makes clear, this apparent churning of governments masked a considerable stability in Italian politics:

The volatility of Italian governments is customarily noted, and the underlying continuity of the postwar record is almost equally commonplace. Italy accounts for a larger number of governments than any other country in my sample ... On the other hand, just as evidently partisan composition and personnel have changed very little from government to government.

Thus, in spite of the very real weaknesses in its political system that have made government survival difficult, Italy has had a stable growth rate (less volatile even than Spain, but more on that below) throughout the post-war period, which is hard to explain via conventional theories that explain growth-rate volatility by focusing on getting policies "right" or risk-averse political agents. Instead, focusing on the stability of policy induced by a system that encouraged the formation of coalition governments, and of the centrality of the Christian Democrats in any viable coalition, yields a more plausible explanation of this apparent paradox of Italian stability.

Spain

The Spanish political experience marks a sharp contrast to the Italian one surveyed above. Political competition in Spain is quintessentially Downsian with two major parties competing for office. On the surface it might seem a strange case to study given the argument made in this book. Yet, Spain is useful on two fronts. First, as a comparison to Italy's chronic coalition and minority governments, it is striking to find that Italy has actually had a lower level of growth-rate volatility than Spain, whether one considers only Spain's democratic era or the entire period for which comparable data exist.[2] A clearer confirmation of the utility of the credible constraints framework is difficult to imagine.

Second, and more relevant to my interests here, the case of Spain allows a clear assessment of the differences between dictatorship and democracy, and of the importance of political competition for understanding national economic performance. In the modern period, Spain was ruled until 1975 by a dictator, Francisco Franco, and after that as a parliamentary monarchy with two major parties – the Union of the Democratic Center (UCD) and the Socialist Party (PSOE) – competing for power. The sharp break with its dictatorial past allows a clear comparison before and after the introduction of democracy, and of the consequences of such a break for growth-rate volatility.

Spain experienced an "economic miracle" during the 1960s and 1970s; from 1960 to 1973, the last decade and half or so of Franco's dictatorship, Spain had the fastest growing economy in Europe. Growth ended abruptly as a result of the 1973 energy crisis, and while the Spanish economy continues to provide a high standard of living to citizens, economic growth rates have been, on average, lower than they were in the 1960s (see Figure 6.2). The slightly lower growth

---

[2] Using the measure of growth-rate volatility described in Chapter 3, the results are as follows. Since 1975, Spain's growth-rate volatility score is 0.52 while Italy's is 0.31.

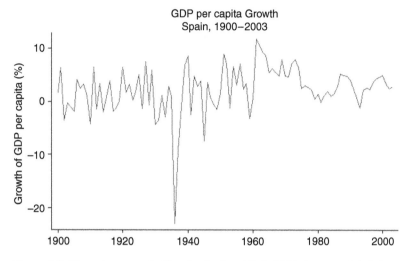

Figure 6.2 Growth-rate volatility in Spain, 1900–2003 (source: Maddison (2007)).

rates in the democratic period are only one part of the story, however. Compared to the Franquist regime, Spain today also has much lower growth-rate volatility than it did under dictatorship (for the 1965–75 non-democratic period, Spain's growth rate-volatility score is 2.14; since 1975, it has been 1.31). In fact, even if one takes the long view and considers the last hundred years of national economic performance, it is quite clear that Spain's economy was least volatile during the twenty-five years at the end of the twentieth century, at which time it had democratic institutions (see Figure 6.2).

Gunther (1996) describes four periods of government from 1977 to 1996 during which two parties dominated politics – the Union of the Democratic Center (UCD) and the Socialist Party (PSOE). During the first period from 1977 to 1979, Spain's newly elected President Adolfo Suarez led a UCD-majority government. The Suarez administration pursued a consensus-building model that incorporated opposition groups as well as labor interests in determining economic policy. The UCD followed traditional Keynesian methods including attempting to stimulate demand in order to pre-empt the effects of recession. As part of this strategy, the UCD negotiated neocorporatist deals with labor and business interests in order to limit the rate of inflation.

The second period (1979 to 1982) was a period of "dissensus" during which there was a UCD-led minority government. The PSOE actively fought the UCD and factions within the UCD in turn battled each other. The UCD led a minority government that was unable to build broad support for economic reforms (Gunther 1996). Despite some policy changes that did decrease inflation, this Socialist regime (1979 to 1982) was unable to alter negative economic outcomes such as rising public spending and increasing unemployment (Perez-Diaz 1986).

From 1982 to 1989 was the third period of Spanish government during which there was a breakdown of neocorporatist, labor–government negotiations under a PSOE majority government. Under the Gonzalez administration, the government had very limited constraints on its policy options and chose to make the Spanish economy a priority. In a switch from the demand-side Keynesian politics of the UCD, the PSOE implemented a strategy that mixed demand- and supply-side strategies (Gunther 1996). The PSOE also pursued a restrictive monetary policy and limited market reform including the curtailment of government regulations thought to hurt competitiveness. The PSOE sought approval from certain groups, negotiating with the centrist Catalan coalition, Convergencia i Unio, as well as the opposition party, Alianza Popular/Partido Popular (AP/PP). Fearing future losses in power, the PSOE at least made an effort to appear to make concessions to these groups. However, these negotiations occurred privately, outside of the public political sphere (Gunther 1996). While decision-making was not entirely centralized, unlike the Brazilian government, the PSOE was not forced to make significant changes in legislation because of opposition pressures. Policymaking was certainly more decentralized than during the Franquist era and democracy did introduce some incentives for the party in power to consider outside criticism, but policymaking was nonetheless dominated by two political parties.

From 1990 to 1996, a PSOE-minority-led government formed a coalition with the Catalans' popular leader, Jordi Pujol. Decision-making was so highly centralized between the PSOE and Pujol that the latter was even referred to by one newspaper as the "Co-President of the Government" (Gunther 1996). Despite this coalition, the PSOE remained a highly disciplined and coherent party (Montero 2001). While the PSOE was forced to include one significant outside interest, the Catalan nationalists, it did not have to form a broad coalition based on multiple, competing parties and could largely pursue its desired policies with limited modifications.

While decision-making power in post-Franquist Spain was substantially less centralized then before, politics was dominated by two parties. After the first period during which the UCD promoted a consensus-based policymaking model, relatively few opposition or outside interests were included in the process. Unlike Brazil, Spain's relatively non-fragmented party system made it easier to change economic policy precisely because the diversity of interests included in the policy process was limited. Although Spanish politics was characterized by centralized decision-making that scholars previously thought facilitated policymaking, the centralization of power coupled with regular democratic alternations in power produced changing economic policies that were not built on a broad consensus. The dangers of such alternation in economic policy, however, were mitigated by the fact that both major parties in Spain are quite similar in their policy preferences, and so policy changes are not dramatic but rather gradual. This is built into the structure of the system to some degree for, as Montero (2001) notes, Spanish institutions, in sharp contrast to those of Brazil, promote coherent, stable party rule that is resistant to particularism and ad hoc coalitions. The benefits of this stability are apparent when one considers the much lower growth-rate volatility enjoyed by Spain compared to Brazil's frequent crises and high instability.

Brazil

Brazil is a classic example of chronic high growth-rate volatility and political gridlock caused by a politically fragmented presidential system. Policymaking has been criticized for being slow and cumbersome as proposals are contested among the diverse interests represented in the Brazilian Congress (Ames 2001). Nonetheless, the package of economic reforms that was ultimately successful required extensive coalition-building and cooperation between the executive and the legislative branches thereby producing widely supported policies that would be difficult to change.[3] As a result, the reforms were successful in reducing inflation, increasing surpluses, and bolstering investor

---

[3] Figueiredo and Limongi (2000) and Limongi (2006) describe in interesting detail the incentives for party discipline and coalition formation in the Brazilian system.

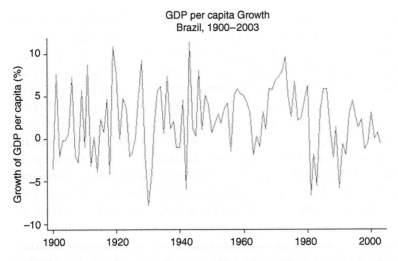

Figure 6.3 Growth-rate volatility in Brazil, 1900–2003 (source: Maddison (2007)).

confidence. Despite Brazil's "governability crisis" resulting from an abundance of veto points (Ames 2001) and some uncertainty when power was transferred to a new president in 2002 (Alston *et al.* 2006), in 2006 *Latin Finance* reported that, "the turbulence and volatility that marked the 2002 elections have been absent this time around as investors feel that regardless of the outcome, Brazil will remain fiscally responsible, market friendly and keep inflation in check" (Brooks and Mosley 2008; Johnson 2006). While Brazil's political institutions arguably could cause a number of serious governance problems, policies that are successfully passed are likely to be quite stable because of the consensus-building required in order to enact any legislation, and growth-rate volatility appears to be declining.

Macroeconomic crises in Brazil have been attributed to high deficit spending at the national and sub-national level (Samuels 2003). In the 1970s, the volatility of growth rates increased rapidly. With the rise of democratization in the 1980s, governors and mayors further increased spending in response to electoral pressures. Still worse, sub-national leaders frequently took advantage of government-owned banks, refusing to pay back loans borrowed to cover rising spending.

Figure 6.3 presents the changes in the levels of GDP per capita from 1900 to 2003. Brazil's growth rates have been volatile throughout the twentieth century, and crises are a fact of life. The 1980s, and the debt crisis that afflicted the entire region, saw frequent crises and high volatility in Brazil that persisted into the 1990s. The most recent decade of growth, however, has been more stable, as policymakers have worked hard to reform some of the pathologies of Brazil's policymaking process. For the period between 1965 and 1985, Brazil's growth-rate volatility was 3.61; in the two decades following that, its volatility dropped to 2.71. This is still considerably higher than the volatility scores of either Italy or Spain, which is to be expected given that we know volatility tends to be higher in the developing world, and because both European countries have political systems that encourage policy compromise relatively. In Brazil's case, the fundamental institutional framework, namely a presidential system that promotes policy "gridlock" and electoral dynamics that promote narrow particularistic interests, remains intact and unlikely to change. Therefore, according to the framework outlined in this book, one should expect volatility to persist into the future, though the maturation of Brazil's parties documented by Figueiredo and Limongi (2000) suggests a more optimistic outlook might also be justified. Whether my pessimism about Brazil's future is more warranted will be for future scholars to evaluate, but for now I turn to the past to consider Brazil's growth experiences in the second half of the twentieth century.

The rampant growth-rate volatility Brazil has experienced in recent decades has severely impacted a population poorly equipped to adjust to such unpredictable economic changes. Brazil has one of the largest rich–poor gaps in the world, and the ability of the poor to influence politics is limited by an extremely fragmented party system (Weyland 1996). Indeed, since 1990, Brazil has had one of the most fragmented party systems in the world. A low electoral threshold in combination with a high district magnitude allows a large number of parties to win representation in the Congress. From 1985 to 1995, Brazil had fifteen major political parties spanning the left-right political spectrum (Mainwaring 1997). The effective number of parties in Brazil's lower house, the Chamber of Deputies, more than doubled from 2.83 in 1986 to 8.13 in 1994. Likewise, in Brazil's upper house the effective number of parties increased from 2.27 in 1986 to 6.08 in 1994 (cited in Mainwaring 1997). While the effective number of electoral parties tells us nothing about the ideological orientation of these parties, it does indicate the trend of increasing

Brazilian party fragmentation. Furthermore, coalition-building is difficult because undisciplined catch-all parties allow politicians to switch their alliances frequently and to act independently of their parties. More importantly, the dynamics of presidentialism exacerbate these pathologies (Ames 2001), though Cheibub's research suggests that these are not inevitable (Cheibub 2007; Cheibub *et al.* 2004). Party system fragmentation, presidentialism, and the absence of any sense of coalition "dharma", poses serious challenges for policymaking. Despite economic crises, failing social services, and rampant crime, legislative proposals are hampered by concessions and delays. In the rare event that legislation passes, it often requires a great deal of patronage and pork to grease its path (Ames 2001).

While the Brazilian president is endowed with a number of significant powers, the Congress also reserves important powers, including veto authority, which make policymaking more difficult than in other presidential systems. The president has broad constitutional powers including veto and partial veto authority, the ability to legislate, and even the power to shape the congressional agenda. Presidential decrees have been used to institute parts of controversial economic policies such as Collor's 1990 economic plan and Cardoso's *Real* Plan in 1994. However, even presidential decrees must be approved by the legislature within thirty days of their passage (Mainwaring 1997).[4] Brazil's institutions ensure that a diverse set of interests are represented and even influential enough to stall policymaking. Long-term policy changes require the cooperation of a broad range of interests.

The need for economic reform was apparent in the late 1980s. In fact, Brazil was the last Latin American country to adopt and maintain a stabilization program (Ames 2001). Cardoso's *Real* Plan provides an example of how fragmentation can produce stable policy outcomes. Despite the consensus on the need for reform, Cardoso's *Real* Plan required significant negotiations between the executive and the legislature before its acceptance in 1994. As the Minister of Finance, Fernando Henrique Cardoso worked to build support for the economic plan. The first major step in the Cardoso Plan required a constitutional amendment to eliminate the constitutionally mandated earmarks for a

---

[4] By law, Congress must pass all presidential decrees within twenty days of issuance. In practice, however, presidential decrees have often been allowed to remain in effect unless the Congress chooses to reject them.

large percentage of tax revenue in order to establish the Social Emergency Fund (FSE). The FSE necessitated a constitutional amendment which required a 60 percent approval from both houses of the Brazilian Congress. To gain the necessary political support, Cardoso's center-left Social Democratic Party (Partido da Social Democracia Brasileira or PSDB) had to gain the support for the large center-right Liberal Front Party (Partido da Frente Liberal or PFL). The PFL and PSDB had electoral incentives to cooperate in order to form a viable opposition to the Worker's Party (Partido dos Trabalhadores, PT) ahead of upcoming presidential elections.

This coalition proved extremely beneficial for President Cardoso after his election enabling him to pass the *Real* Plan as well as additional necessary reforms. A worsening of the finances of Brazil's state governments strengthened the federal government's bargaining power. Cardoso took advantage. For instance, the "Camata Law" required states to limit payroll expenditures if they wished to keep federal funding and additional legislation required states to stop issuing bonds to cover their debt. Reforms also successfully limited the ability of regional governments to rely on loans from state banks to finance expenditures, only to default on these loans later (Samuels 2003).

The *Real* Plan has been credited with reducing inflation, generating budget surpluses (through tax reform), and limiting government expenditures. Despite high fragmentation and the election of the leftist PT party in 2002, the reforms were not reversed. One might argue that Cardoso got lucky and his plan was passed despite high fragmentation. However, the *Real* Plan was unarguably the product of negotiations and concessions. While Cardoso may have been exceptional in his ability to negotiate legislation, once passed the policy proved very difficult to change. Research suggests that only particular types of policies are likely to be volatile in the Brazilian system. Programs such as those with an ideological component (the environment, poverty alleviation, and land reform) or those requiring approval at the Congressional district level are likely to be volatile (Alston *et al.* 2006). In contrast, nationally mandated policies limiting government deficits and implementing tax reforms are actually likely to be quite stable.

Although broadly successful, Cardoso's economic reforms provided no guarantee of long-term growth and investor confidence and were criticized on several accounts. While Cardoso implemented important restrictions on spending, surpluses were primarily generated because of improved tax collection, not reduced spending. Additionally, as part of the negotiations required to pass a reform plan, Cardoso had to offer sub-national governments compensation, a practice derided by some as an unstable bargaining tactic that relied on "horsetrading" (de Souza 1999). Scholars have criticized the reforms because Brazil's debt is still short-term, increasing the risk of a liquidity crisis, and the debt is tied to the dollar (Samuels 2003). Cardoso's policies may also be problematic because they relied on maintaining high interest rates and strict control over the exchange rate (Da Fonseca 1998). In the end, whether or not the particular choices of macroeconomic policy were flawless may be less important than the fact that investors do not fear a sudden reversal. While the run-up to Lula's election in 2002 induced some jitters among investors, markets appear to have grown more confident that fundamental policy changes will not occur, which is reflected in a lowering of Brazil's sovereign risk ratings (Brooks and Mosley 2008).

Brazil appears to have gotten some of its institutions "right" in the sense that the bargaining required to implement long-term changes in economic policy ensured the policy stability desired by investors. Notably, growth-rate volatility has declined since 1995 to 1.85, two points lower than in the previous decade and three points lower than in the disastrous decade between 1975 and 1985. The advantages of Brazilian institutions, however, should not be overstated as its institutions have been touted, with good reason, as an example of how political fragmentation in presidential systems has the potential to hinder efficient policymaking by inducing policy gridlock (Ames 2001). The Brazilian system has also been criticized for its "predatory federalism" under which sub-national governments used their powerful leverage to demand financing from the central government. A hyperpresidential system also allows the executive to take action without legislative approval, at least in the short term. Additionally, a strong presidency with minimal party control may mean that once legislation is passed it is difficult to change, but there is no guarantee that a president (or other political leader) can successfully negotiate a compromise. While Brazil's institutions pose serious challenges on some issues, at least in this instance, slower policymaking due to the inclusion of a broad range of interests ultimately produced stable policies that investors were confident would remain in place for a long time.

Botswana

The final case, Botswana, the other developing country considered here, offers an interesting contrast to the Brazilian political experience. It has had none of the fluctuations in political freedoms that Brazil has experienced, has a parliamentary system of government compared to Brazil's presidential system, and power is largely concentrated in a single ruling party. Africa's record of economic and political development yields precious few success stories, perhaps making clear why observers have hailed Botswana as an example for the rest of the continent. While other states have struggled to develop and maintain legitimate democratic institutions, suffering frequent civil wars and violent coups by would-be dictators, Botswana has managed to sustain uninterrupted democratic rule since its independence from British rule in 1966. Moreover, the country has gone from being one of the poorest countries in the world forty years ago to a solidly middle-income country today with a GDP per capita around $15,000. Botswana's high average growth rates, however, mask a high level of growth-rate volatility for much of the post-independent era, although volatility has declined considerably in the last fifteen years. Between 1995 and 2005, Botswana's growth-rate volatility dropped to 1.17 – comparable to the rates experienced by Italy and Spain and other middle-income countries – which is almost three points lower than it was in the decade prior. Given what we know of volatility's impact on growth in Africa (World Bank 2008), this factor alone might explain Botswana's success. Interestingly, as in Spain, this decline in volatility has coincided with the increasing competitiveness of Botswana's electoral system that has forced the ruling party to consider alternative perspectives in policymaking.

Botswana adopted a parliamentary democracy to organize its politics, and political power in independent Botswana has been centralized in the BDP. Mineral resources, primarily diamonds, drove rapid growth in the 1970s. By the mid-1970s, however, growth rates began to fluctuate wildly and were declining by the early 1980s. Corruption stemming from BDP management ultimately fueled a rash of bankruptcies and defaulted loans. Arguably, concentrated power in a single party allowed flawed economic policies to be enacted without debate. Unlike Brazil, therefore, in Botswana problems with economic policy did not arise because of policy gridlock caused by political parties

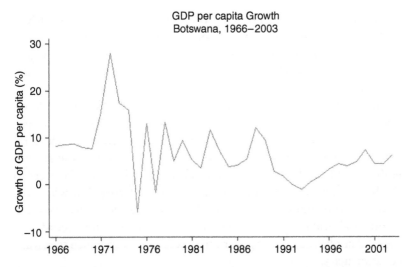

Figure 6.4 Growth-rate volatility in Botswana, 1966–2003 (source: Maddison (2007)).

that refuse to cooperate with each other, but rather from the abuse of resources by the dominant party.

In the early 1970s, growth rates began to fluctuate widely in Botswana and volatility continued to be a problem through the 1980s (see Figure 6.4).

Despite this volatility in the rate of growth, Botswana's overall growth was positive through the 1970s during the natural resource boom and high diamond prices. The country suffered, however, in the early 1980s when the price of diamonds fell. Botswana is often touted as the "African miracle" in which sound macroeconomic policy in combination with natural resources allowed for sustained growth over time. Despite Botswana's relative success in comparison to its African neighbors, growth-rate volatility persisted until 1990 and was in part the product of the misuse of centralized power (Leith 2005).

The first modern political party – the Botswana People's Party (BPP) – came to prominence in the early 1960s. Since its inception, the BPP has been plagued by in-fighting. The Botswana Democratic Party (BDP) formed in response to the BPP and by 1969 had become the country's dominant party due to the internal squabbling in the BPP; two BPP splinter parties – the Botswana Independence Party (BIP) and the Botswana National Front (BNF) – eventually formed (Charlton 1993). Today, although several political parties contest elections in Botswana, the BDP remains dominant, consistently winning a majority of National Assembly seats, though competition has been increasing in recent years.

The BDP dominated politics from 1969 to 1984, because it developed an effective system of centralized patronage. While the opposition, primarily the BPP, argued that the BDP used unfair electoral practices, international sources have argued that elections were generally considered free and fair (Tsie 1996). Charlton (1993) refers to the BDP's tactics as an "alternative patronage strategy" in which the government maintained tight central control over decisions regarding resource allocation. Opposition parties were largely unsuccessful as they did not have access to government resources with which to reward constituencies.

As of 1984, the BDP began to face more significant electoral challenges from a better organized BNF. Despite a more effective opposition, for a decade the BDP used its incumbency advantage to continue winning elections (Charlton 1993). However, in the 1994 parliamentary elections, a two-party system appeared to emerge as the BNF won thirteen of the forty seats in the National Assembly and some hailed the end of a dominant party system (Tsie 1996). In the 1999 elections, the BDP won thirty-three of the forty possible seats in the National Assembly. The BNF won six seats and the remaining seat went to the Botswana Congress Party. In 2004, the BDP still dominated, winning forty-four out of fifty-seven possible seats. However, the BNF fared much better, winning twelve seats with the Botswana Congress Party again winning a single seat (Leith 2005). Thus, while political competition has steadily increased, the BDP's grip on power has not yet been threatened, though its smaller majorities over the last decade or so have necessitated greater cooperation with opposition parties for the purposes of implementing policy.

Decisions about economic reform are made by the ruling BDP party. Botswana has been praised for its role in deepening the Southern African Customs Union (SACU) via the 2002 SACU Agreement, which established new rules for joint decision-making processes and revenue sharing, and which recognized the need for better management of external (non-SACU) trade. When diamond earnings dropped suddenly in 1981, the government of Botswana responded rapidly and effectively by devaluing the currency and avoiding exchange controls (Rodrik 1997c). Two significant policy problems, however, were difficulty in restricting expenditures and in net lending (Leith 2005; Lewis 1993). Government efficiency was brought into question by the irresponsible borrowing practices of the political elite. For instance, Botswana's National Development Bank (NDB) was created to manage the distribution of loans from the government and external sources to the agricultural sector and other high priority development areas. Because of a rapid increase in lending in the 1980s, by 1993 the NDB was nearly bankrupt. The government ultimately spent millions to cover unpaid loans which risked signaling to borrowers that loans need not be repaid. Misuse of the Small Borrowers Fund (SDF) and the Botswana Cooperative Bank were also indicative of the irresponsible borrowing on the part of elites (Good 1994). While BDP dominance may have allowed a coherent macroeconomic policy, it also allowed political elites to take advantage of domestic lending institutions with few consequences.

Botswana has been praised for adhering to sound macroeconomic policy that promoted growth through the 1970s and most of the 1980s. Nonetheless, Botswana's experience was also marked by extreme growth-rate volatility. The level of corruption and mismanagement in Botswana may be lower than in other sub-Saharan countries, but the centralization of power and elite predominance led to a number of bankruptcies and loan defaults in the early 1990s (Good 1994). While the BDP is less dominant than in the past because of the emergence of the BPP and the BNF as successful opposition parties, there has not been significant variation in the number of influential parties over time. As a result, some of Botswana's macroeconomic successes have been undermined by corruption among the elites in the form of irresponsible lending and spending.

Botswana is an interesting case for this book. First, it exemplifies the mixed virtues of concentrated power even in democratic systems, and the advantages of growing competitiveness in the political system. Unchecked by viable opposition, the BDP was able to implement economic policy and begin the process of development, but the same lack of constraints meant that it was able to succumb to the temptations of power and use control over the government apparatus to further its hold over power. Increasing corruption and unilateral policymaking generated high growth-rate volatility through the 1980s and into the 1990s. In the most recent decades, however, the BDP has begun to face genuine competition for office. While its opponents are still some way away from dethroning the BDP, their growing strength has forced the incumbents to consider alternative perspectives when designing policy, and to enact policies that appeal more broadly. Competition thus forces policymaking towards the center, and is correlated with reduced levels of growth-rate volatility. Second, in a comparative perspective, Botswana is also an exemplar for the virtues of genuine political continuity and stability. Compared to its regional neighbors, Botswana has enjoyed uninterrupted democracy over the past forty years, while others have struggled with violent internal conflict and coups that fuel political instability. This core stability of Botswana's political system has played no small part in making it an exemplar for the rest of the continent (Rodrik 1997c). Thus, given the argument of this book, as Botswana's internal political competition continues to grow more robust, the strong institutional framework it possesses will provide a firm basis for continued economic growth and development.

Conclusion

The previous three chapters have provided strong empirical support for the hypothesis that the compromise engendered by coalition governments reduces policy uncertainty and growth-rate volatility while improving overall economic growth. This chapter has applied the main theoretical framework to four different countries, allowing me to explicate important nuances in the argument. Brazil, for instance, makes clear that presidential systems face genuine problems when they are fragmented politically, as the gridlock in policy that is created is qualitatively different from the compromise we see in coalition government systems like India. Botswana demonstrates the virtues of long-term political stability which has enabled it to move comfortably into the category of middle-income states, yet, even as Botswana is appropriately praised for its economic success, a closer look reveals that concentration of political power in a single dominant political party allowed policy excesses to occur and growth-rate volatility to persist. The gradual increase in political competition in recent years appears to be correlated with a reduction in growth volatility.

Finally, two developed democracies, Spain and Italy, show both the tremendous advantages of democracy over dictatorship for providing stable national economic performance, but also how different dynamics of parliamentary politics affect volatility. Spain has a stable two-party system today, but this can generate alternations in economic policy as the parties take turns in power. However, when the Spanish parties work more with other societal groups to build consensus over policy, stability is increased. Italy, by contrast, has an extremely fragmented political system, yet has managed to maintain very stable growth rates in spite of various problems politically because coalition governments have made policy change gradual. These cases thus support the central argument of this book that political fragmentation and the consensus- and coalition-building that it necessitates can produce stable, predictable economic policies on which economic agents can rely, and thereby improve national economic performance. The conclusion develops this point more fully.

7 | Conclusion

India began the twentieth century as the jewel in the crown of the British empire. A hundred years later it begins the new millennium as a success story of economic growth in the developing world. Yet while India appears to have made this transition successfully, the challenges to its continued success are considerable and daunting (Bardhan 2009). Moreover, that many of its fellow former colonies in the developing world remain mired in what seems at times to be inescapable poverty, the stakes for understanding why some countries are able to enjoy better economic performance than others are apparent. While government programs can and do go a long way towards alleviating the suffering caused by poor economic conditions, generating sustainable and inclusive economic growth is possibly the surest way of doing so.

The challenges of economic development are made more difficult by a second normative goal for developing countries: developing democratic institutions that allow citizens to participate in the policymaking process by choosing their own leaders. The past fifty years have seen democracy spread across the globe, at least as a principle accepted by most people (Inglehart and Welzel 2005), and, despite reversals in democratic freedoms in some countries, the fact remains that more people live today in democratic countries than did in 1950. This increase in democracy globally is welcome in its own right, but the twin concerns of political and economic well-being raise an question of obvious pertinence: does democracy help or hurt national economic performance? If democracy increases economic growth, then we have yet another reason to encourage the adoption of democratic norms and principles in developing countries and to shout down defenses of dictatorial rule on the grounds of economic expediency. If, on the other hand, democracy is found to retard economic development, stronger normative justifications for democracy in poor countries must be developed, and discussions of the appropriate "sequencing" of such reforms must return to the center of political science conversations. Finally, should democracy be found to have no effect on national economic performance, the case for democracy remains strong on normative grounds but is slightly weakened on more instrumental bases.

The relationship between democratic political institutions and economic growth has therefore been the focus of much recent research in political science, but the results have been equivocal at best. Przeworski et al. (2000) find little evidence that democracy aids growth, a conclusion borne out by a recent meta-analysis of multiple studies on the topic (Doucouliagos and Ulubasoglu 2008). Even more troubling for pro-democracy arguments, Mulligan et al. (2004) find no evidence of any systematic differences in the types of public policies made by democracies and non-democracies. And Ross (2006) concludes that democracy makes no material difference for the lives of the poor.

This book offers a different perspective on the relationship between politics and economic development. It does so by broadening the investigation to focus not only on the level of economic growth enjoyed by a country, but also the stability of that growth. More volatile economic growth has been found to hurt long-term economic growth prospects (Ramey and Ramey 1995; Sirimaneetham and Temple 2009), and it can have devastating consequences for those on the lowest rung of the economic ladder. Analytically the joint focus on volatility and level of economic growth allows me to distinguish between countries that might otherwise appear to be quite similar, and to build on a recent literature that treats growth-rate volatility as an important dependent variable in its own right (Chandra and Rudra 2008; Mobarak 2005; Quinn and Woolley 2001; Rodrik 1998b, 2000).

Given limited or mixed evidence about differences in policymaking across regime types (Mulligan et al. 2004) or for the effects of policy choices on growth outcomes (Acemoglu et al. 2003b; Easterly 2005; Fatas and Mihov 2005), I argue that cross-national variation in economic growth and volatility, i.e., in national economic performance, must be explained by understanding the behavior of private economic agents in developing countries. Specifically, where governments are unable to commit credibly to long-term policy stability, private economic agents engage in short-term and more liquid forms of investment, which allow them to withdraw their capital at the first signs of trouble. This means that longer-term investment opportunities vital to economic development are foregone because of the risks associated with policy uncertainty, and the economy is deprived of valuable capital and made vulnerable to capital flight. Contrariwise, when governments are able to make credible commitments, economic agents are less likely to perceive policy uncertainty to be an obstacle to the conduct and growth of their businesses, more likely to save and invest their income, less likely to engage in capital flight, and more likely to invest in innovation. In turn, these actions generate higher and more stable economic growth.

The "credible constraints" theoretical framework builds on a vibrant literature in economics on the importance of government credibility for investor behavior. But what makes some countries more credible than others? Rather than rely on "expert" assessments of country credibility, which at any rate describe rather than explain cross-national variation in credibility, I offer a theory of credibility rooted in the relationship between political institutions and societal constituencies. In diverse democratic societies, control over policymaking authority is contested, leading to the possibility of policy fluctuations (and therefore lower credibility of future policy stability) as different groups come to power. In non-democratic societies, leaders face a different version of the same problem: given that they can unilaterally change policy, how do they convince investors that they will not do so?

Theories of credibility developed in the context of the OECD states have typically emphasized the delegation of policymaking authority from partisan political figures to non-partisan technocrats in bureaucracies. Central bank independence is perhaps the most well-studied of such mechanisms, though judicial independence is a close second. In both cases, actors independent of politicians and insulated from the whims and fancies of voters have a say in policymaking. Since these actors have longer time horizons than politicians, their participation in the policymaking process increases expectations of long-term policy stability and therefore bolsters investor confidence (Cukierman *et al.* 1992; Henisz 2002, 2004).

An alternative source of credible commitments to policy stability arises from patterns of party competition within political institutions. Political parties compete for power by differentiating themselves on policy positions. When a single party controls all the levers of the legislative process, it is better able to enact policies closer to its ideal point. The resulting policy might in fact be the preferred outcome for economic agents too (for instance, if the government in question favors a business-friendly policy regime), but the government cannot guarantee that future governments will not reverse course should the opposition win. In this case, even if economic agents respond by investing in the country, they will remain wary of future policy change, and therefore forgo more irreversible investments.

In other situations, however, no one party controls the policymaking process fully; in this case, where policymaking authority is diffused across multiple actors, each controlled by a different party that in turn is accountable to a different societal constituency and therefore with a different ideal point on policy, policy change becomes more difficult as the set of policies on which both (or all) parties with a say in the policymaking process agree shrinks. In presidential systems, this situation arises when different political parties control the executive and legislative branches of government, a situation commonly called "divided government." In parliamentary systems, the situation arises when no one party secures a majority of seats in the legislature, forcing the largest party either to form a "coalition" government, or to rule as a "minority" government with support from outside the government. Divided presidential and coalition or minority parliamentary systems both result in smaller win-sets for policy change, but with important differences. In divided presidentialism, the survival of each branch of government is independent of the other, giving neither party much incentive to cooperate with the other. This leads to "gridlock." In coalition or minority parliamentary systems, by comparison, the survival of all parties in the legislature is contingent on the survival of the government; the government can therefore get policy enacted by threatening a vote of confidence, the failure of which would dissolve parliament and lead to fresh elections. The caveat however is that the government must compromise its preferred policy positions to garner enough support from other parties that passing the legislation is preferred to taking one's chances at the polls in new elections. Thus, the dynamics of parliamentarism generate incentives for "policy compromise" rather than gridlock when coalition or minority governments prevail. The broad implications of this analysis, I argue in the book, are that coalition and minority parliamentary governments are best suited to convince economic agents that policy change will be incremental and based on shared consensus (and therefore stable). To the extent that economic agents are risk-averse, such policy stability should encourage them to invest more in the economy, be less likely to flee at the first sign of trouble, and therefore generate higher and more stable levels of economic growth for the country.

The theoretical framework thus tackles a fundamental question in comparative political economy: how does politics affect national economic performance? Building on well-established theories about the importance of democracy on the one hand and about the importance of policy credibility on the other, I offer a novel and somewhat counterintuitive answer: governments forced to compromise with political opponents are most likely to generate good national economic performance. This answer flies in the face of previous scholarship that has endorsed "strong" governments that push through painful economic reforms at the expense possibly of political freedoms and competition as exemplified by the old dictatorial apologia, "You can't make an omelette without breaking a few eggs."

The core insight also finds support in the literature on ethnic conflict that has long advocated the development of power-sharing institutions that force erstwhile opponents to compromise with each other in order to govern. These arguments have been applied both to the governance of ethnically divided societies (Horowitz 1991), to quelling ethnic violence (Varshney 2002), and to the settlement of violent internal conflicts (Hartzell and Hoddie 2007). Further, it offers a fresh response to an important challenge posed by Samuel Huntington's classic work on political order in developing societies (1968). Huntington argued persuasively that the mobilization of previously marginalized citizens in developing countries would overwhelm weak political-institutional structures, leading to disorder as citizens took the streets to air their grievances in response to an ineffectual state (see also Kohli 1991). Two very different policy responses follow from Huntington's argument: one can either limit the mobilization of citizens into the political sphere or one can increase the channels by which myriad citizens can exercise their voices in politics. My argument makes a case for the latter path, advocating "more democracy" rather than "no democracy." To the extent that this process is in fact messy and disorderly, so be it. Over the long run, I argue, such inefficiencies are more than made up for by the higher economic performance citizens enjoy.[1]

---

[1] Sen (1999) offers a philosophical defense of political freedoms as indistinguishable from the concept of "development."

At the theoretical level, then, my argument seeks to tackle central debates in the political science literature of the past forty years, and to do so by building on that literature by taking a new perspective in the hopes that a change in tack will yield new insights. Do the data validate this exercise? The four empirical chapters suggest they do. Using cross-national time-series data from over a hundred developing countries, I showed in Chapter 3 that, even after controlling for plausible alternative political factors and for theoretically relevant economic factors, coalition governments in parliamentary democracies have higher growth rates than other forms of government, and that such governments experience lower growth-rate volatility too. Importantly, the main findings hold up even when I use matching techniques to address potential endogeneity. Second, separate analyses reported in Chapter 4 show that coalition parliamentary governments encourage more private savings and reduce the level of capital flight experienced by the country. Together these increase the resources available to capital-scarce societies to generate growth and development. Chapter 4 also utilizes firm-level survey data from the EBRD-World Bank Business Environment and Enterprise Performance surveys to show that firms located in countries governed by coalition governments are less likely to consider regulatory and economic policy uncertainty to be major obstacles to their businesses, and that this reduced uncertainty increases their willingness to open new establishments in the near future. These survey-based findings should bolster confidence in the macro-level results by providing micro-level evidence in favor of the causal mechanisms posited by the theory.

Chapters 5 and 6 move away from cross-national analyses to country-specific analyses in order to delve deeper into the argument. Chapter 5 provides a new interpretation of India's recent economic successes based on the theoretical framework and cross-national economic results that find in favor of coalition governments. As anticipated by those findings, a cross-temporal analysis of India's national economic performance finds that India's rapid growth began only after its political system fragmented allowing more parties a chance to influence the policymaking process. Since the 1970s, India's once-indomitable Congress Party has slowly lost its grip on power at the national and state levels, beginning with a steady erosion in the number of state governments it controlled. The main loss of vote share for the Congress occurred at the hands of regional parties (Chhibber and Nooruddin 2000). This increasing regionalization of Indian politics has had an important consequence for national-level politics: no one party is competitive throughout the country, making coalition politics a virtual inevitability today. Indeed since 1989 India has been governed either by minority or coalition governments, and there is little to suggest that this will change any time soon. Many public commentators have decried coalition governments for stalling the economic reform process (conveniently ignoring that the major economic reforms of the past twenty years were enacted by a minority government!), but my analysis suggests that the opposite conclusion might be more apt. Clearly my "credible constraints" hypothesis fits the Indian experience, but to offer an independent test of the hypothesis, I use both state-level economic data and a business survey jointly conducted by the Confederation of Indian Industries and the World Bank to identify the determinants of firm competitiveness. The results make clear once more that coalition governments reduce the probability that firms consider economic policy uncertainty an obstacle, and increase the probability that firms invest resources in research and development. Finally, Chapter 6 re-examines the growth patterns of Italy, Spain, Brazil, and Botswana in light of the theoretical model. In each case, the data are consistent with the predictions of the argument, confirming both the plausibility and the generalizability of the theoretical framework.

The credible constraint institutions identified in this book are more commonly found in democratic societies. While nothing in principle prevents dictators from delegating responsibility for policymaking to independent bureaucrats, experience suggests that they are loathe to do so. Even more to the point, situations in which dictators must share power akin to those in parliamentary coalition or minority governments or presidential divided governments simply do not arise. This does not mean, of course, that all dictators are equally strong, or that they can exercise unchecked power. Rather, even where leaders are not chosen by the people, they still need to satisfy a core constituency of supporters in order to retain power, what Bueno de Mesquita *et al.* (2003) call a "winning coalition." But, from the perspective of economic agents, the existence of such "checks" on dictator power are comparatively weaker, and more opaque, increasing uncertainty about future policy and affecting investment decisions (Jensen 2006).

The relative credibility disadvantage of dictatorial regimes masks the fact that there exists interesting variation in the design of political institutions within these countries (Gandhi 2008b; Gandhi and Przeworski

2006; Geddes 1999). Joseph Wright argues that dictators recognize the limits of their credibility, and therefore create "binding legislatures" to assuage economic agents' uncertainties (2008). Scott Gehlbach and Philip Keefer argue that well-institutionalized ruling parties, such as the Chinese Communist Party, provide a similar check on individual leader power (n.d.). Their argument echoes one made two decades ago by Kenneth Lieberthal and Michael Oksenberg, who described the Chinese political system as one of "fragmented authority." Their analysis suggests that "the fragmented, segmented, and stratified structure of the [Chinese] state promotes a system of negotiations, bargaining, and the seeking of consensus," leading to an "incremental" policy process (Lieberthal and Oksenberg 1988: 1). Such language is not that dissimilar from the language I use to describe my credible constraints framework, and offers the possibility that, while the particulars might be different in each case, the fundamental reasons that both China and India are growing so rapidly today are similar.

While still underdeveloped compared to our understanding of politics in developed democracies, theoretical efforts such as those described above are exciting for their potential ability to unite our understanding of how politics is conducted within democratic and non-democratic societies under a common theoretical framework. I have offered one such framework in this book. By making the inherent credibility problem faced by any political leader seeking to encourage investments and generate growth the central focus of the inquiry, we generate a coherent explanation for variation in how political institutions are designed around the globe, as well as for why some states are better able to provide superior national economic performance to their citizens than others.

So where do we go from here? What lessons can be taken from the analyses presented in these pages that might inform advice given to developing countries seeking to reduce growth-rate volatility and increase economic growth? The first implication is that governments must find ways to incorporate diverse perspectives into their policy-making, and to do so via formal institutional channels that allow opponents to exercise genuine control over the content of eventual policy outcomes. Doing so carries the obvious downside of slowing down reform processes that might be desirable, but it must be emphasized that reform is not impossible under coalition or minority government.

It is simply more difficult and requires a commitment to consensus-building. Indeed, one might well argue that reforms that do not enjoy such consensus are doomed to failure in the long run as their negative consequences generate protests from those who were marginalized during their formulation, and who therefore seek to reverse the policies if possible (Gehlbach and Malesky 2009).

The second implication is more optimistic, and suggests the conditions required for this process to work ideally. Democracy is a process by which different societal constituencies compete for control of the reins of power. At its core, therefore, it is unpredictable because the power lies in the hands of the masses, rather than being purely concentrated in the hands of a few technocrats. Kaushik Basu sarcastically (and, in my opinion, astutely) comments on the tendency of experts to advocate democratic governance in developing countries while simultaneously advocating a particular course of policy reform as if to do so was their prerogative rather than that of the country's citizens and their elected leaders (Basu 2008). Free and fair elections can result in the election of an explicitly reform-oriented government such as the BJP-led National Democratic Alliance in 1999 in India, and its ouster five years later *in spite of* a record of high growth rates during its tenure in office. In the absence of incentives that promote consensus-building and power-sharing, such democratic unpredictability can induce policy swings that increase investor uncertainty and hurt growth prospects. But, in turn, the process of building consensus and sharing power does not come easily or automatically to political parties. Rather those who seek to lead must come to terms with the principles of "coalition dharma," treating their partners as co-equals and committing sincerely to consensual policymaking. As India's recent experience attests, when parties do so, politicians can make policy, economic agents can conduct business, and a sleeping elephant can be induced to trot, and indeed to run.

A | *Appendix to Chapter 2*

Summary of review of empirical growth literature

See Klomp and de Haan (2009) for a review of research exclusively on the determinants of macroeconomic volatility.

Table A.1 *Review of literature*

Authors	Dependent variable	Political-institutional variables (if any)	Political-institutional findings
Abrams and Lewis (1995)	Economic growth per capita	Regime (democratic/ non-democratic)	Democracy is positively correlated with growth through an intervening variable of liberty
Adams (2004)	Poverty (poverty line headcount, poverty gap index)		
Agenor et al. (2007)	Income growth per capita		
Aghion et al. (1999)	Economic growth, income inequality (use many measures for both)		
Alesina and La Ferrara (2004)	GDP per capita growth		
Alesina et al. (1992)	Per capita GDP growth		
Alfaro (2004)	Average annual per capita growth rate		

Study	Variables	Findings
Almeida and Ferreira (2002)	Average annual per capita GDP growth rate, growth rate of real per capita GDP	Regime type (measured with Gastil Index and Polity III)	Authoritarian regimes have more variance in growth rates both within and across countries, more variance in policies, and both the highest and lowest growth rate countries are more likely to be autocracies than democracies
Ang and McKibbin (2007)	Financial development, economic growth		
Arayama and Miyoshi (2004)	Real GDP		
Aron (2000)	Real per capita growth	Beri disaggregated business risk indicators; ICRG disaggregated business risk indicators; Business International disaggregated risk indicators; Gastil's political rights index; Putnam's Social Capital and Local Government and Institutional Performance Measures; Clague *et al.*'s Political Regime Indicator; DeVarrsay and Spindler's constitutional rights indicators	Finds an existent, but not robust, correlation between "institutional quality" and economic growth

179

Table A.1 (*cont.*)

Authors	Dependent variable	Political-institutional variables (if any)	Political-institutional findings
Awokuse (2005)	Real GDP growth		
Azam et al. (2002)	Economic growth (lit review)		
Bahmani-Oskooee and Niroomand (1999)	Real GDP		
Baier et al. (2006)	Average output growth per worker		
Balaguer and Cantavella-Jorda (2004)	Real domestic output		
Baqir et al. (2005)	Real GDP growth		
Barrell and Pain (1997)	Foreign direct investment (in $ and as % of GDP)		
Barro (1995)	Real per capita GDP growth		
Barro (1996)	Real per capita GDP growth		
Barro and Lee (2003)	IMF lending and five-year growth rates of per capita GDP		
Barro and McCleary (2003)	Average growth rate of real per capita GDP		
Baum and Lake (2003)	Annual growth rate in real GDP	Regime type (derived from Polity 98)	Democracy increases life expectancy and education which in turn increases growth

Reference	Dependent variable	Independent variable	Result
Bekaert et al. (2001a)	Investment/GDP ratio and others		
Bekaert et al. (2001b)	Real per capita GDP growth		
Berend (2002)	Development (subjective definition)		
Berggren and Jordahl (2005)	Real per capita GDP growth	Legal structure and property rights index (may or may not include institutional variables)	Positive significant relationship with growth
Bertocchi and Canova (1996)	Growth (average growth rate per capita)		
Bhattacharyya (2004)	Growth in income per capita		
Bjornskov (2005)	Decadal growth		
Blomstrom et al. (1996)	Five-year growth rate in per capita GDP		
Bloom and Sachs (1998)	Growth in GDP per capita		
Borensztein et al. (1998)	Average annual growth rate of per capita real GDP		

Table A.1 (*cont.*)

Authors	Dependent variable	Political-institutional variables (if any)	Political-institutional findings
Breen (1997)	Economic performance, equality (modeled)		
Bruno and Easterly (1998)	Per capita growth rate, per capita growth rate differed from the world average		
Bueno de Mesquita *et al.* (2001)	Average annual real growth rate in per capita income	Size of selectorate (who can choose the leader), size of winning coalition (whose support is needed to stay in office) (both of these are correlates of democracy)	Democracy positively impacts growth
Burdekin *et al.* (2004)	Percent change in real GDP per capita (sometimes lagged)		
Butkiewicz and Yanikkaya (2005)	Growth rate in real GDP per capita	Democracy (regime type) (measured by the Gastil Index)	Gastil Index not significant
Campos and Coricelli (2002)	Growth rate in real GDP per capita	Rule of Law Index by Campos (includes type of law and non-institutional variables), Rule of Law Index by Karatnycky *et al.* (includes adoption of a constitution, constitutional rights, and non-institutional	No results, article is literature review and stylized history (stylized is their self description)

Study	Dependent variable	Independent variable	Result
Cannon (2000)	Review of Frankel piece on economic growth		
Carlsson and Lundstrom (2001)	GDP growth	Legal structure and property rights index	Significant and positive
Castello and Domenech (2002)	Gini coefficient, average growth rate per capita		
Chang (2002)	GDP		
Chang and Caudill (2005)	Real GDP per capita		
Chatterjee et al. (2003)	GDP		
Chen and Feng (2000)	Per capita GDP growth		
Choe and Moosa (1999)	Real GDP		
Chong and Zanforlin (2004)	Per capita GDP growth	Institutional Quality Index (including independence of bureaucracy, and other variables)	Index is significant but not robust to changes in specification
Chow and loh Lin (2002)	Real GDP		
Coclanis and Doshi (2000)	Economic performance (case studies)		

183

Table A.1 (*cont.*)

Authors	Dependent variable	Political-institutional variables (if any)	Political-institutional findings
Collier (2000)	Average per capita GDP growth	Interaction between regime type and ethnic fragmentation (regime measured with Gastil Index)	Democracy is positively correlated with growth. Democracy mitigates the negative effects of ethnic fragmentation on growth
Collins *et al.* (1996)	Growth of per capita GDP		
Crafts (2004)	GDP per capita purchasing power parity, international inequality		
Crenshaw *et al.* (1997)	Real GDP per capita growth		
Crotty and Lee (2001)	Economic growth (measured in wide variety of ways)		
Dakurah *et al.* (2001)	GNP		
Davoodi and fu Zou (1998)	Per capita GDP growth	Fiscal decentralization	Decentralized fiscal power is not correlated with growth in developed countries, in developing countries it is negatively correlated with growth
Dawson and Hubbard (2004)	GDP at market prices, gross capital formation		

de Haan and Siermann (1998)	GDP per capita	Gastil Civil Rights Index (put into an index of economic freedom)	The effect of economic freedom on growth depends on what you use to measure economic freedom
de Haan and Stürm (2000)	Average growth of per capita GDP	Civil rights indexes (put into indexes of economic freedom)	Economic freedom will speed a nation to its steady state of economic growth, but not alter that steady state of economic growth
Demetriades and Hussein (1996)	Real GDP		
Demetriades and Luintel (1996)	Real GDP per capita		
Demurger (2001)	GDP growth rate		
Devarajan et al. (1996)	Five-year forward moving average of per capita rel GDP		
Dougherty and Jorgenson (1996)	GNP		
Dudley (1999)	Economic growth (modeled)		
Dunning (2005)	Economic performance (per capita GDP, real per capita GDP, and other indicators)		
Durham (1999)		Regime type/discretion (number of effective parties and constitutional framework measure)	Discretion decreases growth in advanced areas, inhibits investments in poor (not advanced) areas. Single-party dictatorships have higher investment ratios

185

Table A.1 (*cont.*)

Authors	Dependent variable	Political-institutional variables (if any)	Political-institutional findings
Easterly (1991)	Per capita GDP (PPP where available)		
Easterly (2007)	Change in per capita GDP		
Edwards (2001)	Average real GDP growth		
Ehrlich and Lui (1999)	Real per capita GDP	Communist regime	Communist regime has negative impact on growth
Evans and Rauch (1999)	Total growth of real GDP per capita from 1970–90	Weberian bureaucratic structure (use of meritocracy, predictable career ladder)	Weberian bureaucratic structure contributed to increased growth. It also tends to pattern by region
Ezcurra (2007)	Annual growth rate		
Fagerberg *et al.* (2007)	Real GDP growth		
Fatas (2000)	GNP average growth rate		
Fedderke *et al.* (1999)	Economic growth (not specifically measured, goal of the article is to define social capital in a way that shows how it contributes to economic growth)		

Study	Dependent variable	Independent variable	Findings
Feiock *et al.* (2008)	Economic development (discussed)	Quality of governance	Level of governance matters for the shape of economic development. Quality of regional governance can spread economic development more evenly, preventing "spikes" but not achieving complete "flatness" (geographically speaking)
Feng (1997)	Real per capita GDP growth	Regime type (Gurr's Index, Bollen Index, Gastil Index), regularity of government change	Irregular government change negatively effects growth, democracy indirectly acts through regular government change to improve growth, but its direct effect is negative
Fidrmuc (2003)	Growth rate of GDP		
Fogel (2005)	(Not an empirical article/no causal argument)		
Fosu (2002)	Mean annual percent growth rate of GDP		
Freire-Seren (2002)	Gross value added (regional output)		
Frye (2002)	Real rate of year to year change in GDP	Regime type (Freedom House)	With proper controls, democracy has no impact on growth

Table A.1 (*cont.*)

Authors	Dependent variable	Political-institutional variables (if any)	Political-institutional findings
Galor and Moav (2002)	Economic growth (output per capita, and others)		
Galor and Tsiddon (1997)	Output growth (modeled)		
Gao (2005)	World growth rate (modeled)		
Gapinski (1996)	Output growth (a function of real GDP and labor)		
Garrison and Lee (1995)	Growth of per capita real GDP		
Gerring et al. (2006)	Percentage change in real GDP per capita in constant dollars	Regime type, democratic stock (regime since 1900)	The higher a country's democratic stock, the higher its growth rate
Ghirmay et al. (2001)	Real GDP		
Glaeser et al. (1995)	GDP per capita growth, urban growth		
Gounder (2004)	Economic growth, political stability	Regime type, rule of law, quality of institutions (Gastil Index)	(Case study) democracy, rule of law, and quality of institutions increases growth
Gradstein and Justman (2002)	Individual income (modeled)		
Granato et al. (1996)	Mean rate of per capita economic growth		

Gregorio and Guidotti (1995)	GDP per capita		
Greiner (1996)	Economic growth (modeled)		
Greiner et al. (2004)	Wage inequality (wage premium, college premium)		
Grier (1999)	Average real GDP growth		
Gupta and Sommers (1999)	GNP per capita		
Guseh (1997)	Logged annual rates of growth		
Gyimah-Brempong (2002)	GDP, per capita income, income inequality		
Haggard (2005)	Economic growth (lit review style)	Regime type, property rights, ability to credible commitment	Institutions effect economic growth by solving collective action problems. Many different institutions could solve the same problem.
Haile et al. (2003)	Ten-year average GDP growth per capita		
Hall and Jones (1999)	Output per worker		
Hall and Leeson (2007)	GDP per capita PPP		

Table A.1 (*cont.*)

Authors	Dependent variable	Political-institutional variables (if any)	Political-institutional findings
Hanushek and Kim (1995)	Average annual growth in real per capita GDP		
Hazan and Berdugo (2002)	Economic development (modeled)		
Henderson (2003)	Output per worker (in purchasing power parity)		
Henisz (2000)	Real per capita GDP growth	Political Constraints Index	Institutions that allow credible commitment increase growth rates
Henry (2003)	Economic development (growth rate of output per worker, growth rate of capital stock)		
Heo (1998)	Growth in GDP		
Heo (1999)	Growth in GDP		
Heo and DeRouen (1998)	Growth in GDP		
Hojman (2002)	Economic and political performance	Quality of institutions	
Holtz-Eakin *et al.* (2004)	Public spending (modeled)		(case study)

Isham *et al.* (2005)	Per capita growth rate	Rule of law, law and order tradition, civil liberties, quality of bureaucracy, political rights, rule-based governance	All institutional variables have positive and significant coefficients.
Islam (1995)	Growth covergence (constructed with log of per capita GDP)		
Iwata *et al.* (2003)	Percent growth of output, capital, and labor		
Jalilian *et al.* (2007)	GDP per capita growth		
Jones (1995a)	Per capita GDP, annual growth rate, total factor productivity growth		
Jones (1995b)	US total factor productivity growth rate		
Jones (2002)	Stability of US growth rate		
Jorgenson and Stiroh (1999)	Total factor productivity growth		
Jorgenson and Stiroh (2000)	Real output (created for this paper)		
Kalaitzidakis (2001)	Per capita GDP growth		
Kalemli-Ozcan (2002)	Population growth		

191

Table A.1 (*cont.*)

Authors	Dependent variable	Political-institutional variables (if any)	Political-institutional findings
Kaneko (2000)	Interaction between specialization and growth rate		
Kentor (1998)	GDP per capita		
Kentor (2001)	Income inequality, fertility rates, population growth, economic development (GNP per capita, GNP per capita growth)		
Kentor and Boswell (2003)	Growth in GNP per capita		
Khatkhate (1997)	(lit review of other works)		
King (1998)	Welfare provision		
Kirkpatrick and Weiss (1995)	GNP per capita		
Kneller (2007)	GDP growth five-year average		
Koren and Tenreyro (2007)	Real GDP per capita		
Krebs (2003)	Average growth rate		
Krueger and Lindahl (2001)	Annualized change in log GDP		

Study	Dependent variable	Independent variable	Findings
Krusell *et al.* (1997)	Economic growth (modeled)		
Kurtz and Schrank (2007)	GDP per capita growth, government effectiveness	Government effectiveness	Growth causes the changes/improvements in government effectiveness, government effectiveness does not cause growth
Kurzman *et al.* (2002)	Annual log difference of real GDP per capita	Democracy	Democracy has a statistically significant indirect and generally positive effect on economic growth. Democracy shows no long-term, direct effect on growth
Le and Suruga (2005)	Five-year forward moving average of per capita real GDP		
Leblang (1996)	Per capita growth rate	Regime type (Polity II)	Democracy affects growth indirectly through property rights
Leblang (1997)	Ten-year average growth rate	Regime type (Polity II)	Democracy increases growth
Levine (1997)	Real GDP per capita		
Levine (1998)	Real per capita GDP growth		
Levine (1999)	Real per capita GDP growth		
Levitt and Poterba (1999)	Growth rate of real per capita personal income (US States)		
Li and Liu (2005)	GDP growth		

Table A.1 (*cont.*)

Authors	Dependent variable	Political-institutional variables (if any)	Political-institutional findings
Liu *et al.* (2002)	GDP (calculated with gross industrial output)		
Lundberg and Squire (2003)	Growth (GDP growth) and inequality (adjusted Gini Index)		
Mah (2005)	Real GNP growth rate		
Mangeloja (2005)	GDP per capita growth		
Martin (2000)	Per capita growth rate		
Mauro (1995)	GDP growth	Bureaucratic efficiency index (bureaucracy and red tape, judiciary efficiency, and corruption)	Bureaucratic efficiency is positively correlated with GDP growth
Mauro (2004)	Corruption persistance (modeled)		
Mazumdar (1996)	Per capita real GDP		
Mazur and Alexander (2001)	Growth in real per capita GDP, real per capita GDP		
Mello (2002)	GDP		
Milbourne *et al.* (2003)	Output		
Mintz and Stevenson (1995)	Economic growth		

Study		Dependent variable	Notes
Miwa and Ramseyer (2002)		Economic growth (stock market capitalization divided by firm accounting equity)	
Mo (2001)		GDP growth rate	
Monte and Papagni (2001)		Per capita GDP growth	
Moon (1998)		Real GDP per capita growth	
Mulligan et al. (2004)	Regime type (polity scores)	Policy differences across regimes	
Murdoch and Sandler (2002)		Income per capita growth	
Murdoch and Sandler (2004)		Income per capita growth	
Nahar and Inder (2002)		Convergence	
Nelson (2007)	Institutions and technologies supported by those institutions	Economic growth (descriptive)	The field does not have a coherent view of institutions, and this definition needs to be developed. There is not one set of institutions that is the be-all and end-all for growth, but rather the details of the institutions and how they support technologies that lead to economic growth must be studied

Table A.1 (*cont.*)

Authors	Dependent variable	Political-institutional variables (if any)	Political-institutional findings
Neusser (2001)	Total factor productivity		
Nunn (2004)	Log of real per capita GDP		
Oliva and Rivera-Batiz (2002)	Real per capita annual GDP growth	Quality of democracy (Polity IV), rule of law (Kaufmann Index)	Democracy affects growth through promoting education, rule of law affects growth through increasing FDI
Onafowora and Owoye (1998)	Co integration vectors of real output, investment, exports, and trade policy		
Ozlu (1996)	Output		
Palmer and Whitten (1999)	Vote choice		
Parai (2003)	Per capita domestic capital, consumption		
Pedersen and Elmer (2003)	Real GDP		
Peretto (2003)	Growth (modeled)		
Peretto (2007)	Growth (modeled)		
Petrucci (2003)	Growth (modeled)		

Study	Dependent variable	Independent variable	Findings
Pfeifer et al. (1999)	(discussion of economic situation and possible courses of action in the Middle East)		
Pickering and Kisangani (2006)	GDP per capita, GDP per capita growth		
Pinto and Timmons (2005)	Sources of growth (factor capital accumulation, human capital accumulation, and productivity)	Political competition and regime type (Polity 98)	While political competition does affect the sources of growth, the substantive effect in the short run is small. A long-run approach may be needed
Plumper and Martin (2003)	GDP per capita growth PPP	Level of democracy (Polity 98)	Level of democracy has a U-shaped relationship with growth (growth is highest with mid-levels of democracy)
Quinn and Woolley (2001)	Real per capita GDP growth	Regime type (Gastil Index)	Democracy creates stronger growth by punishing the government for economic volatility
Ran et al. (2007)	Output growth		
Rauch (1995)	Share of infrastructure expenditure in total municipal expenditure	Merit-based civil service, city manager form of government, commission form of government	Investment is higher with merit-based civil service, investment is lower with commission or manager form of government
Rivera-Batiz (2001)	Economic growth (modeled)		

Table A.1 (*cont.*)

Authors	Dependent variable	Political-institutional variables (if any)	Political-institutional findings
Rivera-Batiz (2002)	Total factor productivity, growth in GDP per capita	Regime type	Democracy increases total factor productivity, and GDP per capita growth
Roberts and Rodriguez (1997)	Economic growth (modeled)		
Rodriguez and Rodrik (1999)	Economic progress (growth of GDP per capita, convergence)		
Rodrik (1997a)	Economic growth (per worker output, total factor production, growth rate, change in growth rate)		
Rodrik (2003a)	Per capital GDP growth	Economic principles (liberalization of agricultural markets, abolition of the state order system, privatization of land, tax reform, etc.)	Economic principles that contribute to economic success do not map on to one set of institutions, rather many different institutions can embrace the same principles
Rowley (2000)	Economic growth rate	Institutions	Case studies
Sachs and Warner (1995)	Real GDP	Rule of law, bureaucratic quality	Both significant and positive

Savvides (1995)	Per capita growth rate		
Scarpetta et al. (2000)	GDP per capita growth, GDP per capita growth disparities		
Schatz (1996)	Economic performance		
Schofer et al. (2000)	Annualized growth of real GDP per capita		
Scruggs (2001)	Real average GDP growth, average per capita GDP growth	Political democracy Index (Polity III)	Democracy has no direct impact on economic growth
Scully (2002)	Inequality (Gini coefficient), economic growth (real growth rate in per capita GDP)	Economic Freedom Index (Gwartney, Lawson and Block)	Economic Freedom increases economic growth and reduces inequality
Scully (2003)	GDP growth rate		
Senhadji (2000)	GDP per capita		
Shan (2005)	GDP		
Stafford (1999)	Real wage growth		
Stern et al. (1996)	Environmental degradation		

Table A.1 (*cont.*)

Authors	Dependent variable	Political-institutional variables (if any)	Political-institutional findings
Stiglitz (2000)	Economic growth and stability		
Stokey (1998)	Growth, capital accumulation (modeled)		
Storm and Naastepad (2005)	Economic growth (per capita GDP)		
Strauss and Thomas (1998)	Wages and productivity		
Stürm and de Haan (2001b)	Average GDP per capita growth		
Swank (1996)	GDP per capita growth	Communitarian polities (Confucian states, social corporatist states)	Confucian states and social corporatist states have higher growth rates, but more work needs to be done
Tang and Hedley (1998)	Average GNP growth rate		
Teboul and Moustier (2001)	Per capita income growth		
Teles (2005)	Per capita GNP		

Temple and Johnson (1998)	Log difference GDP per capita	
Ventura (1997)	Economic growth (modeled)	
Voitchovsky (2005)	Five-year difference in real GDP per capita	
Wahab (2004)	Government expenditure	
Weede (1996)	GDP growth	
Whiteley (2000)	Mean GDP growth rate	
Wu and Davis (1999)	Real per capita GDP, real per capita GDP growth	Economic Freedom Index, Political Freedom Index	Economic freedom contributes to economic growth.
Yao (2006)	GDP, exports, FDI	
Yoo (2003)	Real GDP per person of working age in purchasing power parity	
Yu (1997)	Growth rate of money aggregates, bank credit, industrial output, retail price index	

B | *Appendix to Chapter 3*

List of countries in growth-rate volatility analysis

Albania, Algeria, Angola, Argentina, Armenia, Azerbaijan, Bangladesh, Belarus, Benin, Bolivia, Botswana, Brazil, Bulgaria, Burkina Faso, Burundi, Cambodia, Cameroon, Cape Verde, Central African Republic, Chad, Chile, China, Colombia, Comoros, Congo (Rep. of), Costa Rica, Côte d'Ivoire, Croatia, Dominican Republic, Ecuador, Egypt, El Salvador, Eritrea, Equatorial Guinea, Estonia, Ethiopia, Gabon, Gambia, Georgia, Ghana, Guatemala, Guinea, Guinea-Bissau, Honduras, India, Indonesia, Iran, Jamaica, Jordan, Kazakhstan, Kenya, Kuwait, Kyrgyzstan, Laos, Latvia, Lebanon, Lesotho, Libya, Lithuania, Macedonia, Madagascar, Malawi, Malaysia, Mali, Mauritania, Mauritius, Moldova, Mongolia, Morocco, Mozambique, Namibia, Nepal, Nicaragua, Niger, Nigeria, Oman, Pakistan, Panama, Papua New Guinea, Paraguay, Peru, Philippines, Romania, Russian Federation, Rwanda, Saudi Arabia, Senegal, Slovakia, Slovenia, South Africa, Sri Lanka, Swaziland, Syria, Tanzania, Thailand, Togo, Trinidad and Tobago, Tunisia, Uganda, Ukraine, United Arab Emirates, Uruguay, Venezuela, Vietnam, Yemen, Zaire, Zambia, Zimbabwe.

Summary statistics for variables included in analysis

Table B.1 *Summary statistics*

Variable	Mean	Std. Dev.	Min.	Max.	N
Growth-rate volatility	4.368	3.847	0	40.145	1968
Extreme volatility	0.156	0.224	0	1	1986
Average growth	1.74	4.089	−42.271	57.057	1986

Table B.1 (*cont.*)

Variable	Mean	Std. Dev.	Min.	Max.	N
Africa growth types	0.52	0.5	0	1	415
Coalition/minority	0.075	0.231	0	1	2472
Divided govt	0.029	0.131	0	1	2472
Judicial indep.	0.22	0.394	0	1	2472
Federalism	0.053	0.219	0	1	2472
Central bank indep.	0.241	0.408	0	1	2472
Democracy	0.431	0.471	0	1	2156
Binding legislatures	0.67	0.424	0	1	424
Conflict index	5.664	3.268	0	11.469	1954
Civil wars	0.212	0.409	0	1	1937
GDP growth	3.67	4.146	−42.451	54.879	2003
Population growth	1.83	1.529	−20.359	16.619	2293
Inflation (Log)	2.922	0.940	−0.99	8.849	1996
GDP per capita (Log)	7.48	1.552	4.44	10.808	1929
GDP fractionalization index	2.339	0.358	1.291	2.997	1812
Trade openness (% GDP)	75.012	43.211	2.351	315.49	1946
Agriculture (% GDP)	20.34	15.618	0.078	87.901	1843
Primary commodity exporter	0.136	0.343	0	1	2472
Terms-of-trade adjustment	1.086	13.477	−95.291	191.852	1201
Govt. consumption (% GDP)	16.35	6.909	3.915	56.338	1892
Liquidity (M2 % GDP)	38.262	30.298	4.107	362.63	1687

Construction of credible constraint indicators

Divided presidential government

In order to create a divided presidential government variable I integrate the variables h_alignl1, chga_hinst, and dpi_maj. h_alignl1 indicates whether the same party controls both the executive and the lower chamber. If chga_hinst classifies a government as a presidential democracy or a mixed democracy, and h_alignl1 indicates that the party in control of the executive is not in control of the lower house, the divided/minority government variable is set to 1. If the case is classified as a presidential or mixed democracy and the same party controls both the executive and the lower chamber, it is set to 0.

Minority and coalition parliamentary government

For minority parliamentary government, dpi_maj is the number of seats held by the government divided by the total number of seats. If this is below 50 percent, and the chga_hinst classifies the government as a parliamentary democracy, we assume it is a minority government and set the indicator to 1. If the percentage of seats held by the government is greater than 50 percent and it is a parliamentary democracy, we set it to 0 unless there is a coalition in place. For an indicator of coalition government, I use dpi_gs, which measures the number of seats held by the government, and dpi_gps1, which measures the number of seats held by the largest party in the government. I divide the number of seats held by the largest party in government by the number of seats held by the government. If the largest party in the government holds less than 90 percent of the seats, I consider it a coalition government and set the indicator to 1. Otherwise the government is treated as a majority government, and the indicator is set to 0.

Judicial independence

I use a variable constructed by Witold Henisz and archived in the Quality of Government dataset (h_j). This is coded 1 if there is an independent judiciary (which Henisz bases on information collected for the Polity Index's Executive Constraints variable and the ICRG Rule and Law variable), and 0 if not.

Federalism

To create the federal variable I use pt_federal from the Quality of Government data set. It is already a dummy variable classifying systems as either federalist or non-federalist structures.

Central bank independence

The final institution on which I collect data is the central bank. The data here are from Cukierman *et al.* (1992) who collect information

on various aspects of central bank independence for seventy-two countries. (To conserve space I refer the reader to the original article by
Cukierman *et al.* for a detailed description and justification of the
various dimensions of central bank independence.) Cukierman *et al.*
(1992) then combine these various dimensions to create a single Central
Bank Independence Score, ranging from 0 to 1, where 1 is the highest
value or most independent. However, *de jure* independence of central
banks does not always correlate very highly with their de facto independence (especially in developing countries), which suggests a need
for some caution. Cukierman *et al.* (1992) suggest that the turnover
rate of the head of the central bank, measured by the average number of changes per year, might be a better indicator of the de facto
independence enjoyed by the central bank such that more frequent
changes are suggestive of greater political interference. Stürm and de
Haan (2001a) concur with this view and extend the original central
bank chief executive officer turnover data to 2000. I utilize both indicators of central bank independence in the construction of my central
bank independence variable. Because the central bank independence
score is designed to capture the *de jure* independence of the bank while
previous research has found that the turnover rate is a better proxy for
de facto independence, I require that a state's central bank score above
the mean on both variables before I code. The mean for the central
bank independence is 0.25 (while the theoretical range is 0 to 1, the
highest value for any state is earned by the German central bank which
scores 0.69). The mean for the turnover rates is 0.20, or approximately
one change every five years.

Regression results: volatility hurts growth

Table B.2 *Volatility hurts growth in the developing world*

	DV: economic growth	
Economic growth lagged	0.13 $(0.04)^{0.00}$	0.07 $(0.06)^{0.27}$
Growth-rate volatility	−0.61 $(0.07)^{0.00}$	−0.37 $(0.11)^{0.00}$

Table B.2 *(cont.)*

	DV: economic growth	
Growth-rate volatility squared	0.03 $(0.001)^{0.00}$	0.02 $(0.01)^{0.00}$
Democracy		−0.01 $(0.34)^{0.97}$
Political instability		−0.19 $(0.04)^{0.00}$
Population (Log)		0.30 $(0.15)^{0.04}$
GDP per capita lagged		−0.51 $(0.31)^{0.10}$
Trade openness (% GDP)		0.14 $(0.01)^{0.02}$
Agriculture (% GDP)		−0.05 $(0.02)^{0.02}$
Government consumption (% GDP)		−0.11 $(0.03)^{0.00}$
Net FDI inflows (% GDP)		0.24 $(0.06)^{0.00}$
Constant	3.03 $(0.27)^{0.00}$	3.56 $(3.94)^{0.37}$
No. of observations	793	510
No. of countries	157	123
Root mean square error	3.60	3.13

Note: Sample of non-OECD states. Each observation is a five-year period. Cell entries are OLS coefficients, with standard errors corrected for clustering by country reported in parentheses and two-sided p-values superscripted.

C | Appendix to Chapter 4

Countries included in Tables 4.2 and 4.3

Using the EBRD-World Bank Business Environment and Enterprise Performance Survey (BEEPS), Tables 4.2 and 4.3 analyze the effect of credible constraint institutions on the probability that a firm considers regulatory uncertainty a major obstacle to conducting business.

The countries included in these analyses are: Albania, Armenia, Azerbaijan, Bangladesh, Belarus, Brazil, Bulgaria, Cambodia, China, Croatia, Czech Republic, Ecuador, El Salvador, Estonia, Ethiopia, Georgia, Guatemala, Honduras, Hungary, Indonesia, India, Kazakhstan, Kenya, Kyrgyzstan, Latvia, Lithuania, Macedonia, Mali, Moldova, Nicaragua, Peru, Philippines, Poland, Romania, Russian Federation, Senegal, Slovakia, Slovenia, South Africa, Syria, Tajikistan, Tanzania, Turkey, Uganda, Ukraine, Uzbekistan, Yugoslavia, and Zambia.

D | *Appendix to Chapter 5*

Governments and prime ministers of independent India, 1947–present

Table D.1 *Governments and prime ministers of independent India, 1947–present*

Prime minister	Party	Coalition	Dates
J. Nehru	INC		8/15/47–5/27/64
G.L. Nanda	(Interim)	INC	–6/9/64
L.B. Shastri	INC		–1/11/66
G.L. Nanda	(Interim)	INC	–1/24/66
I. Gandhi	INC		–3/24/77
M. Desai	INC (O)	Janata Dal (minority)	–7/28/79
C. Singh	Lok Dal	Janata Party (minority)	–1/14/80
I. Gandhi	INC (I)		–10/31/84
R. Gandhi	INC (I)		–12/2/89
V.P. Singh	Janata Dal	National Front (minority)	–11/10/90
C. Shekhar	Samajwadi Party (minority)		–6/21/91
P.V. Narasimha Rao	INC (I) (minority)		–5/16/96
A.B. Vajpayee	BJP (minority)		–6/1/96
H.D. Deve Gowda	Janata Dal	United Front (minority)	–4/21/97
I.K. Gujral	Janata Dal	United Front (minority)	–3/19/98

Table D.1 (*cont.*)

Prime Minister	Party	Coalition	Dates
A.B. Vajpayee	BJP (minority)	National Democratic Alliance	–5/22/04
Dr. M. Singh	INC	United Progressive Alliance (minority)	–5/16/09
Dr. M. Singh	INC	United Progressive Alliance	–present

Source: Panagariya 2008: xi–xii.
Note: INC=Indian National Congress; BJP=Bharatiya Janata Party.

References

Abrams, Burton A. and Kenneth A. Lewis. 1995. "Cultural and Institutional Determinants of Economic Growth: A Cross-Section Analysis." *Public Choice* 83(3–4):273–89.

Acemoglu, Daron, Simon Johnson, and James Robinson. 2003a. "An African Success Story: Botswana." In *In Search of Prosperity: Analytical Narratives on Economic Growth*, ed. Dani Rodrik. Princeton University Press.

Acemoglu, Daron, Simon Johnson, James Robinson, and Yunyong Thaicharoen. 2003b. "Institutional Causes, Macroeconomic Symptoms: Volatility, Crises and Growth." *Journal of Monetary Economics* 50:49–123.

Adams, Richard Jr. 2004. "Economic Growth, Inequality and Poverty: Estimating the Growth Elasticity of Poverty." *World Development* 32(12):1989–2014.

Agenor, Pierre-Richard and Peter J. Montiel. 1999. *Development Macroeconomics*. Princeton University Press.

Agenor, Pierre-Richard, C. John McDermott, and Eswar S. Prasad. 2000. "Macroeconomic Fluctuations in Developing Countries: Some Stylized Facts." *The World Bank Economic Review* 14(2):251–85.

Agenor, Pierre-Richard, Mustapha Nabli, Tarik Yousef, and Henning Tarp Jensen. 2007. "Labor Market Reforms, Growth, and Unemployment in Labor-Exporting Countries in the Middle East and North Africa." *Journal of Policy Modeling* 29(2):277–309.

Aghion, Philippe, and Abhijit Banerjee. 2005. *Volatility and Growth*. New York: Oxford University Press.

Aghion, Philippe and Peter Howitt. 1998. *Endogenous Growth Theory*. Cambridge, MA: MIT Press.

Aghion, Philippe, Eve Caroli, and Cecilia Garcia-Penalosa. 1999. "Inequality and Economic Growth: The Perspective of the New Growth Theories." *Journal of Economic Literature* 37(4):1615–60.

Ahlquist, John S. 2006. "Economic Policy, Institutions, and Capital Flows: Portfolio and Direct Investment Flows in Developing Countries." *International Studies Quarterly* 50:681–704.

Ahluwalia, Isher Judge and John Williamson, eds. 2003. *The South Asian Experience with Growth*. New Delhi: Oxford University Press.

Aizenman, Joshua and Nancy Marion. 1993. "Macroeconomic Uncertainty and Private Investment." *Economics Letters* 41(2):207–10.

Aizenman, Joshua and Nancy Marion. 1999. "Volatility and the Investment Response." *Economica* 66:157–79.

Alesina, Alberto and Eliana La Ferrara. 2004. "Ethnic Diversity and Economic Performance." *National Bureau of Economic Research Working Paper Series* No. 10313.

Alesina, Alberto, Sule Ozler, Nouriel Roubini, and Phillip Swagel. 1992. "Political Instability and Economic Growth." *National Bureau of Economic Research Working Paper Series* No. 4173. Published in 1996 as *Journal of Economic Growth* 1(2):189–212.

Alfaro, Laura. 2004. "Capital Controls: A Political Economy Approach." *Review of International Economics* 12(4):571–90.

Almeida, Heitor and Daniel Ferreira. 2002. "Democracy and the Variability of Economic Performance." *Economics and Politics* 14(3):1954–85.

Alston, Lee, Marcus Andres Melo, Bernardo Mueller, and Carlos Pereira. 2006. *Political Institutions, Policy-making Processes, and Policy Outcomes in Brazil*. Washington, DC: Inter-American Development Bank.

Ames, Barry. 2001. *The Deadlock of Democracy in Brazil*. Ann Arbor: University of Michigan Press.

Amsden, Alice. 1989. *Asia's Next Giant: South Korea and Late Industrialization*. New York: Oxford University Press.

Andersen, Jørgen Juel and Silje Aslaksen. 2008. "Constitutions and the Resource Curse." *Journal of Development Economics* 87:227–46.

Ang, James B. and Warwick J. McKibbin. 2007. "Financial Liberalization, Financial Sector Development and Growth: Evidence from Malaysia." *Journal of Development Economics* 84(1):215–33.

Arayama, Yuko and Katsuya Miyoshi. 2004. "Regional Diversity and Sources of Economic Growth in China." *The World Economy* 27(10):1583–607.

Arbache, Jorge Saba and John Page. 2007. "More Growth or Fewer Collapses? A New Look at Long-Run Growth." *World Bank Policy Research Working Paper* No. WPS 4384.

Aron, Janine. 2000. "Growth and Institutions: A Review of the Evidence." *The World Bank Research Observer* 1:99–135.

Atinc, Tamar M. 2002. "Facts about East Asian Vulnerability and Poverty." Technical report, Washington, DC: World Bank.

Auty, Richard M. 2001. *Resource Abundance and Economic Development*. Oxford University Press.

Awokuse, Titus O. 2005. "Exports, Economic Growth and Causality in Korea." *Applied Economics Letters* 12(11):693–96.

Azam, Jean-Paul, Augustin Fosu, and Njuguna S. Ndung'u. 2002. "Explaining Slow Growth in Africa." *African Development Review* 14:177–220.

Bahmani-Oskooee, Mohsen and Farhang Niroomand. 1999. "Openness and Economic Growth: An Empirical Investigation." *Applied Economics Letters* 6(9):557.

Baier, Scott L., Gerald P. Dwyer, and Robert Tamura. 2006. "How Important are Capital and Total Factor Productivity for Economic Growth?" *Economic Inquiry* 44(1):23–49.

Balaguer, Jacint and Manuel Cantavella-Jorda. 2004. "Export Composition and Spanish Economic Growth: Evidence from the 20th Century." *Journal of Policy Modeling* 26(2):165–79.

Balakrishnan, Pulapre. 2007. "The Recovery of India: Economic Growth in the Nehru Era." *Economic &Political Weekly* November 17:52–66.

Balakrishnan, Pulapre and M. Parameswaran. 2007. "Understanding Economic Growth in India: A Prerequisite." *Economic & Political Weekly* 42(27/28):2915–22.

Banks, Arthur S. 2001. *Cross-national Time Series Data Archive.* [CD-Rom].

Baqir, Reza, Rodney Ramcharan, and Ratna Sahay. 2005. "IMF Programs and Growth: Is Optimism Defensible?" *IMF Staff Papers* 52(2):267–86.

Bardhan, Pranab. 2006. "Awakening Giants, Feet of Clay: A Comparative Assessment of the Rise of China and India." *Journal of South Asian Development* 1(1):1–17.

Bardhan, Pranab. 2009. "India and China: Governance Issues and Development." *Journal of Asian Studies* 68(2):347–57.

Barrell, Ray and Nigel Pain. 1997. "Foreign Direct Investment, Technological Change, and Economic Growth Within Europe." *The Economic Journal* 107(445):1770–86.

Barro, Robert J. 1991. "Economic Growth in a Cross Section of Countries." *Quarterly Journal of Economics* 106(2):407–43.

Barro, Robert J. 1995. "Inflation and Economic Growth." Technical report, National Bureau of Economic Research, Inc.

Barro, Robert J. 1996. "Determinants of Economic Growth: A Cross-Country Empirical Study." *NBER Working Paper 5698.*

Barro, Robert J. 1997. *Determinants of Economic Growth.* Cambridge, MA: MIT Press.

Barro, Robert J. and Jong-Wha Lee. 2003. "IMF Programs: Who Is Chosen and What Are the Effects?" Departmental Working Papers 2003-9, Australian National University, Economics RSPAS.

Barro, Robert J. and Rachel M. McCleary. 2003. "Religion and Economic Growth across Countries." *American Sociological Review* 68(5): 760–81.

Barro, Robert J. and Xavier Sala-i-Martin. 1995. *Economic Growth*. Cambridge, MA: MIT Press.

Bartels, Larry M. 1991. "Instrumental and 'Quasi-Instrumental' Variables." *American Journal of Political Science* 35(3):777–800.

Basu, Kaushik. 2008. "India's Dilemmas: The Political Economy of Policymaking in a Globalised World." *Economic & Political Weekly* 43(5): 53–62.

Bates, Robert H. 1981. *Markets and States in Tropical Africa*. Berkeley: University of California Press.

Bates, Robert H. 2001. *Prosperity and Violence*. New York: W.W. Norton & Company.

Baum, Matthew A. and David A. Lake. 2003. "The Political Economy of Growth: Democracy and Human Capital." *American Journal of Political Science* 47(2):333–47.

Bechtel, Michael M. and Roland Füss. 2008. "When Investors Enjoy Less Policy Risk: Divided Government, Economic Policy Change, and Stock Market Volatility in Germany, 1970–2005." *Swiss Political Science Review* 14(2):278–314.

Beck, Thorsten, George Clarke, Alberto Groff, Philip Keefer, and Patrick Walsh. 2001. "New Tools in Comparative Political Economy: The Database of Political Institutions." *World Bank Economic Review* 15(1):165–76.

Bekaert, Geert, Campbell R. Harvey, and Christian Lundblad. 2001a. "Does Financial Liberalization Spur Growth?" *NBER Working Paper Series* No. 8245.

Bekaert, Geert, Campbell R. Harvey, and Christian Lundblad. 2001b. "Emerging Equity Markets and Economic Development." *Journal of Development Economics* 66(2):465–504.

Berend, Ivan T. 2002. "Economic Fluctuation Revisited." *European Review* 10(3):305–16.

Berggren, Niclas and Henrik Jordahl. 2005. "Does Free Trade Really Reduce Growth? Further Testing Using the Economic Freedom Index." *Public Choice* 122(1):99–114.

Bertocchi, Graziella and Fabio Canova. 1996. "Did Colonization Matter for Growth? An Empirical Exploration into the Historical Causes of Africa's Underdevelopment." *C.E.P.R. Discussion Papers*.

Bhagwati, Jagdish. 2004. *In Defense of Globalization*. Oxford University Press.

Bhattacharyya, Sambit. 2004. "Deep Determinants of Economic Growth." *Applied Economics Letters* 11(9):587–90.

Biglaiser, Glen and Karl DeRouen. 2006. "Economic Reforms and Inflows of Foreign Direct Investment in Latin America." *Latin American Research Review* 41(1):51–75.

Bjornskov, Christian. 2005. "Does Political Ideology Affect Economic Growth?" *Public Choice* 123(1):133–46.

Bleaney, Michael F. 1996. "Macroeconomic Stability, Investment and Growth in Developing Countries." *Journal of Development Economics* 48:461–77.

Bleaney, Michael and David Fielding. 2002. "Exchange Rate Regimes, Inflation and Output Volatility in Developing Countries." *Journal of Development Economics* 68:233–45.

Blomstrom, Magnus, Robert E. Lipsey, and Mario Zejan. 1996. "Is Fixed Investment the Key to Economic Growth?" *The Quarterly Journal of Economics* 111(1):269–76.

Bloom, David E. and Jeffrey D. Sachs. 1998. "Geography, Demography, and Economic Growth in Africa." *Brookings Papers on Economic Activity* 29(2):207–96.

Borensztein, Eduardo, Jose De Gregorio, and Jong-Wha Lee. 1998. "How Does Foreign Direct Investment Affect Economic Growth?" *Journal of International Economics* 45:115–35.

Borner, Silvio, Aymo Brunetti, and Beatrice Weder. 1995. *Political Credibility and Economic Development*. New York: St. Martin's Press.

Bosworth, Barry and Susan M. Collins. 1999. "Capital Inflows, Investment and Growth." *Tokyo Club Papers* 12.

Bosworth, Barry, Susan M. Collins, and Arvind Virmani. 2006. "Sources of Growth in the Indian Economy." Technical report, India Policy Forum.

Bound, John, David A. Jaeger, and Regina M. Baker. 1995. "Problems with Instrumental Variables Estimation When the Correlation Between the Instruments and the Endogenous Explanatory Variable Is Weak." *Journal of the American Statistical Association* 90(430):443–50.

Boyce, James K. and Léonce Ndikumana. 2000. "Is Africa a Net Credit? New Estimates of Capital Flight from Severely Indebted Sub-Saharan African Countries, 1970–1996." University of Massachusetts, Amherst.

Breen, Richard. 1997. "Inequality, Economic Growth and Social Mobility." *The British Journal of Sociology* 48(3):429–49.

Brooks, Sarah M. and Layna Mosley. 2008. "Risk, Uncertainty, and Autonomy: Financial Market Constraints in Developing Countries." The Ohio State University and University of North Carolina.

Brunetti, Aymo. 1998. "Policy Volatility and Economic Growth: A Comparative, Empirical Analysis." *European Journal of Political Economy* 14:35–52.

Bruno, Michael. 1995. "Development Issues in a Changing World: New Lessons, Old Debates, Open Questions." *Proceedings of the World Bank Conference on Development Economics 1994.*

Bruno, Michael and William Easterly. 1998. "Inflation Crises and Long-Run Growth." *Journal of Monetary Economics* 41(1):3–26.

Bueno de Mesquita, Bruce. 1975. *Strategy, Risk and Personality in Coalition Politics: The Case of India.* Cambridge University Press.

Bueno de Mesquita, Bruce, James D. Morrow, Randolph Siverson, and Alastair Smith. 2001. "Political Competition and Economic Growth." *Journal of Democracy* 12(1):58–72.

Bueno de Mesquita, Bruce, Alastair Smith, Randolph M. Siverson, and James D. Morrow. 2003. *The Logic of Political Survival.* Cambridge, MA: MIT Press.

Burdekin, Richard C.K., Arthur T. Denzau, Manfred W. Keil, Thitithep Sitthiyot, and Thomas D. Willett. 2004. "When Does Inflation Hurt Economic Growth? Different Nonlinearities for Different Economies." *Journal of Macroeconomics* 26(3):519–32.

Burkhart, Ross E. and Michael S. Lewis-Beck. 1994. "Comparative Democracy: The Economic Development Thesis." *American Political Science Review* 88(4):903–10.

Butkiewicz, James L. and Halit Yanikkaya. 2005. "The Impact of Sociopolitical Instability on Economic Growth: Analysis and Implications." *Journal of Policy Modeling* 27(5):629–45.

Caballero, Ricardo J. 2000a. "Aggregate Investment: Lessons from the Previous Millennium." Paper presented at the Annual Meeting of the American Economics Association, January.

Caballero, Ricardo J. 2000b. "Aggregate Volatility in Modern Latin America: Causes and Cures." Policy report prepared for the World Bank's FY00 flagship report "Dealing with Economic Insecurity in Latin American," April.

Caballero, Ricardo J. 2000c. "Macroeconomic Volatility in Latin America: A View and Three Case Studies." *Economia* 1(1):31–108.

Caballero, Ricardo J. 2001. "Coping with Chile's External Vulnerability: A Financial Problem." Working Paper No. 154, Banco Central de Chile.

Campos, Nauro F. and Fabrizio Coricelli. 2002. "Growth in Transition: What We Know, What We Don't, and What We Should." *Journal of Economic Literature* 40(3):793–836.

Cannon, Edmund S. 2000. "Economies of Scale and Constant Returns to Capital: A Neglected Early Contribution to the Theory of Economic Growth." *The American Economic Review* 90(1):292–5.

Carlsson, Fredrik and Susanna Lundstrom. 2001. "Economic Freedom and Growth: Decomposing the Effects." Working Papers in Economics 33, Department of Economics, Gothenburg University.

Castello, Amparo and Rafael Domenech. 2002. "Human Capital Inequality and Economic Growth: Some New Evidence." *The Economic Journal* 112:187–200.

Cerra, Valerie, Meenakshi Rishi, and Sweta C. Saxena. 2008. "Robbing the Riches: Capital Flight, Institutions and Debt." *Journal of Development Studies* 44(8):1190–213.

Chandra, Siddharth. 1998. "Democratic Institutions and Economic Growth." University of Pittsburgh.

Chandra, Siddharth and Nita Rudra. 2008. "Regime Type and Economic Performance: Why Democracies Just 'Muddle Through'." University of Pittsburgh.

Chang, Tsangyao. 2002. "Financial Development and Economic Growth in Mainland China: a Note on Testing Demand-following or Supply-leading Hypothesis." *Applied Economics Letters* 9(13):869.

Chang, Tsangyao and Steven B. Caudill. 2005. "Financial Development and Economic Growth: The Case of Taiwan." *Applied Economics* 37(12):1329–35.

Charlton, Roger. 1993. "The Politics of Elections in Botswana." *Africa: Journal of the International African Institute* 63(3):330–70.

Chatterjee, Santanu, Georgios Sakoulis, and Stephen J. Turnovsky. 2003. "Unilateral Capital Transfers, Public Investment, and Economic Growth." *European Economic Review* 47(6):1077–103.

Cheibub, José Antonio. 2007. *Presidentialism, Parliamentarism, and Democracy*. New York: Cambridge University Press.

Cheibub, José Antonio and Jennifer Gandhi. 2004. "Classifying Political Regimes: A Sixfold Classification of Democracies and Dictatorships." Paper presented at the Annual Meeting of the American Political Science Association.

Cheibub, José Antonio, Adam Przeworski, and Sebastian M. Saiegh. 2004. "Government Coalitions and Legislative Success Under Presidentialism and Parliamentarism." *British Journal of Political Science* 34: 565–87.

Chen, Bai-Zhu and Yi Feng. 2000. "Determinants of Economic Growth in China: Private Enterprise, Education, and Openness." *China Economic Review* 11(1):1–15.

Chhibber, Pradeep K. 1999. *Democracy without Associations: Transformation of the Party System and Social Cleavages in India*. Ann Arbor: University of Michigan Press.

Chhibber, Pradeep K. and Ken Kollman. 1998. "Party Aggregation and the Number of Parties in India and the United States." *American Political Science Review* 92(2):329–42.

Chhibber, Pradeep K. and Ken Kollman. 2004. *The Formation of National Party Systems*. Princeton University Press.

Chhibber, Pradeep K. and Irfan Nooruddin. 2000. "Party Competition and Fragmentation in Indian Elections, 1957–1998." In *Indian Politics and the 1998 Elections*, ed. Ramashray Roy and Paul Wallace. New Delhi: Sage Publications.

Chhibber, Pradeep K. and Irfan Nooruddin. 2004. "Do Party Systems Count? Party Competition and Government Performance in the Indian States." *Comparative Political Studies* 37:153–87.

Chhibber, Pradeep K. and Irfan Nooruddin. 2007. "Ideology, Party Fragmentation, and Public Sector Employment in the Indian States." University of California, Berkeley, and The Ohio State University.

Chibber, Vivek. 2003. *Locked in Place: State-Building and Late Industrialization in India*. Princeton University Press.

Chinn, Menzie D. and Hiro Ito. 2006. "What Matters for Financial Development? Capital Controls, Institutions, and Interactions." *Journal of Development Economics* 81:163–92.

Choe, Chongwoo and Imad A. Moosa. 1999. "Financial System and Economic Growth: The Korean Experience." *World Development* 27(6):1069–82.

Chong, Alberto and Luisa Zanforlin. 2004. "Inward-Looking Policies, Institutions, Autocrats, and Economic Growth in Latin America: An Empirical Exploration." *Public Choice* 121(3):335–61.

Chow, Gregory and An loh Lin. 2002. "Accounting for Economic Growth in Taiwan and Mainland China: A Comparative Analysis." *Journal of Comparative Economics* 30(3):507–30.

Clague, Christopher, Philip Keefer, Stephen Knack, and Mancur Olson. 1996. "Property and Contract Rights in Autocracies and Democracies." *Journal of Economic Growth* 1:243–76.

Clague, Christopher, Philip Keefer, Stephen Knack, and Mancur Olson. 1999. "Contract-Intensive Money: Contract Enforcement, Property Rights, and Economic Performance." *Journal of Economic Growth* 4:185–11.

Coclanis, Peter A. and Tilak Doshi. 2000. "Globalization in Southeast Asia." *Annals of the American Academy of Political and Social Science* 570:49–64.

Cohen, Stephen P. 2002. *India: Emerging Power.* Washington, DC: Brookings Institution Press.

Coleman, John J. 1999. "Unified Government, Divided Government, and Party Responsiveness." *American Political Science Review* 93(4): 821–35.

Collier, Paul. 2000. "Ethnicity, Politics and Economic Performance." *Economics and Politics* 12(3):225–45.

Collier, Paul. 2002. "Primary Commodity Dependence and Africa's Future." Technical report, World Bank Working Paper.

Collins, Susan M., Barry P. Bosworth, and Dani Rodrik. 1996. "Economic Growth in East Asia: Accumulation versus Assimilation." *Brookings Papers on Economic Activity* 1996(2):135–203.

Crafts, Nicholas. 2004. "Globalisation and Economic Growth: A Historical Perspective." *The World Economy* 27(1):45–58.

Crenshaw, Edward M., Ansari Z. Ameen, and Matthew Christenson. 1997. "Population Dynamics and Economic Development: Age-Specific Population Growth Rates and Economic Growth in Developing Countries, 1965 to 1990." *American Sociological Review* 62(6):974–84.

Crotty, James and Kang-Kook Lee. 2001. "Economic Performance in Post-Crisis Korea: A Critical Perspective on Neoliberal Restructuring." Technical Report Working Paper 23 Political Economy Research Institute, University of Massachusetts at Amherst.

Cukierman, Alex, Steven B. Webb, and Bilin Neyapti. 1992. "Measuring the Independence of Central Banks and its Effect on Policy Outcomes." *World Bank Economic Review* 6(3):353–98.

Da Fonseca, Manuel A.R. 1998. "Brazil's Real Plan." *Journal of Latin American Studies* 30:619–39.

Dakurah, A. Henry, Stephen P. Davies, and Rajan K. Sampath. 2001. "Defense Spending and Economic Growth in Developing Countries: A Causality Analysis." *Journal of Policy Modeling* 23(6):651–8.

Das, Gurcharan. 2002. *India Unbound: The Social and Economic Revolution from Independence to the Global Information Age.* New York: Anchor Books.

Davoodi, Hamid and Heng fu Zou. 1998. "Fiscal Decentralization and Economic Growth: A Cross-Country Study." *Journal of Urban Economics* 43(2):244–57.

Dawson, P.J. and L.J. Hubbard. 2004. "Exports and Economic Growth in Central and East European Countries During Transition." *Applied Economics* 36(16):1819–24.

de Haan, Jakob and Clemens L.J. Siermann. 1998. "Further Evidence on the Relationship between Economic Freedom and Economic Growth." *Public Choice* 95(3–4):363–80.

de Haan, Jakob and Jan-Egbert Stürm. 2000. "On the Relationship between Economic Freedom and Economic Growth." *European Journal of Political Economy* 16(2):215–41.

De Long, J. Bradford. 2003. "India since Independence: An Analytical Growth Narrative." In *In Search of Prosperity: Analytical Narratives on Economic Growth*, ed. Dani Rodrik. Princeton University Press.

de Souza, Amaury. 1999. "Cardoso and the Struggle for Reform in Brazil." *Journal of Democracy* 10(3):49–63.

Demetriades, Panicos O. and Khaled A. Hussein. 1996. "Does Financial Development Cause Economic Growth? Time-series Evidence from 16 Countries." *Journal of Development Economics* 51(2): 387–411.

Demetriades, Panicos O. and Kul B. Luintel. 1996. "Financial Development, Economic Growth and Banker Sector Controls: Evidence from India." *Economic Journal* 106(435):359–74.

Demurger, Sylvie. 2001. "Infrastructure Development and Economic Growth: An Explanation for Regional Disparities in China?" *Journal of Comparative Economics* 29(1):95–117.

Devarajan, Shantayanan, Vinaya Swaroop, and Heng fu Zou. 1996. "The Composition of Public Expenditure and Economic Growth." *Journal of Monetary Economics* 37(2):313–44.

Diermeier, Daniel, Joel M. Ericson, Timothy Frye, and Steven Lewis. 1997. "Credible Commitment and Property Rights: The Role of Strategic Interaction Between Political and Economic Actors." In *The Political Economy of Property Rights: Institutional Change and Credibility in the Reform of Centrally Planned Economies*, ed. David L. Weimer. Cambridge University Press, pp. 20–42.

Doucouliagos, Hristos and Mehmet Ali Ulubasoglu. 2008. "Democracy and Economic Growth: A Meta-Analysis." *American Journal of Political Science* 52:61–83.

Dougherty, Chrys and Dale W. Jorgenson. 1996. "International Comparisons of the Sources of Economic Growth." *The American Economic Review* 86(2):25–9.

Dudley, Leonard. 1999. "Communications and Economic Growth." *European Economic Review* 43(3):595–619.

Dunning, Thad. 2005. "Resource Dependence, Economic Performance, and Political Stability." *Journal of Conflict Resolution* 49(4): 451–82.

Durham, J. Benson. 1999. "Economic Growth and Political Regimes." *Journal of Economic Growth* 4(1):81–111.

Dutz, Mark A., ed. 2007. *Unleashing India's Innovation: Toward Sustainable and Inclusive Growth*. Washington, DC: World Bank.

Easterly, William. 1991. "Economic Policy and Economic Growth: A Critical Examination of the Negative Roles of Culture, Technological Advances, and Economic Policies." *Finance and Development* 28(3):10–13.

Easterly, William. 2005. "National Policies and Economic Growth: A Reappraisal." In *Handbook of Economic Growth*, vol. 1A, ed. Philippe Aghion and Steven Durlauf. Amsterdam: Elsevier, pp. 1–47.

Easterly, William. 2007. "Was Development Assistance a Mistake?" *American Economic Review* 97(2):328–32.

Easterly, William and Aart Kraay. 2000. "Small States, Small Problems? Income, Growth, and Volatility in Small States." *World Development* 28(11):2013–27.

Easterly, William, Roumeen Islam, and Joseph E. Stiglitz. 2001. "Shaken and Stirred: Explaining Growth, Volatility." *Annual World Bank Conference on Development Economics 2000*, 191–211.

EBRD-World Bank. 2005. *EBRD-World Bank Business Environment and Enterprise Performance Survey (BEEPS)*. London: European Bank for Reconstruction and Development. Online, available at: www.ebrd.com/country/sector/econo/surveys/beeps.htm   www.enterprisesurveys.org/.

Edwards III, George C., Andrew Barrett, and Jerrey Peake. 1997. "The Legislative Impact of Divided Government." *American Journal of Political Science* 41(2):545–63.

Edwards, Sebastian. 2001. "Capital Mobility and Economic Performance: Are Emerging Economies Different?" NBER Working Papers 8076, National Bureau of Economic Research, Inc.

Ehrlich, Isaac and Francis T. Lui. 1999. "Bureaucratic Corruption and Endogenous Economic Growth." *The Journal of Political Economy* 107(6):S270–S293.

Ehrlich, Sean D. 2007. "Access to Protection: Domestic Institutions and Trade Policies in Democracies." *International Organization* 61(3): 571–606.

Election Commission of India. 1987–98. *Reports on State Elections*. New Delhi: Government of India.

Elgie, Robert. 2001. *Divided Government in Comparative Perspective*. Oxford University Press.

Evans, Peter and James E. Rauch. 1999. "Bureaucracy and Growth: A Cross-National Analysis of the Effects of 'Weberian' State Structures on Economic Growth." *American Sociological Review* 64(5):748–65.

Ezcurra, Roberto. 2007. "Is Income Inequality Harmful for Regional Growth? Evidence from the European Union." *Urban Studies* 44(10):1953–71.

Fagerberg, Jan, Martin Srholec, and Mark Knell. 2007. "The Competitiveness of Nations: Why Some Countries Prosper While Others Fall Behind." *World Development* 35(10):1595–620.

Fatas, Antonio. 2000. "Do Business Cycles Cast Long Shadows? Short-Run Persistence and Economic Growth." *Journal of Economic Growth* 5:147–62.

Fatas, Antonio and Ilian Mihov. 2005. "Policy Volatility, Institutions and Economic Growth." *CEPR Discussion Papers.*

Fedderke, Johannes, Raphael De Kadt, and John Luiz. 1999. "Economic Growth and Social Capital: A Critical Reflection." *Theory and Society* 28(5):709–45.

Feiock, Richard C., Jae Moon, and Hyung Jun Park. 2008. "Is the World 'Flat' or 'Spiky'? Rethinking the Governance Implications of Globalization for Economic Development." *Public Administration Review* 68(1):24–35.

Feng, Yi. 1997. "Democracy, Political Stability and Economic Growth." *British Journal of Political Science* 27:391–418.

Fidrmuc, Jan. 2003. "Economic Reform, Democracy and Growth during Post-communist Transition." *European Journal of Political Economy* 19(3):583–604.

Figueiredo, Argelina Cheibub and Fernando Limongi. 2000. "Presidential Power, Legislative Organization, and Party Behavior in Brazil." *Comparative Politics* 32(2):151–70.

Findlay, Ronald. 1978. "Relative Backwardness, Direct Foreign Investment, and the Transfer of Technology." *Quarterly Journal of Economics* 92:1–16.

Flores, Thomas Edward and Irfan Nooruddin. 2009. "Democracy Under the Gun: Understanding Post-Conflict Economic Recovery." *Journal of Conflict Resolution* 53(1):3–29.

Fogel, Robert W. 2005. "Reconsidering Expectations of Economic Growth After World War II from the Perspective of 2004." *IMF Staff Papers* 52:6–14.

Fosu, Augustin Kwasi. 2002. "Political Instability and Economic Growth: Implications of Coup Events in Sub-Saharan Africa." *American Journal of Economics and Sociology* 61(1):329–48.

Fowler, James H. 2006. "Elections and Markets: The Effect of Partisanship, Policy Risk, and Electoral Margins on the Economy." *Journal of Politics* 68(1):89–103.

Franzese, Jr., Robert J. 2007. "Fiscal Policy with Multiple Policy: Veto Actors and Deadlock, Collective Action and Common Pools, Bargaining and Compromise." In *Veto Players and Policy Change*, ed. Hideko Magara. Tokyo: Waseda University Press, pp. 118–61.

Freire-Seren, M.J. 2002. "On the Relationship Between Human Capital Accumulation and Economic Growth." *Applied Economics Letters* 9(12):805.

Frye, Timothy. 2002. "The Perils of Polarization: Economic Performance in the Postcommunist World." *World Politics* 54:308–37.

Fudenberg, Drew and Jean Tirole. 1991. *Game Theory*. Cambridge, MA: MIT Press.

Galor, Oded and Omer Moav. 2002. "Natural Selection and the Origin of Economic Growth." *The Quarterly Journal of Economics* 117(4): 1133–91.

Galor, Oded and Daniel Tsiddon. 1997. "Technological Progress, Mobility, and Economic Growth." *American Economic Review* 87(3):363–82.

Gandhi, Jennifer. 2008a. *Political Institutions under Dictatorship*. New York: Cambridge University Press.

Gandhi, Jennifer. 2008b. "Dictatorial Institutions and their Impact on Economic Growth." *European Journal of Sociology* 49(1):3–30.

Gandhi, Jennifer and Adam Przeworski. 2006. "Cooperation, Cooptation, and Rebellion Under Dictatorships." *Economics and Politics* 18(1): 1–26.

Ganguly, Sumit. 2003. *India as an Emerging Power*. London: Routledge.

Gao, Ting. 2005. "Foreign Direct Investment and Growth Under Economic Integration." *Journal of International Economics* 67:157–74.

Gapinski, James H. 1996. "Heterogeneous Capital, Economic Growth, and Economic Development." *Journal of Macroeconomics* 18(4):561–85.

Garrison, Charles B. and Feng-Yao Lee. 1995. "The Effect of Macroeconomic Variables on Economic Growth Rates: A Cross-Country Study." *Journal of Macroeconomics* 17(2):303–17.

Geddes, Barbara. 1999. "Authoritarian Breakdown: Empirical Test of a Game Theoretic Argument." Technical report, UCLA.

Gehlbach, Scott and Philip Keefer. n.d. "Investment Without Democracy: Ruling-Party Institutionalization and Credible Commitment in Autocracies."

Gehlbach, Scott and Edmund J. Malesky. 2009. "The Contribution of Veto Players to Economic Reform." Technical report, University of Wisconsin and University of California at San Diego. Online, available at: http://ssrn.com/abstract=1315870.

Gerring, John, Philip Bond, William T. Barndt, and Carola Moreno. 2006. "Democracy and Economic Growth: A Historical Perspective." *World Politics* 57:323–64.

Ghirmay, Teame, Richard Grabowski, and Subhash C. Sharma. 2001. "Exports, Investment, Efficiency and Economic Growth in LDC: An Empirical Investigation." *Applied Economics* 33(6):689–700.

Glaeser, Edward L., Jose A. Scheinkman, and Andrei Shleifer. 1995. "Economic Growth in a Cross-Section of Cities." *National Bureau of Economic Research Working Paper Series* No. 5013. published in 1995 in *Journal on Monetary Economics* 36: 117–44.

Goldberg, Ellis, Eric Mvukiyehe, and Erik Wibbels. 2008. "Lessons from Strange Cases: Democracy, Development, and the Resource Case in the U.S. States." *Comparative Political Studies.* 41(4–5):477–514.

Good, Kenneth. 1994. "Corruption and Mismanagement in Botswana: A Best-Case Example?" *The Journal of Modern African Studies* 32(3):499–521.

Gounder, Rukmani. 2004. "Fiji's Economic Growth Impediments." *Journal of the Asia Pacific Economy* 9:301–24.

Gradstein, Mark and Moshe Justman. 2002. "Education, Social Cohesion, and Economic Growth." *American Economic Review* 92(4): 1192–204.

Granato, Jim, Ronald Inglehart, and David Leblang. 1996. "The Effect of Cultural Values on Economic Development: Theory, Hypotheses, and Some Empirical Tests." *American Journal of Political Science* 40(3):607–31.

Gregorio, Jose De and Pablo E. Guidotti. 1995. "Financial Development and Economic Growth." *World Development* 23(3):433–48.

Greiner, Alfred. 1996. "Endogenous Growth Cycles: Arrow's Learning by Doing Reconsidered." *Journal of Macroeconomics* 18(4):587–604.

Greiner, Alfred, Jens Rubart, and Willi Semmler. 2004. "Economic Growth, Skill-biased Technical Change and Wage Inequality: A Model and Estimations for the US and Europe." *Journal of Macroeconomics* 26(4):597–621.

Grier, Robin M. 1999. "Colonial Legacies and Economic Growth." *Public Choice* 98(3–4):317–35.

Gunther, Richard. 1996. "The Impact of Regime Change on Public Policy: The Case of Spain." *Journal of Public Policy* 16(2):157–201.

Gupta, Sandeep K. and Paul M. Sommers. 1999. "A Simple Cross-Section Model of Economic Growth Stands the Test of Time." *Applied Economics Letters* 6(9):601–3.

Guseh, James S. 1997. "Government Size and Economic Growth in Developing Countries: A Political-Economy Framework." *Journal of Macroeconomics* 19(1):175–92.

Gyimah-Brempong, K. 2002. "Corruption, Economic Growth, and Income Inequality in Africa." *Economics of Governance* 3(3):183–209.

Haggard, Stephan. 1990. *Pathways from the Periphery.* Ithaca: Cornell University Press.

Haggard, Stephan. 2005. "Globalization, Democracy and the Evolution of Social Contracts in East Asia." *Taiwan Journal of Democracy* 1(1): 21–48.

Haile, Daniel, Abdolkarim Sadrieh, and Harrie A.A. Verbon. 2003. "Self-Serving Dictators and Economic Growth." CESifo working Paper Series No. 1105, Center for Economic Studies and Ifo Institute for Economic Research, Tilburg University.

Hall, Joshua T. and Peter T. Leeson. 2007. "Good for the Goose, Bad for the Gander: International Labor Standards and Comparative Development." *Journal of Labor Research* 28(4):658–76.

Hall, Robert E. and Charles I. Jones. 1999. "Why Do Some Countries Produce So Much More Output Per Worker Than Others?" *The Quarterly Journal of Economics* 114(1):83–116.

Hamilton, Alexander, James Madison, and John Jay. 1987[1788]. *The Federalist Papers*. London: Penguin Books.

Hamori, Shigeyuki and Naoko Hamori. 2000. "An Empirical Analysis of Economic Fluctuations in Japan: 1885–1940." *Japan and the World Economy* 12:11–19.

Hanushek, Eric A. and Dongwook Kim. 1995. "Schooling, Labor Force Quality, and Economic Growth." *National Bureau of Economic Research Working Paper Series* No. 5399.

Hartzell, Caroline A. and Matthew Hoddie. 2007. *Crafting Peace: Power-Sharing Institutions and the Negotiated Settlement of Civil Wars*. University Park: Pennsylvania State University Press.

Hatekar, Neeraj and Ambrish Dongre. 2005. "Structural Breaks in India's Growth: Revisiting the Debate with Longer Perspective." *Economic & Political Weekly* 40(14):1432–5.

Hazan, Moshe and Binyamin Berdugo. 2002. "Child Labour, Fertility, and Economic Growth." *Economic Journal* 112(482):810–28.

Heckman, J.J., H. Ichimura, and P.E. Todd. 1997. "Matching as an Econometric Evaluation Estimator: Evidence from Evaluating a Job Training Programme." *Review of Economic Studies* 64:605–54.

Heckman, J.J., H. Ichimura, and P.E. Todd. 1998. "Matching as an Econometric Evaluation Estimator." *Review of Economic Studies* 65:261–94.

Henderson, Vernon. 2003. "The Urbanization Process and Economic Growth: The So-What Question." *Journal of Economic Growth* 8(1):47–71.

Henisz, Witold J. 2000. "The Institutional Environment for Economic Growth." *Economics and Politics* 12(1):1–31.

Henisz, Witold J. 2002. *Politics and International Investment: Measuring Risk and Protecting Profits*. London: Edward Elgar.

Henisz, Witold. 2004. "Political Institutions and Policy Volatility." *Economics and Politics* 16:1954–85.

Henisz, Witold J. and Bennet A. Zelner. 2002. "Measures of Political Risk." Technical report, University of Pennsylvania.

Henry, Peter Blair. 2003. "Capital-Account Liberalization, the Cost of Capital, and Economic Growth." *American Economic Review* 93(2):91–6.

Heo, Uk. 1998. "Modeling the Defense-Growth Relationship around the Globe." *Journal of Conflict Resolution* 42(5):637–57.

Heo, Uk. 1999. "Defense Spending and Economic Growth in South Korea: The Indirect Link." *Journal of Peace Research* 36(6):699–708.

Heo, Uk and Karl DeRouen Jr. 1998. "Military Expenditures, Technological Change, and Economic Growth in the East Asian NICs." *Journal of Politics* 60(3):830–46.

Hermes, Niels and Robert Lensink. 2002. "Capital Flight and the Uncertainty of Government Policies." Technical report.

Hibbs, Jr., Douglas A. 1987. *The American Political Economy: Macroeconomics and Electoral Politics*. Cambridge, MA: Harvard University Press.

Hojman, David E. 2002. "The Political Economy of Chile's Fast Economic Growth: An Olsonian Interpretation." *Public Choice* 111(1):155–78.

Holtz-Eakin, Douglas, Mary E. Lovely, and Mehmet S. Tosun. 2004. "Generational Conflict, Fiscal Policy, and Economic Growth." *Journal of Macroeconomics* 26(1):1–23.

Horowitz, Donald L. 1991. *A Democratic South Africa? Constitutional Engineering in a Divided Society*. Berkeley: University of California Press.

Howell, William, Scott Adler, Charles Cameron, and Charles Riemann. 2000. "Divided Government and the Legislative Productivity of Congress, 1945–94." *Legislative Studies Quarterly* 25(2):285–312.

Huff, W.G., G. Dewit, and C. Oughton. 2001. "Credibility and Reputation in the Developmental State: A Model with East Asian Applications." *World Development* 29(4):711–24.

Huntington, Samuel P. 1968. *Political Order in Changing Societies*. New Haven: Yale University Press.

Imbens, Guido. 2000. "The Role of Propensity Score in Estimating Dose-Response Functions." *Biometrika* 87(3):706–10.

Imbs, Jean. 2007. "Growth and Volatility." *Journal of Monetary Economics* 54:1848–62.

Inglehart, Ronald and Christian Welzel. 2005. *Modernization, Cultural Change, and Democracy: The Human Development Sequence*. New York: Cambridge University Press.

International Monetary Fund. 1999. *World Economic Outlook: Safe-guarding Macroeconomic Stability at Low Inflation.* Washington, DC: International Monetary Fund.

Isham, Jonathan, Michael Woolcock, Lant Pritchett, and Gwen Busby. 2005. "The Varieties of Resource Experience: Natural Resource Export Structures and the Political Economy of Economic Growth." *World Bank Economic Review* 19(2):141–74.

Islam, Nazrul. 1995. "Growth Empirics: A Panel Data Approach." *The Quarterly Journal of Economics* 110(4):1127–70.

Iwata, Shigeru, Mohsin S. Khan, and Hiroshi Murao. 2003. "Sources of Economic Growth in East Asia: A Nonparametric Assessment." *IMF Staff Papers* 50(2).

Jalilian, Hossein, Colin Kirkpatrick, and David Parker. 2007. "The Impact of Regulation on Economic Growth in Developing Countries: A Cross-Country Analysis." *World Development* 35(1):87–103.

Jenkins, Rob. 1999. *Democratic Politics and Economic Reform in India.* Cambridge University Press.

Jenkins, Rob. 2005. "The NDA and the Politics of Economic Reform." In *Coalition Politics and Hindu Nationalism,* ed. Katharine Adeney and Lawrence Sáez. New York: Routledge, pp. 173–92.

Jensen, Nathan M. 2003. "Democratic Governance and Mutinational Corporations: Political Regimes and Inflows of Foreign Direct Investment." *International Organization* 57:587–616.

Jensen, Nathan M. 2004. "Crisis, Conditions, and Capital: The Effect of International Monetary Fund Agreements on Foreign Direct Investment Inflows." *Journal of Conflict Resolution* 48 (2):194–210.

Jensen, Nathan M. 2006. *Nation-States and the Multinational Corporation: A Political Economy of Foreign Direct Investment.* Princeton University Press.

Jensen, Nathan and Fiona McGillivray. 2005. "Federal Institutions and Multinational Investors: Federalism, Government Credibility, and Foreign Direct Investment." *International Interactions* 31(4):303–25.

Johnson, Chalmers. 1982. *MITI and the Japanese Miracle: The Growth of Industrial Policy, 1925–1975.* Palo Alto: Stanford University Press.

Johnson, Elizabeth. 2006. "Stability Dividend." *Latin Finance* 180.

Jones, Charles I. 1995a. "Time Series Tests of Endogenous Growth Models." *The Quarterly Journal of Economics* 110(2):495–525.

Jones, Charles I. 1995b. "R and D Based Models of Economic Growth." *The Journal of Political Economy* 103(4):759–84.

Jones, Charles I. 2002. "Sources of U.S. Economic Growth in a World of Ideas." *American Economic Review* 92(1):220–39.

Jones, Mark P. 1995. *Electoral Laws and the Survival of Presidential Democracies*. Notre Dame, IN: Notre Dame University Press.

Jorgensen, Nickolas E. 2006. "Cleavages, Court, and Credible Commitments: The Politics of Judicial Independence." PhD thesis, University of Michigan.

Jorgenson, Dale W. and Kevin J. Stiroh. 1999. "Information Technology and Growth." *The American Economic Review* 89(2):109–15.

Jorgenson, Dale W. and Kevin J. Stiroh. 2000. "Raising the Speed Limit: US Economic Growth in the Information Age." OECD Economics Department Working Paper 261.

Joshi, Sharad. 2004. "Coalition Dharma and Economic Progress." *The Hindu Business Line*, May 12. Online, available at: www.thehindu businessline.com/2004/05/12/stories/2004051200101100.htm.

Kalaitzidakis, Pantelis. 2001. "Measures of Human Capital and Nonlinearities in Economic Growth." *Journal of Economic Growth* 6(3):229–54.

Kalemli-Ozcan, Sebnem. 2002. "Does the Mortality Decline Promote Economic Growth?" *Journal of Economic Growth* 7(4):411–39.

Kaneko, Akihiko. 2000. "Terms of Trade, Economic Growth, and Trade Patterns: A Small Open-economy Case." *Journal of International Economics* 52(1):169–81.

Kapur, Devesh. 2002. "The Causes and Consequences of India's IT Boom." *India Review* 1(2):91–110.

Kapur, Devesh. 2005. "Explaining Democratic Durability and Economic Performance: The Role of India's Institutions." In *Public Institutions in India: Performance and Design*, ed. Devesh Kapur and Pratap Bhanu Mehta. New York: Oxford University Press, pp. 28–76.

Keeler, John T.S. 1993. "Opening the Window for Reform: Mandates, Crises, and Extraordinary Policy-Making." *Comparative Political Studies* 25(4):433–86.

Kenny, Charles and David Williams. 2001. "What Do We Know About Economic Growth? Or, Why Don't We Know Very Much?" *World Development* 29(1):1–22.

Kentor, Jeffrey. 1998. "The Long-Term Effects of Foreign Investment Dependence on Economic Growth, 1940–1990." *The American Journal of Sociology* 103(4):1024–46.

Kentor, Jeffrey. 2001. "The Long Term Effects of Globalization on Income Inequality, Population Growth, and Economic Development." *Social Problems* 48(4):435–55.

Kentor, Jeffrey and Terry Boswell. 2003. "Foreign Capital Dependence and Development: A New Direction." *American Sociological Review* 68(2):301–13.

Kenyon, Thomas and Megumi Naoi. 2006. "Policy Uncertainty in Hybrid Regimes: Evidence from Firm Level Surveys." Technical report, World Bank and UCSD.

Khatkhate, Deena R. 1997. "India's Economic Growth: A Conundrum." *World Development* 25(9):1551–59.

Khatkhate, Deena. 2005. "Reserve Bank of India: A Study in the Separation and Attrition of Powers." In *Public Institutions in India: Performance and Design*, ed. Devesh Kapur and Pratap Bhanu Mehta. New York: Oxford University Press, pp. 320–50.

King, Loren A. 1998. "Economic Growth and Basic Human Needs." *International Studies Quarterly* 42:385–400.

King, Robert, Charles Plosser, and Sergio Rebello. 1988. "Production, Growth, and Business Cycles, II: New Directions." *Journal of Monetary Economics* 21(2/3):309–43.

Kirkpatrick, Colin and John Weiss. 1995. "Trade Policy Reforms and Performance in Africa in the 1980s." *The Journal of Modern African Studies* 33(2):285–98.

Klomp, Jeroen and Jakob de Haan. 2009. "Political Institutions and Economic Volatility." *European Journal of Political Economy* 25:311–26.

Kneller, Richard. 2007. "No Miracles Here: Trade Policy, Fiscal Policy and Economic Growth." *Journal of Development Studies* 43(7):1248–69.

Kohli, Atul. 1991. *Democracy and Discontent: India's Growing Crisis of Governability*. Cambridge University Press.

Kohli, Atul. 2004. *State-Directed Development: Political Power and Industrialization in the Global Periphery*. New York: Cambridge University Press.

Kohli, Atul. 2006a. "Politics of Economic Growth in India, 1980–2005. Part I: The 1980s." *Economic & Political Weekly* 41(13):1251–59.

Kohli, Atul. 2006b. "Politics of Economic Growth in India, 1980–2005. Part II: The 1990s and Beyond." *Economic & Political Weekly* 41(14): 1361–70.

Kohli, Atul. 2007. "State, Business, and Economic Growth in India." *Studies in Comparative International Development* 42:87–114.

Koren, Miklos and Silvana Tenreyro. 2007. "Volatility and Development." *The Quarterly Journal of Economics* 122(1):243–87.

Krebs, Tom. 2003. "Human Capital Risk and Economic Growth." *The Quarterly Journal of Economics* 118(2):709–44.

Krehbiel, Keith. 1996. "Institutional and Partisan Source of Gridlock: A Theory of Divided and Unified Government." *Journal of Theoretical Politics* 8(1):7–40.

Krehbiel, Keith. 1998. *Pivotal Politics: A Theory of U.S. Lawmaking*. University of Chicago Press.

Krueger, Alan B. and Mikael Lindahl. 2001. "Education for Growth: Why and For Whom?" *Journal of Economic Literature* 39(4):1101–36.

Krueger, Anne O. 1990. "Government Failures in Development." *Journal of Economic Perspectives* 4(3):9–23.

Krueger, Anne O. and Sajjid Z. Chinoy, eds. 2003. *Reforming India's External, Financial, and Fiscal Policies*. Palo Alto: Stanford University Press.

Krusell, Per, Vincenzo Quadrini, and Jose-Victor Rios-Rull. 1997. "Politico-economic Equilibrium and Economic Growth." *Journal of Economic Dynamics and Control* 21(1):243–72.

Kurtz, Marcus J. and Andrew Schrank. 2007. "Growth and Governance: Models, Measures, and Mechanisms." *Journal of Politics* 69(2): 538–54.

Kurzman, Charles, Regina Werum, and Ross E. Burkhart. 2002. "Democracy's Effect on Economic Growth: A Pooled Time-Series Analysis, 1951–1980." *Studies in Comparative International Development* 37(1):3–33.

Kydland, Finn E. and Edward C. Prescott. 1977. "Rules Rather than Discretion: The Inconsistancy of Optimal Plans." *The Journal of Political Economy* 85(3):473–92.

Lake, David A. and Matthew A. Baum. 2001. "The Invisible Hand of Democracy." *Comparative Political Studies* 34(6):587–621.

Le, Manh Vu and Terukazu Suruga. 2005. "Foreign Direct Investment, Public Expenditure and Economic Growth: The Empirical Evidence for the Period 1970–2001." *Applied Economics Letters* 12(1):45–9.

Leblang, David A. 1996. "Property Rights, Democracy and Economic Growth." *Political Research Quarterly* 49(1):5–26.

Leblang, David A. 1997. "Political Democracy and Economic Growth: Pooled Cross-Sectional and Time-Series Evidence." *British Journal of Political Science* 27:453–72.

Lee, Keun and Byung-Yeon Kim. 2009. "Both Institutions and Policies Matter but Differently for Different Income Group of Countries: Determinants of Long-Run Economic Growth Revisited." *World Development* 37(3):533–54.

Leith, J. Clark. 2005. *Why Botswana Prospered*. Montreal: McGill-Queen's University Press.

Leuven, E. and B. Sianesi. 2003. "PSMATCH2: Stata Module to Perform Full Mahalanobis and Propensity Score Matching, Common Support Graphing, and Covariate Imbalance Testing." Online, available at: http://ideas.repec.org/c/boc/bocode/s432001.html.

Levi, Margaret. 1988. *Of Rule and Revenue*. Berkeley: University of California Press.

Levine, Ross. 1997. "Financial Development and Economic Growth: Views and Agenda." *Journal of Economic Literature* 35(2):688–726.

Levine, Ross. 1998. "The Legal Environment, Banks, and Long-Run Economic Growth." *Journal of Money, Credit and Banking* 30(3):596–613.

Levine, Ross. 1999. "Law, Finance, and Economic Growth." *Journal of Financial Intermediation* 8(1–2):8–35.

Levine, Ross and David Renelt. 1992. "A Sensitivity Analysis of Cross-Country Growth Regressions." *American Economic Review* 82(4): 942–63.

Levitt, Steven D. and James M. Poterba. 1999. "Congressional Distributive Politics and State Economic Performance." *Public Choice* 99(1–2): 185–216.

Lewis, Stephen. 1993. "Policymaking and Economic Performance: Botswana in Comparative Perspective." In *Botswana: The Political Economy of Democratic Development*. Boulder: Lynne Rienner Publishers.

Li, Quan and Adam Resnick. 2003. "Reversal of Fortunes: Democratic Institutions and Foreign Direct Investment Inflows to Developing Coutries." *International Organization* 57:175–211.

Li, Xiaoying and Xiaming Liu. 2005. "Foreign Direct Investment and Economic Growth: An Increasingly Endogenous Relationship." *World Development* 33(3):393–407.

Lieberthal, Kenneth and Michel Oksenberg. 1988. *Policy Making in China: Leaders, Structure, and Processes*. Princeton University Press.

Lijphart, Arend. 2004. "Constitutional Design for Divided Societies." *Journal of Democracy* 15(2):96–109.

Limongi, Fernando. 2006. "Democracy in Brazil: Presidentialism, Party Coalitions and the Decision Making Process." *Novos Estudos Cebrap* 3:17–41.

Linden, Leigh L. 2004. "Are Incumbents Really Advantaged? The Preference for Non-Incumbents in Indian National Elections." Technical report, Columbia University, Department of Economics.

Lindert, Peter H. 2004. *Growing Public: Social Spending and Economic Growth Since the Eighteenth Century*. New York: Cambridge University Press.

Linz, Juan J. 1978. *The Breakdown of Democratic Regimes: Crisis, Breakdown, and Reequilibration*. Baltimore: Johns Hopkins University Press.

Linz, Juan J. 1990a. "The Perils of Presidentialism." *Journal of Democracy* 1(1):51–69.

Linz, Juan J. 1990b. "The Virtues of Parliamentarism." *Journal of Democracy* 1(4):84–91.

Linz, Juan J. 1994. "Presidential or Parliamentary Democracy: Does It Make a Difference?" In *The Failure of Presidential Democracy: The Case of Latin America*, ed. Juan J. Linz and Arturo Valenzuela. Baltimore: Johns Hopkins University Press, pp. 3–90.

Linz, Juan J. and Alfred Stepan. 1996. *Problems of Democratic Transition and Consolidation: Southern Europe, South America, and Post-Communist Europe*. Baltimore: Johns Hopkins University Press.

Liu, Xiaohui, Peter Burridge, and P.J.N. Sinclair. 2002. "Relationships between Economic Growth, Foreign Direct Investment and Trade: Evidence from China." *Applied Economics* 34(11):1433–40.

Locke, Richard M. 1995. *Remaking the Italian Economy*. Ithaca: Cornell University Press.

Lohmann, Susanne and Sharyn O'Halloran. 1994. "Divided Government and U.S. Trade Policy: Theory and Evidence." *International Organization* 48(4):595–632.

Lokniti. 2004. National Election Survey. Technical report, New Delhi: CSDS-Lokniti.

Lucas, Robert. 1988. "On the Mechanics of Economic Development." *Journal of Monetary Economics* 22:3–42.

Lucas, Robert and Edward C. Prescott. 1971. "Investment under Uncertainty." *Econometrica* 39(5):659–81.

Luce, Edward. 2008. *In Spite of the Gods: The Rise of Modern India*. New York: Anchor Books.

Lundberg, Mattias and Lyn Squire. 2003. "The Simultaneous Evolution of Growth and Inequality." *Economic Journal* 113(487):326–44.

MacIntyre, Andrew. 2003. *The Power of Institutions: Political Architecture and Governance*. Ithaca: Cornell University Press.

MacIntyre, Andrew, T.J. Pempel, and John Ravenhill, eds. 2008. *Crisis as Catalyst: Asia's Dynamic Political Economy*. Ithaca, NY: Cornell University Press.

McMillan, Alistair. 2005. "The BJP Coalition: Partisanship and Power-sharing in Government." In *Coalition Politics and Hindu Nationalism*, ed. Katharine Adeney and Lawrence Sáez. New York: Routledge, pp. 13–35.

Maddison, Angus. 2007. "World Population, GDP and Per Capita GDP, 1-2003 AD." Technical report, University of Groningen.

Mah, Jai S. 2005. "Export Expansion, Economic Growth and Causality in China." *Applied Economics Letters* 12:105–7.

Mainwaring, Scott. 1993. "Presidentialism, Multipartism, and Democracy: The Difficult Combination." *Comparative Political Studies* 26(2): 198–228.

Mainwaring, Scott. 1997. "Multipartism, Robust Federalism, and Presidentialism in Brazil." In *Presidentialism and Democracy in Latin America*, ed. Scott Mainwaring and Mathew Soberg Shugart. Cambridge University Press.

Mainwaring, Scott and Timothy R. Scully. 1995. "Introduction: Party Systems in Latin America." In *Building Democratic Party Systems in Latin America*, ed. Scott Mainwaring and Timothy R. Scully. Stanford University Press, pp. 1–34.

Malik, Adeel and Jonathan R.W. Temple. 2009. "The Geography of Output Volatility." *Journal of Development Economics* 90(2):163–78.

Mangeloja, Esa. 2005. "Economic Growth and Religious Production Efficiency." *Applied Economics* 37(20):23–49.

Markusen, James R. 2001. "Commitment to Rules on Investment: The Developing Countries' Stake." *Review of International Economics* 9(2):287–302.

Martin, Lisa L. 2000. *Democratic Commitments*. Princeton University Press.

Mauro, Paolo. 1995. "Corruption and Growth." *The Quarterly Journal of Economics* 110(3):681–712.

Mauro, Paolo. 2004. "The Persistence of Corruption and Slow Economic Growth." *IMF Staff Papers* 51(1).

Mayhew, David R. 1991a. *Divided We Govern: Party Control, Lawmaking and Investigations, 1946–1990*. New Haven: Yale University Press.

Mayhew, David R. 1991b. "Divided Party Control: Does It Make a Difference?" *PS: Political Science and Politics* 24(4):637–40.

Mazumdar, Krishna. 1996. "An Analysis of Causal Flow between Social Development and Economic Growth: The Social Development Index." *American Journal of Economics and Sociology* 55(3):361–83.

Mazur, Emilia A. and W. Robert J. Alexander. 2001. "Financial Sector Development and Economic Growth in New Zealand." *Applied Economics Letters* 8(8):545–9.

Mehlum, Halvor. 2002. "Zimbabwe: Investments, Credibility, and the Dynamics Following Trade Liberalization." *Economic Modelling* 19:565–84.

Mehta, Pratap Bhanu. 2005. "India's Judiciary: The Promise of Uncertainty." In *Public Institutions in India: Performance and Design*, ed. Devesh Kapur and Pratap Bhanu Mehta. New York: Oxford University Press, pp. 158–93.

Mello, Luiz R. De. 2002. "Public Finance, Government Spending and Economic Growth: The Case of Local Governments in Brazil." *Applied Economics* 34(15):1871–83.

Mershon, Carol. 1996. "The Costs of Coalition: Coalition Theories and Italian Governments." *American Political Science Review* 90(3): 534–54.

Mershon, Carol. 2002. *The Costs of Coalition*. Stanford University Press.

Milbourne, R., G. Otto, and G. Voss. 2003. "Public Investment and Economic Growth." *Applied Economics* 35(5):527.

Milner, Helen V. and Peter B. Rosendorff. 1996. "Democratic Politics and International Trade Negotiations: Elections and Divided Government as Constraints on Trade Liberalization." *Journal of Conflict Resolution* 41(1):117–46.

Mintz, Alex and Randolph T. Stevenson. 1995. "Defense Expenditures, Economic Growth, and the 'Peace Dividend': A Longitudinal Analysis of 103 Countries." *The Journal of Conflict Resolution* 39(2):283–305.

Miwa, Yoshiro and J. Mark Ramseyer. 2002. "Banks and Economic Growth: Implications from Japanese History." *Journal of Law & Economics* 45(1):127–64.

Mo, Pak Hung. 2001. "Corruption and Economic Growth." *Journal of Comparative Economics* 29(1):66–79.

Mobarak, Ahmed Mushfiq. 2005. "Democracy, Volatility, and Development." *The Review of Economics and Statistics* 87(2):348–61.

Monte, Alfredo Del and Erasmo Papagni. 2001. "Public Expenditure, Corruption, and Economic Growth: The Case of Italy." *European Journal of Political Economy* 17:1–16.

Montero, Alfred. 2001. "Decentralizing Democracy: Spain and Brazil in Comparative Perspective." *Comparative Politics* 33(2):149–69.

Moon, Bruce E. 1998. "Exports, Outward-Oriented Development, and Economic Growth." *Political Research Quarterly* 51(1):7–36.

Morlino, Leonardo. 2001. "The Three Phases of Italian Parties." In *Political Parties and Democracy*, ed. Larry Diamond and Richard Gunther. Baltimore: Johns Hopkins University Press.

Müller, Wolfgang C. and Kaare Strøm, eds. 2000. *Coalition Governments in Western Europe*. Oxford University Press.

Mulligan, Casey B, Ricard Gil, and Xavier X. Sala-i-Martin. 2004. "Do Democracies Have Different Public Policies than Nondemocracies?" *Journal of Economic Perspectives* 18:51–74.

Muralidharan, Sukumar and Sudha Mahalingam. 1999. "Big Business and Elections." *Frontline* 16(16). Online, available at: www.thehindu.com/fline/fl1616/16160040.htm.

Murdoch, James C. and Todd Sandler. 2002. "Economic Growth, Civil Wars, and Spatial Spillovers." *The Journal of Conflict Resolution* 46(1):91–110.

Murdoch, James C. and Todd Sandler. 2004. "Civil Wars and Economic Growth: Spatial Dispersion." *American Journal of Political Science* 48(1):138–51.

Nahar, S. and B. Inder. 2002. "Testing Convergence in Economic Growth for OECD Countries." *Applied Economics* 34(16):2011.

Ndikumana, Léonce and James K. Boyce. 2003. "Public Debts and Private Assets: Explaining Capital Flight from Sub-Saharan African Countries." *World Development* 31(1)107–30.

Nelson, Joan M. 2007. "Elections, Democracy, and Social Services." *Studies in Comparative International Development* 41(4):79–97.

Neusser, Klaus. 2001. "A Multisectoral Log-Linear Model of Economic Growth with Marshallian Externalities." *Journal of Macroeconomics* 23(4):537–64.

Newfarmer, Richard. 1998. *East Asia: The Road to Recovery.* Washington, DC: World Bank.

Nikolenyi, Csaba. 2009. *Minority Governments in India: The Puzzle of Elusive Majorities.* London: Routledge.

Nooruddin, Irfan. 2009. "Coalition Dharma: Explaining Support for Coalition Politics in the Indian Electorate." Technical report, The Ohio State University.

Nooruddin, Irfan and Pradeep Chhibber. 2008. "Unstable Politics: Electoral Volatility in the Indian State." *Comparative Political Studies* 41: 1069–91.

Nooruddin, Irfan and Joel W. Simmons. 2006. "The Politics of Hard Choices: IMF Programs and Government Spending." *International Organization* 60(4):1001–33.

North, Douglass C. 1981. *Structure and Change in Economic History.* New York: W.W. Norton & Company.

North, Douglass C. 1990. "A Transaction Cost Theory of Politics." *Journal of Theoretical Politics* 2(4):355–67.

North, Douglass C. 1994. "Economic Performance Through Time." *American Economic Review* 84(3):359–68.

North, Douglass C. 2005. *Understanding of the Process of Economic Change.* Princeton University Press.

North, Douglass C. and Robert Paul Thomas. 1973. *The Rise of the Western World: A New Economic History.* Cambridge University Press.

North, Douglass C. and Barry R. Weingast. 1989. "Constitutions and Commitment: The Evolution of Institutions Governing Public Choice in Seventeenth-Century England." *Journal of Economic History* 49(4):803–32.

Nunn, Nathan. 2004. "Slavery, Institutional Development, and Long-Run Growth in Africa, 1400–2000." International Trade 0411007, EconWPA.

Oliva, Maria-Angels and Luis A. Rivera-Batiz. 2002. "Political Institutions, Capital Flows, and Developing Country Growth: An Empirical Investigation." *Review of Development Economics* 6(2):248–62.

Olson, Mancur. 1982. *The Rise and Decline of Nations*. New Haven: Yale University Press.

Onafowora, Olugbenga A. and Oluwole Owoye. 1998. "Can Trade Liberalization Stimulate Economic Growth in Africa?" *World Development* 26(3):497–506.

Organski, A.F.K. and Jacek Kugler. 1980. *The War Ledger*. University of Chicago Press.

Ozlu, Elvan. 1996. "Aggregate Economic Fluctuations in Endogenous Growth Models." *Journal of Macroeconomics* 18(1):27–47.

Palmer, Harvey D. and Guy D. Whitten. 1999. "The Electoral Impact of Unexpected Inflation and Economic Growth." *British Journal of Political Science* 29(4):623–39.

Panagariya, Arvind. 2008. *India: The Emerging Giant*. New York: Oxford University Press.

Parai, Amar K. 2003. "Foreign Capital Inflow and Economic Growth in LDCs." *Applied Economics Letters* 10(6):377.

Pedersen, Torben Mark and Anne Marie Elmer. 2003. "International Evidence on the Connection Between Business Cycles and Economic Growth." *Journal of Macroeconomics* 25(2):255–75.

Peretto, Pietro F. 2003. "Endogenous Market Structure and the Growth and Welfare Effects of Economic Integration." *Journal of International Economics* 60(1):177–201.

Peretto, Pietro F. 2007. "Schumpeterian Growth with Productive Public Spending and Distortionary Taxation." *Review of Development Economics* 11(4):699–722.

Perez, Sofia A. 2000. "From Decentralization to Reorganization: Explaining the Return to National Bargaining in Italy and Spain." *Comparative Politics* 32(4):437–58.

Perez-Diaz, Victor. 1986. "Economic Policies and Social Pacts in Spain during the Transition: The Two Faces of Neo-Corporatism." *European Sociological Review* 2(1):1–19.

Persson, Torsten. 2005. "Forms of Democracy, Policy and Economic Development." Technical report, NBER Working Paper No. 11171.

Petrucci, Alberto. 2003. "Money, Endogenous Fertility and Economic Growth." *Journal of Macroeconomics* 25:527–39.

Pfeifer, Karen, Marsha Pripstein-Posusney, Djavad Salehi-Isfahani, and Steve Niva. 1999. "Reform or Reaction? Dilemmas of Economic Development in the Middle East." *Middle East Report* (210):14–15.

Pickering, Jeffrey and Emizet F. Kisangani. 2006. "Political, Economic, and Social Consequences of Foreign Military Intervention." *Political Research Quarterly* 59(3):363–76.

Pinto, Pablo and Jeffrey E. Timmons. 2005. "The Political Determinants of Economic Performance. Political Competition and the Sources of Growth." *Comparative Political Studies* 38(1):26–50.

Plumper, Thomas and Christian W. Martin. 2003. "Democracy, Government Spending, and Economic Growth: A Political-Economic Explanation of the Barro-Effect." *Public Choice* 117(1–2):27–50.

Posner, Alan. 1977. "Italy: Dependence and Political Fragmentation." *International Organization* 31(4):809–38.

Poterba, James M. 1994. "State Responses to Fiscal Crisis: The Effects of Budgetary Institutions and Policies." *Journal of Political Economy* 102(4):799–821.

Prasad, Eswar S., Kenneth Rogoff, Shang-Jin Wei, and M. Ayhan Kose. 2006. "Financial Globalization, Growth, and Volatility in Developing Countries." In *Globalization and Poverty*, ed. Ann E. Harrison. University of Chicago Press, pp. 457–511.

Pritchett, Lant. 2000. "Understanding Patterns of Economic Growth: Searching for Hills among Plateaus, Mountains, and Plains." *World Bank Economic Review* 14(2):221–50.

Przeworski, Adam and Fernando Limongi. 1993. "Political Regimes and Economic Growth." *The Journal of Economic Perspectives* 7(3):51–69.

Przeworski, Adam, Susan C. Stokes, and Bernard Manin, eds. 1999. *Democracy, Accountability, and Representation*. New York: Cambridge University Press.

Przeworski, Adam, Michael E. Alvarez, José A. Cheibub, and Fernando Limongi. 2000. *Democracy and Development: Political Institutions and Well-Being in the World, 1950–1990*. New York: Cambridge University Press.

Quinn, Dennis P. and John T. Woolley. 2001. "Democracy and National Economic Performance: The Preference for Stability." *American Journal of Political Science* 45(3):634–57.

Ramaswamy, K.V. 2007. "Regional Dimension of Growth and Employment." *Economic & Political Weekly* 42(49):47–56.

Ramey, Garey and Valerie Ramey. 1991. "Technology Commitment and the Cost of Economic Fluctuations." Technical report, NBER *Working Paper* No. 3755.

Ramey, Garey and Valerie Ramey. 1995. "Cross-Country Evidence on the Link Between Volatility and Growth." *American Economic Review* 85:1138–51.

Ran, Jimmy, Jan P. Voon, and Guangzhong Li. 2007. "How Does FDI Affect China? Evidence from Industries and Provinces." *Journal of Comparative Economics* 35(4):774–99.

Rao, M. Govinda and Nirvikar Singh. 2005. "India's Federal Institutions and Economic Reform." In *Public Institutions in India: Performance and Design*, ed. Devesh Kapur and Pratap Bhanu Mehta. New York: Oxford University Press, pp. 351–405.

Rauch, James E. 1995. "Bureaucracy, Infrastructure, and Economic Growth: Evidence from U.S. Cities During the Progressive Era." *American Economic Review* 85(4):968–79.

Reserve Bank of India. 1967–2004. *Bulletin*. New Delhi: Government of India.

Rivera-Batiz, Francisco L. 2001. "International Financial Liberalization, Corruption, and Economic Growth." *Review of International Economics* 9(4):727–37.

Rivera-Batiz, Francisco L. 2002. "Democracy, Governance, and Economic Growth: Theory and Evidence." *Review of Development Economics* 6(2):225–47.

Roberts, Bryan W. and Alvaro Rodriguez. 1997. "Economic Growth Under a Self-Interested Central Planner and Transition to a Market Economy." *Journal of Comparative Economics* 24(2):121–39.

Roberts, Tyson. 2006. "Political Institutions and Foreign Direct Investment in Developing Countries: Does Policy Stability Matter More than Democracy and Property Rights?" Technical report. Paper presented at the 2006 Annual Meeting of the American Political Science Association, Philadelphia.

Rock, Michael T. 2009. "Has Democracy Slowed Growth in Asia?" *World Development* 37(5):941–52.

Rodriguez, Francisco and Dani Rodrik. 1999. "Trade Policy and Economic Growth: A Sceptic's Guide to the Cross-National Evidence." Technical report, CEPR. Discussion Papers.

Rodrik, Dani. 1997a. "Democracy and Economic Performance." Unpublished paper, Harvard University.

Rodrik, Dani. 1997b. *Has Globalization Gone Too Far?* Institute for International Economics.

Rodrik, Dani. 1997c. "Trade Policy and Economic Performance in Sub-Saharan Africa." Technical report, Swedish Ministry for Foreign Affairs.

Rodrik, Dani. 1998a. "Globalisation, Social Conflict and Economic Growth." *The World Economy* 21(2):143–58.

Rodrik, Dani. 1998b. "Where Did All the Growth Go? External Shocks, Social Conflict, and Growth Collapse." *Journal of Economic Growth* 4(4):385–412.

Rodrik, Dani. 2000. "Participatory Politics, Social Cooperation, and Economic Stability." *American Economics Review* 90.

Rodrik, Dani. 2003a. "Growth Strategies." *National Bureau of Economic Research Working Paper Series* No. 10050.

Rodrik, Dani, ed. 2003b. *In Search of Prosperity: Analytic Narratives on Economic Growth*. Princeton University Press.

Rodrik, Dani. 2007. *One Economics, Many Recipes: Globalization, Institutions, and Economic Growth*. Princeton University Press.

Rodrik, Dani and Arvind Subramanian. 2004. "From 'Hindu Growth' to Productivity Surge: The Mystery of the Indian Growth Transition." Technical report, *NBER Working Paper* No. W10376.

Rose, Andrew K. and Mark M. Spiegel. 2009. "International Financial Remoteness and Macroeconomic Volatility." *Journal of Development Economics* 89(2):250–7.

Rosenbaum, Paul R. and Donald B. Rubin. 1983. "The Central Role of the Propensity Score in Observational Studies for Causal Effects." *Biometrika* 70(1):41–55.

Rosenbaum, Paul R. and Donald B. Rubin. 1985. "Constructing a Control Group Using Multivariate Matched Sampling Methods that Incorporate the Propensity Score." *The American Statistician* 39(1):33–8.

Ross, Michael. 2006. "Is Democracy Good For the Poor?" *American Journal of Political Science* 50(4):860–74.

Ross, Michael L. 2004a. "What Do We Know About Natural Resources and Civil War?" *Journal of Peace Research* 41(3):337–56.

Ross, Michael L. 2004b. "How Do Natural Resources Influence Civil War? Evidence from Thirteen Cases." *International Organization* 58(Winter):35–67.

Rostow, W.W. 1971. *The Stages of Economic Growth*. New York: Cambridge University Press.

Roubini, Nouriel and Jeffrey D. Sachs. 1989. "Political and Economic Determinants of Budget Deficits in the Industrial Democracies." *European Economic Review* 33(5):903–38.

Rowley, Charles K. 2000. "Political Culture and Economic Performance in Sub-Saharan Africa." *European Journal of Political Economy* 16(1):133–58.

Rubin, Donald B. 1974. "Estimating Causal Effects of Treatments in Randomised and Non-Randomised Studies." *Journal of Educational Psychology* 66:688–701.

Rubin, Donald B. 1980. "Bias Reduction Using Mahalanobis-Metric Matching." *Biometrics* 36:293–8.

Rubin, Donald B. 2006. *Matched Sampling for Causal Effects*. New York: Cambridge University Press.

Russett, Bruce M. and John Oneal. 2001. *Triangulating Peace: Democracy, Interdependence, and International Organizations*. New York: W.W. Norton.

Sachs, Jeffrey D. and Andrew M. Warner. 1995. "Natural Resource Abundance and Economic Growth." Technical report, *NBER Working Paper*.

Sala-i-Martin, Xavier X. 1997. "I Just Ran Two Million Regressions." *American Economic Review* 87(2):178–83.

Samuels, Richard J. 2003. *Machiavelli's Children: Leaders and their Legacies in Italy and Japan*. Ithaca: Cornell University Press.

Savvides, Andreas. 1995. "Economic Growth in Africa." *World Development* 23:449–58.

Scarpetta, Stefano, Andrea Bassanini, Dirk Pilat, and Paul Schreyer. 2000. "Economic Growth in the OECD Area: Recent Trends at the Aggregate and Sectoral Level." *OECD Economics Department Working Papers* No. 248.

Schatz, Sayre P. 1996. "The World Bank's Fundamental Misconception in Africa." *The Journal of Modern African Studies* 34(2):239–47.

Schineller, Lisa M. 1997. "An Econometric Model of Capital Flight from Developing Countries." Technical report, Board of Governors of the Federal Reserve System, International Finance Discussion Paper No. 579.

Schofer, Evan, Francisco O. Ramirez, and John W. Meyer. 2000. "The Effects of Science on National Economic Development, 1970 to 1990." *American Sociological Review* 65(6):866–87.

Schultz, Kenneth A. and Barry R. Weingast. 2003. "The Democratic Advantage: Institutional Foundations of Financial Power in International Competition." *International Organization* 57:3–42.

Scruggs, Lyle. 2001. "The Politics of Growth Revisited." *The Journal of Politics* 63(1):120–40.

Scully, Gerald W. 2002. "Economic Freedom, Government Policy and the Trade-Off between Equity and Economic Growth." *Public Choice* 113(1–2):77–96.

Scully, Gerald W. 2003. "Optimal Taxation, Economic Growth and Income Inequality." *Public Choice* 115(3–4):299–312.

Sen, Amartya. 1999. *Development as Freedom*. New York: Alfred A. Knopf.

Sen, Kunal. 2007. "Why Did the Elephant Start to Trot? India's Growth Acceleration Re-examined." *Economic & Political Weekly* 42(43): 37–47.

Sengupta, Mitu. 2008. "How the State Changed Its Mind: Power, Politics and the Origins of India's Market Reforms." *Economic & Political Weekly* 43(21):35–42.

Senhadji, Abdelhak S. 2000. "Sources of Economic Growth: An Extensive Growth Accounting Exercise." *IMF Staff Papers* 47(1):129–58.

Shan, Jordan. 2005. "Does Financial Development 'Lead' Economic Growth? A Vector Auto-regression Appraisal." *Applied Economics* 37(12):1353–67.

Shugart, Matthew Soberg and John M. Carey. 1992. *Presidents and Assemblies: Constitutional Design and Electoral Dynamics*. New York: Cambridge University Press.

Shugart, Matthew Soberg and Stephan Haggard. 2001. "Institutions and Public Policy in Presidential Systems." In *Presidents, Parliaments, and Policy*, ed. Stephan Haggard and Mathew D. McCubbins. New York: Cambridge University Press, pp. 64–102.

Simmons, Joel W. 2008. "Parties, Time Horizons, and the Pursuit of Economic Growth through Technological Development." PhD thesis, University of Michigan.

Sirimaneetham, Vatcharin and Jonathan R.W. Temple. 2009. "Macroeconomic Stability and the Distribution of Growth Rates." *World Bank Economic Review* 23(3):443–79.

Stadler, George W. 1990. "Business Cycle Models with Endogenous Technology." *American Economic Review* 80(4):763–78.

Stafford, Frank P. 1999. "Economic Growth: How Good Can It Get?" *The American Economic Review* 89(2):40–4.

Stasavage, David. 2002. "Private Investment and Political Institutions." *Economics and Politics* 14(1):41–63.

Stasavage, David. 2003. *Public Debt and the Birth of the Democratic State: France and Great Britain, 1688–1789*. New York: Cambridge University Press.

Stepan, Alfred and Cindy Skach. 1993. "Constitutional Frameworks and Democratic Consolidation." *World Politics* 46(1):1–22.

Stern, David I., Michael S. Common, and Edward B. Barbier. 1996. "Economic Growth and Environmental Degradation: The Environmental Kuznets Curve and Sustainable Development." *World Development* 24(7):1151–60.

Stiglitz, Joseph. 1993. "Financial Market Imperfections and Business Cycles." *Quarterly Journal of Economics* 108(1):77–114.

Stiglitz, Joseph. 2000. "Capital Market Liberalization, Economic Growth, and Instability." *World Development* 28(6):1075–86.

Stokes, Susan C. 2001. *Mandates and Democracy: Neoliberalism by Surprise in Latin America.* New York: Cambridge University Press.

Stokey, Nancy L. 1998. "Are There Limits to Growth?" *International Economic Review* 39(1):1–31.

Stone, Randall W. 2002. *Lending Credibility: The International Monetary Fund and the Post-Communist Transition.* Princeton University Press.

Storm, Servaas and C.W.M. Naastepad. 2005. "Strategic Factors in Economic Development: East Asian Industrialization 1950–2003." *Development and Change* 36(6):1059–94.

Strauss, John and Duncan Thomas. 1998. "Health, Nutrition, and Economic Development." *Journal of Economic Literature* 36(2):766–817.

Strøm, Kaare. 1990. *Minority Government and Majority Rule.* Cambridge University Press.

Strøm, Kaare and Wolfgang C. Müller. 1999. "The Keys to Togetherness: Coalition Agreements in Parliamentary Democracies." *Journal of Legislative Studies* 5(3/4):255–82.

Stürm, Jan-Egbert and Jacob de Haan. 2001a. "Inflation in Developing Countries: Does Central Bank Independence Matter? New Evidence Based on a New Data Set." Kof Working Paper 07-167, Kof Swiss Economic Institute, ETH Zurich.

Stürm, Jan-Egbert and Jakob de Haan. 2001b. "How Robust is the Relationship between Economic Freedom and Economic Growth?" *Applied Economics* 33(7):839–44.

Swank, Duane. 1996. "Culture, Institutions, and Economic Growth: Theory, Recent Evidence, and the Role of Communitarian Polities." *American Journal of Political Science* 40(3):660–79.

Tang, Eddie Wing Yin and R. Alan Hedley. 1998. "Distributional Coalitions, State Strength, and Economic Growth: Toward a Comprehensive Theory of Economic Development." *Public Choice* 96(3–4):295–323.

Teboul, Rene and Emmanuelle Moustier. 2001. "Foreign Aid and Economic Growth: The case of the Countries South of the Mediterranean." *Applied Economics Letters* 8(3):187.

Teles, Vladimir K. 2005. "The Role of Human Capital in Economic Growth." *Applied Economics Letters* 12(9):583.

Temple, Jonathan and Paul A. Johnson. 1998. "Social Capability and Economic Growth." *The Quarterly Journal of Economics* 113(3):965–90.

Teorell, Jan, Nicholas Charron, Marcus Samanni, Sören Holmberg, and Bo Rothstein. 2009. *Quality of Government Dataset, version 17June09.* University of Gothenburg: The Quality of Government Institute, www.qog.pol.gu.se.

Tsebelis, George. 1995. "Decision Making in Political Systems: Veto Players in Presidentialism, Parliamentarism, Multicameralism, and Multipartyism." *British Journal of Political Science* 25(3):289–325.

Tsebelis, George. 1999. "Veto Players and Law Production in Parliamentary Democracies: An Empirical Analysis." *American Political Science Review* 93(3):591–608.

Tsebelis, George. 2002. *Veto Players: How Political Institutions Work.* Princeton: Russell Sage Foundation and Princeton University Press.

Tsie, Balefi. 1996. "The Political Context of Botswana's Development Performance." *Journal of Southern African Studies* 22(4):599–616.

UNCTAD. 2002. "Statistical Annex to Diversification of Production and Exports in Commodity Dependent Countries, Including Single Commodity Exporters, for Industrialization and Development, Taking into Account the Special Needs of LDCs." Technical report, United Nations Conference on Trade and Development.

USAID. 2000. "Working Without a Net: Women and the Asian Financial Crisis." *Gender Matters Quarterly* 2.

Valenzuela, Arturo. 1994. "Party Politics and the Crisis of Presidentialism in Chile: A Proposal for a Parliamentary Form of Government." In *The Failure of Presidential Democracy: The Case of Latin America*, ed. Juan J. Linz and Arturo Valenzuela. Baltimore: Johns Hopkins University Press, pp. 91–150.

Varshney, Ashutosh. 1998. *Democracy, Development, and the Countryside: Urban-Rural Struggles in India.* New York: Cambridge University Press.

Varshney, Ashutosh. 2002. *Ethnic Conflict and Civic Life: Hindus and Muslims in India.* New Haven: Yale University Press.

Ventura, Jaume. 1997. "Growth and Interdependence." *The Quarterly Journal of Economics* 112(1):57–84.

Vernon, Raymond. 1980. "The Obsolescing Bargain: A Key Factor in Political Risk." In *The International Essays for Business Decision Makers 5*, ed. Mark B. Winchester. Houston: Center for International Business.

Virmani, Arvind. 2004. "Sources of India's Economic Growth: Trends in Total Factor Productivity." *Working Paper* No. 131. Indian Council for Research on International Economic Relations.

Virmani, Arvind. 2006. "India's Economic Growth History: Fluctuations, Trends, Break Points and Phases." *Indian Economic Review* 41: 81–103.

Voitchovsky, Sarah. 2005. "Does the Profile of Income Inequality Matter for Economic Growth?" *Journal of Economic Growth* 10(3): 273–96.

Vreeland, James Raymond. 2003. *The IMF and Economic Development.* New York: Cambridge University Press.

Wahab, Mahmoud. 2004. "Economic Growth and Government Expenditure: Evidence from a New Test Specification." *Applied Economics* 36:2125–35.

Wallack, Jessica Seddon. 2003. "Structural Breaks in Indian Macroeconomic Data." *Economic & Political Weekly* 38:4312–15.

Weede, Erich. 1996. "Legitimacy, Democracy, and Comparative Economic Growth Reconsidered." *European Sociological Review* 12(3):217–25.

Weyland, Kurt. 1996. "Obstacles to Social Reform in Brazil's New Democracy." *Comparative Politics* 29:1–22.

Whiteley, Paul F. 2000. "Economic Growth and Social Capital." *Political Studies* 48(3):443–66.

Widner, Jennifer A. 2001. *Building the Rule of Law.* New York: W.W. Norton.

Wong, Kit Pong. 2010. "The Effects of Irreversibility on the Timing and Intensity of Lumpy Investment." *Economic Modelling* 27(1):97–102.

World Bank. 1987. *World Development Report 1987: Barriers to Adjustment and Growth in the World Economy; Industrialization and Foreign Trade.* Washington, DC: The World Bank.

World Bank. 1993. *The East Asian Miracle: Economic Growth and Public Policy.* Washington, DC: World Bank Publications.

World Bank. 1996. *India: Five Years of Stabilization and Reform and the Challenges Ahead.* Washington, DC: World Bank Publications.

World Bank. 2006. *World Development Indicators 2006.* Washington, DC: World Bank.

World Bank. 2007. *Global Development Finance: The Globalization of Corporate Finance in American Countries.* Washington, DC: The World Bank.

World Bank. 2008. *Africa Development Indicators 2007: Spreading and Sustaining Growth in Africa.* Washington, DC: World Bank Publications.

Wright, Joseph. 2008. "Do Authoritarian Political Institutions Constrain? How Legislatures Affect Economic Growth and Investment." *American Journal of Political Science* 52(2):322–43.

Wu, Chang Hao and Pedro Rapallo. 1997. "Macroeconomic Determinants of Output Growth Volatility: A Cross-Country Regression Analysis 1961–1988." Working Paper, Department of Economics, University of California, San Diego.

Wu, Wenbo and Otto A Davis. 1999. "The Two Freedoms, Economic Growth and Development: An Empirical Study." *Public Choice* 100 (1–2):39–64.

Yago, Milton and Wyn Morgan. 2008. "The Impact of Policy Reversal on Economic Performance in Sub-Saharan Africa." *European Journal of Political Economy* 24:88–106.

Yao, Shujie. 2006. "On Economic Growth, FDI and Exports in China." *Applied Economics* 38(3):339–351.

Yoo, Seung-Hoon. 2003. "Does Information Technology Contribute to Economic Growth in Developing Countries? A Cross-Country Analysis." *Applied Economics Letters* 10(11):679.

Yu, Qiao. 1997. "Economic Fluctuation, Macro Control, and Monetary Policy in the Transitional Chinese Economy." *Journal of Comparative Economics* 25(2):180–95.

Zariski, Raphael. 1965. "Intra-Party Conflict in a Dominant Party: The Experience of Italian Christian Democracy." *Journal of Politics* 27(1): 3–34.

Index

245

For EU product safety concerns, contact us at Calle de José Abascal, 56–1°,
28003 Madrid, Spain or eugpsr@cambridge.org.

www.ingramcontent.com/pod-product-compliance
Ingram Content Group UK Ltd.
Pitfield, Milton Keynes, MK11 3LW, UK
UKHW020332140625
459647UK00018B/2118